# PERSPECTIVES 2

## Workbook

D1518584

**NATIONAL GEOGRAPHIC**
**LEARNING**

Australia · Brazil · Mexico · Singapore · United Kingdom · United States

**Perspectives 2**

Publisher: Sherrise Roehr

Executive Editor: Sarah Kenney

Assistant Editor: Becky Long

Media Researcher: Leila Hishmeh

Senior Technology Product Manager: Lauren Krolick

Director of Global Marketing: Ian Martin

Sr. Director, ELT & World Languages: Michael Burggren

Production Manager: Daisy Sosa

Senior Print Buyer: Mary Beth Hennebury

Composition: Lumina Datamatics, Inc.

Cover/Text Design: Brenda Carmichael

Art Director: Brenda Carmichael

Cover Image: ©JR-art.net/Redux Pictures

For product information and technology assistance, contact us at
**Cengage Learning Customer & Sales Support, cengage.com/contact**

For permission to use material from this text or product,
submit all requests online at **cengage.com/permissions**
Further permissions questions can be emailed to
**permissionrequest@cengage.com**

Perspectives 2 Workbook

ISBN: 978-1-337-29729-5

**National Geographic Learning**
20 Channel Center Street
Boston, MA 02210
USA

National Geographic Learning, a Cengage Learning Company, has a mission to bring the world to the classroom and the classroom to life. With our English language programs, students learn about their world by experiencing it. Through our partnerships with National Geographic and TED Talks, they develop the language and skills they need to be successful global citizens and leaders.

Locate your local office at **international.cengage.com/region**

Visit National Geographic Learning online at **NGL.Cengage.com/ELT**
Visit our corporate website at **www.cengage.com**

Printed in the United States of America
Print Number: 01   Print Year: 2018

# 1 In Touch with Your Feelings

## 1A Show Your Emotions

### VOCABULARY Describing emotions

**1** **Review** Unscramble the letters to make adjectives about emotions.

1 d r i a f a      __ __ __ __ __ d
2 y a p n u h p      __ n __ __ p __ __
3 g r a y n      __ __ g __ __
4 t u p e s      u __ __ __ __
5 r o d e b      __ __ r __ __
6 d o r w e i r      w __ __ __ __ __ __
7 y a p h p      __ __ __ __ y
8 x e i d e t c      __ __ c __ __ __ d

**2** **Review** Complete the sentences with the adjectives from Activity 1.

1 Anja was really _____ when she heard that the dog had died.
2 Have you always been _____ of spiders?
3 Max told me he's _____ about failing the test.
4 He hated the school and had a very _____ childhood.
5 We're so _____ that you can come to the wedding!
6 The trip sounds amazing—are you getting _____ about it?
7 I think he was really _____ with her for not offering to help.
8 Were you as _____ as I was during that movie? I almost fell asleep!

**3** **Review** Listen and choose the correct emotions. 🎧 **1**

| 1 | angry | afraid | worried |
| 2 | excited | bored | happy |
| 3 | bored | worried | upset |
| 4 | afraid | excited | worried |
| 5 | worried | upset | angry |
| 6 | relaxed | afraid | unhappy |

**4** Read the sentences (1–8) and match the words in bold with their definitions (a–h).

1 When it's very dark he sometimes gets **scared**. _____
2 I was very **confused** when he started speaking in German. _____
3 You must be **delighted** that you won! _____
4 I was so **embarrassed** when Jack started to sing. _____
5 Living here can be really **lonely** at times. _____
6 Please don't be **annoyed**—I'm sorry I forgot. _____
7 I always feel **nervous** before job interviews. _____
8 She was **relaxed** and enjoying the sunshine. _____

a not able to understand
b afraid
c feeling happy and calm
d unhappy because you are not with other people
e angry or impatient
f worried
g ashamed or shy
h very happy

**5** Match the adjectives with similar meanings.

| 1 | embarrassed | a | afraid |
| 2 | delighted | b | angry |
| 3 | scared | c | worried |
| 4 | annoyed | d | ashamed |
| 5 | anxious | e | happy |

**6** Choose the correct options to complete the sentences.

1 I'm worried *about / for / with* failing the exam.
2 She was embarrassed *with / by / of* Richard's silly comments.
3 Jamal seems very nervous *with / by / about* the interview.
4 There's no need to get annoyed *of / to / with* Jasmine—she was only trying to help.
5 Are you feeling anxious *over / about / of* your driving test?
6 He was ashamed *by / for / of* his bad grade on the test.
7 Don't be scared *for / of / with* Jason—he's really nice when you get to know him.
8 I'm confused *of / by / from* your text. Can you call me?

**7** Put the words in the correct order to make sentences.

1 My / makes / feel / me / stressed / job / .

   _____

2 scared / you / Are / heights / of / very / ?

   _____

3 lonely / be / your / on / own / Living / can / .

   _____

4 was / She / her / score / with / delighted / test / .

   _____

5 about / I'm / the meaning / this / of / confused / word / .

   _____

6 came / very / We're / that / happy / you / .

   _____

7 have / nothing / of / ashamed / to be / They / .

   _____

8 worried / moving / I'm / a / about / to / city / new / .

   _____

**8** Choose the correct adjectives to complete the sentences.

1 I'm often really *nervous / embarrassed* at the start of a test, but after I've answered a couple of questions, I begin to feel more *excited / relaxed*.

2 We were so *excited / stressed* when we heard the news! You must be absolutely *ashamed /delighted*.

3 **A** So was Mike *annoyed / pleased* with Eve for being so late?

   **B** Yes, and Eve was really *bored / upset* when he shouted at her.

4 With her family far away, Amy often feels a bit *scared / lonely* during the holidays, so she's really *grateful / relaxed* that you invited her.

5 Sorry, I'm *delighted / embarrassed* to admit this, but I'm *confused / worried* about what this sentence means.

6 Rosa's working late—she's feeling really *stressed / pleased* about getting everything finished on time and is *nervous / lonely* about doing the presentation.

**9** Complete the sentences so they are true for you.

1 I got really angry when _____.

2 I sometimes get confused about _____.

3 _____ always makes me feel stressed.

4 One thing I'm happy about is _____.

5 I felt so embarrassed when _____.

6 The time I feel most relaxed is _____.

**10** **Extension** Complete the sentences with these words. There are two adjectives you don't need.

| cheerful | disappointed | grateful | impatient |
|----------|--------------|----------|-----------|
| jealous | proud | scared | selfish |

1 I'm very _____ of Ava's new phone—it's so much better than mine.

2 You shouldn't be so _____ with him when he makes a mess—he's only four.

3 We're extremely _____ to you for being so generous.

4 I'm really _____ with my grade—I only got a B.

5 Javier has been incredibly successful, but we're very _____ of all our children.

6 Pete never helps out with the chores. It's really _____ of him.

**11** **Extension** Choose the adjective that <u>can't</u> be followed by the preposition.

1 *proud / jealous / cheerful* + **of**

2 *impatient / selfish / disappointed* + **with**

3 *lonely / worried / nervous* + **about**

4 *upset / ashamed / scared* + **of**

5 *annoyed / angry / embarrassed* + **with**

6 *excited / proud / happy* + **about**

**12** **Extension** Are these adjectives positive or negative? Complete the chart.

| angry | ashamed | bored | cheerful |
|-------|---------|-------|----------|
| confused | excited | friendly | grateful |
| happy | impatient | lonely | relaxed |
| scared | selfish | upset | worried |

| Positive | Negative |
|----------|----------|
|          |          |
|          |          |
|          |          |
|          |          |

## PRONUNCIATION  -ed adjectives

**13** Listen to each adjective and choose the correct pronunciation of -ed. 🎧 **2**

| | | /t/ | /d/ | /ɪd/ |
|---|---|---|---|---|
| **1** | annoyed | /t/ | /d/ | /ɪd/ |
| **2** | stressed | /t/ | /d/ | /ɪd/ |
| **3** | relaxed | /t/ | /d/ | /ɪd/ |
| **4** | delighted | /t/ | /d/ | /ɪd/ |
| **5** | bored | /t/ | /d/ | /ɪd/ |
| **6** | excited | /t/ | /d/ | /ɪd/ |
| **7** | scared | /t/ | /d/ | /ɪd/ |

**14** Choose the correct options. Then listen and check your answers. 🎧 **3**

1 Yes, I was terrified.
  **a** Were you scared of him?
  **b** Were you annoyed with him?
  **c** Were you ashamed of him?

2 Yes, he was. He thought she'd had an accident.
  **a** Was he worried about her?
  **b** Was he scared of her?
  **c** Was he bored by her?

3 Yes, she is. The test is worth 50% of her grade.
  **a** Is she annoyed with him?
  **b** Is she disappointed with them?
  **c** Is she stressed about it?

4 Yes, they are. They can't wait!
  **a** Are they confused about it?
  **b** Are they excited about it?
  **c** Are they scared by it?

5 Yes, it helps me sleep.
  **a** Does that make you feel relaxed?
  **b** Does that make you feel stressed?
  **c** Does that make you feel scared?

## LISTENING

**15** Do you have a funny habit? Think of something about yourself that only a close friend or family member might know.

*Soccer player Wayne Rooney turns on a vacuum cleaner to help him fall asleep.*

*Author Stephen King eats a slice of cheesecake before writing.*

*Actress Jennifer Aniston touches the outside of a plane before getting on.*

**16** Listen and choose the correct answers. 🎧 **4**

1 In the show *Tell Me Straight*…
  **a** Charlie talks to celebrities.
  **b** Charlie talks to people who know celebrities well.
  **c** Charlie talks to people who know a lot of celebrities.

2 Why does Sandra Rind eat a carrot?
  **a** Because it makes her feel relaxed.
  **b** Because she's hungry before she goes on stage.
  **c** Because it's good for her voice.

3 Bruce Collins sometimes finds it difficult…
  **a** to count to 100.
  **b** to fall asleep.
  **c** to know the difference between left and right.

4 Which celebrity sang in a car?
  **a** Jamie Cawley.
  **b** Gerri Pennington.
  **c** Ralph Powell.

5 Who told a secret about Gerri Pennington?
  **a** Her driving instructor.
  **b** Her best friend.
  **c** Her boyfriend.

6 Charlie thinks that…
  **a** everyone has a few secrets.
  **b** the celebrities feel very embarrassed.
  **c** Fred is going to tell her a secret.

**17** Listen again and complete the sentences. 🎧 **4**

1 Fred is surprised to hear that a soccer player is _____ of spiders.

2 Ralph Powell was _____ that he passed his test.

3 Sandra Rind feels very _____ before she goes on stage.

4 Eating a carrot helps Sandra to be more _____.

5 If he says the wrong numbers, Bruce Collins feels _____ and he becomes more _____.

6 Gerri Pennington writes *left* and *right* on her hands so that she isn't _____.

7 Charlie is _____ to the celebrities and hopes they aren't too _____.

**18** Think about what you heard about the celebrities and decide who said the things below. There is one name you don't need.

| | | |
|---|---|---|
| Bruce Collins | Gerri Pennington | Jamie Cawley |
| Ralph Powell | Sandra Rind | |

1 "Yes, I've finally done it! No more lessons!"
_____

2 "Sorry, did you mean this side of the street, or the other side?" _____

3 "One hundred, ninety-nine, ninety-eight…"
_____

4 "Camp in the forest? No way! Not with all those insects!"
_____

## GRAMMAR  Subject / object questions

**19** Match the questions (1–6) with the answers (a–f).

1 Who brought the chocolate cake? _____
2 How much does Gary earn? _____
3 Why was Priya so angry? _____
4 Who earns the most? _____
5 Who was angry? _____
6 What did she bring? _____

a Gary does; he earns about $90,000.
b Priya. She was angry because Duane was late.
c Gary earns about $90,000, I think.
d Anna brought it. She made it herself.
e Priya was angry because Duane was late.
f Anna brought a chocolate cake.

**20** Correct the mistakes in the questions. Each question contains one mistake.

1 What TV shows do make you angry?
2 Who you talk to when you are confused?
3 Who does laughs most in your family?
4 Why they feel excited?
5 How many people do think this is wrong?
6 Whose cake does taste the best?

**21** Put the words in the correct order to make questions.

1 look / why / angry / so / Jo / does / ?
_____

2 food / did / eat / how much / they / ?
_____

3 a / has / bike / flat tire / whose / ?
_____

4 what / them / did / Pepé / say / to / ?
_____

5 swimming / go / do / how often / you / ?
_____

6 people / came / how many / the / party / to / ?
_____

**22** Read the answers and complete the questions.

1 **A** How much money _____?
   **B** They collected more than $500.
2 **A** Who _____?
   **B** Lena gave us the flowers.
3 **A** How often _____?
   **B** She cries every once in a while.
4 **A** What _____?
   **B** Work makes me feel stressed.
5 **A** Why _____?
   **B** I listen to music to help me relax.
6 **A** How many _____?
   **B** He invited twenty people.

**23** Write answers that are true for you.

1 What is your favorite type of movie?
_____

2 How often do you go out to eat?
_____

3 How many English classes have you taken?
_____

4 When is your mother's birthday?
_____

5 How many times have you seen your favorite movie?
_____

# 1B Fake It until You Feel It

## VOCABULARY BUILDING  Suffixes

**1** How are nouns formed from these adjectives? Complete the chart.

| confused | depressed | disappointed | embarrassed |
|----------|-----------|--------------|-------------|
| excited | exhausted | friendly | happy |
| lonely | nervous | sad | selfish |

| +ment | +ness | +ion |
|-------|-------|------|
|       |       |      |
|       |       |      |
|       |       |      |
|       |       |      |

**2** Complete each sentence with a noun formed from the adjective in parentheses.

**1** Your _____*happiness*_____ is what's most important. (happy)

**2** Not being picked for the team was a big _____. (disappointed)

**3** There seems to be some _____ about the result. (confused)

**4** Having to wait only added to the _____. (excited)

**5** It's with great _____ that we announce the death of Anna Jackson. (sad)

**6** John has always suffered from _____. (depressed)

**7** She could see the _____ on his face. (embarrassed)

## READING

**3** Read the text. What is the World Happiness Report?

**a** A description of how to make the world happier.
**b** A comparison of levels of happiness in different countries.
**c** A list of the 156 happiest places on Earth.

**4** Look at the words in bold in the text and match them with their definitions.

| benchmark | consistently | corruption | evaluation |
|-----------|--------------|------------|------------|
| imaginary | life expectancy | rank | stark |

**1** in a way that does not change _____
**2** not real _____
**3** a level used as a standard when comparing other things _____
**4** the length of time that a person is likely to live _____
**5** obvious in an unpleasant way _____
**6** to put something into a position on a list according to importance, success, size, etc. _____
**7** dishonest or illegal behavior _____
**8** the act of deciding how good or bad something is _____

**5** Read the statements. Are the sentences true (T), false (F), or is the information not given (NG)?

**1** The World Happiness Report is only read by governments. _____
**2** In the survey, people are asked to decide how happy their lives are. _____
**3** Dystopia is an imaginary country where people are extremely happy. _____
**4** Children are not included in the survey. _____
**5** Some people think that the number of people surveyed is too small. _____
**6** The World Happiness Report doesn't consider economic factors. _____
**7** In Iceland and Denmark, people don't pay for medical treatment. _____
**8** People live longer in Madagascar than in Togo. _____

**6** Match the statements and countries.

| Australia | Denmark | Iceland |
|-----------|---------|---------|
| Madagascar | Switzerland | United States |

**1** Most of its citizens know more than one language. _____

**2** It's ranked 13th in the 2016 World Happiness Report. _____

**3** Higher education is free here. _____
**4** It's an island and one of the world's unhappiest countries. _____

**5** Its citizens live nine years longer than the global average. _____

**6** It usually has pleasant weather. _____

# The World Happiness Report

**5** The World Happiness Report is a survey of happiness in different countries published by the United Nations. First produced in 2012, it **ranks** 156 countries by their happiness levels. The report is attracting increasing interest because many governments are now using happiness data to develop policies that support people more effectively.

In the survey, which is available to the public on the World Happiness Report website, leading experts in fields such as economics, psychology, health, and statistics describe how measurements of happiness can be used to assess the progress of a country. The report reviews the state of happiness in the world today and explains national variations. For example, in 2016, Denmark was the world's happiest country, with the US ranked 13th, and the United Kingdom 23rd. The island country of Madagascar, with a ranking of 148, is among the world's unhappiest nations.

So, how do researchers decide on these rankings? They are, in fact, based on answers to a life **evaluation** question called "The Cantril Ladder." People are asked to think of a ladder, in which the best possible life for them is ranked 10, and the worst 0, and decide where their current life is on this 0 to 10 scale. Their answers are then adjusted based on six other factors: levels of GDP (Gross Domestic Product, the value of goods and services that a country produces in a year), **life expectancy**, generosity, social support, freedom, and **corruption**. The results are compared to those of Dystopia, an **imaginary** country that has the world's least happy people. Dystopia is the lowest

**benchmark** of happiness, so that all other countries will be higher than it in relation to those six factors.

One criticism of the report is that it only examines two to three thousand people per country, but researchers believe this is a large enough sample. They also think the report is helpful because, unlike many other world surveys, it doesn't only look at economic factors.

Why, then, is Denmark the world's happiest country? One thing is its life expectancy of 80 years, when the global average is only 71. It also has free health care and an excellent welfare system, which means that wealth is spread fairly across the population. Another country in the top ten is Australia, with its beaches and **consistently** warm temperatures. Melbourne has even been named the best city in the world to live in, because of low crime levels, good climate, medical care, and public transportation. The country of Iceland came in third, offering its citizens low taxes, free higher education, and free health care. It is also rated as the most peaceful nation on Earth. Switzerland, where the majority of citizens understand French, German, and English, is currently in second place, enjoying healthy public finances, low taxes, an average life expectancy of nearly 83, and beautiful scenery connected by efficient railroads. By **stark** contrast, African countries are among the least happy nations in the world, many affected by civil war and extreme poverty. The country of Togo, ranked in 155th place, has a life expectancy of just 58.

# 1C Do you always...?

## GRAMMAR Talking about the present

**1** Match the rules (1–7) with the sentences (a–g).

1 Use the simple present to talk about things that are generally true. _____
2 Use the present perfect to describe actions that started in the past and continue to the present. _____
3 Use the simple present to describe habits and routines. _____
4 Use the present continuous with *always* to describe actions that happen often and may cause an emotional response in the speaker. _____
5 Use the present continuous to talk about actions happening at or around the present time. _____
6 Use the simple present with stative verbs, e.g., *enjoy*, *agree*, *think*. _____
7 Use the present continuous to talk about changing situations. _____

a We're sending cards less often these days.
b Riku is speaking to another customer at the moment.
c Karen and I have known each other for over 30 years.
d I definitely agree with your decision.
e Niamh is always making silly comments.
f She goes to a karate class on Tuesdays.
g Planets closer to the sun have shorter years than Earth.

**2** Are the verbs in bold correct or incorrect? Correct those that are incorrect.

1 Water **is freezing** at 32 degrees Fahrenheit.
2 The phone **rings**. Can you answer it?
3 If it's not raining, she usually **walks** to work.
4 I'm bored. I **am wanting** to watch TV.
5 A It's 6 o'clock already. We need to go.
  B Sorry, Freya, **I've come.**
6 Koala bears **sleep** for more than twenty hours a day.
7 Ahmed's often confused. He's always **asking** questions.
8 I **feed** the cat while Jade and Lee are on vacation this month.

**3** Choose the correct options to complete the sentences.

1 Chris usually *reads / is reading* before going to sleep.
2 I often *am enjoying / enjoy* a cup of tea at bedtime.
3 *We're shopping / We've shopped* online for two hours.
4 Beth is so angry all the time. *She's always shouting / She shouts.*
5 The sun *doesn't set / isn't setting* in Iceland in June.
6 Some people *think / are thinking* this is a good idea.
7 They *never go / are never going* to bed before midnight.
8 *I laugh / I'm laughing* because he told me a joke.

**4** Put the words in the correct order to make sentences and questions.

1 bakes / Blanca / every / bread / day / .

_____

2 long / how / you / have / truth / known / the / ?

_____

3 Jack / always / to / me / asking / help / him / is / .

_____

4 right / now / feeling / are / how / you / ?

_____

5 the / internet / changing / the / communicate / we / way / is / .

_____

6 moon / the / at / per hour / ten / miles / rotates / .

_____

7 become / recently / life / very / has / difficult / .

_____

8 usually / to / TV / I / watch / relax / .

_____

**5** Complete the conversations using *always* + the present continuous form of the verbs in parentheses.

1 A There's a problem with my car again.
  B No way! _____ . (break down)
2 A Sarah finds it difficult to get up in the morning.
  B I'm not surprised. She _____ to bed late. (go)
3 A Amy was really angry with her parents.
  B I don't blame her. _____ . (interfere)
4 A Kira wants to borrow $20.
  B Typical! _____ for money. (ask)
5 A I can't read the menu without my glasses.
  B Where are they? _____ to bring them. (forget)
6 A It's going to be another long night at the office.
  B Really? _____ late. (work)
7 A Li has a stomach bug and can't come out tonight.
  B Poor Li! _____ sick. (feel)
8 A Dean is the worst roommate. He never helps with the cleaning.
  B Maybe you should move. _____ about him. (complain)

**6** Complete the text with the simple present, present continuous, or present perfect form of the verb in parentheses.

Kenji and I **(1)** _____ (share) an apartment for about a year. He **(2)** _____ (enjoy) exercise and every morning he **(3)** _____ (run) around the park. He **(4)** _____ (always ask) me to go with him, but I really **(5)** _____ (not like) getting up early, so sometimes I **(6)** _____ (swim) in the local pool after work. In the evenings, I usually just **(7)** _____ (watch) TV, but Kenji is the sort of person who **(8)** _____ (read) a book or **(9)** _____ (do) a crossword puzzle. Right now, he **(10)** _____ (cook) a meal for the two of us and **(11)** _____ (listen) to the radio. He **(12)** _____ (find) it very difficult to relax, so he often **(13)** _____ (clean) the kitchen after dinner, too. That's great for me, though, since I **(14)** _____ (always be) very lazy.

**7** Choose the correct options. Then listen and check your answers. 🎧 **6**

**1** Do you know Jason?
  **a** Yes, we're knowing him for a couple of years.
  **b** Yes, we've known him for a couple of years.

**2** Are you ready yet?
  **a** Almost, I just come.
  **b** Almost, I'm coming now.

**3** Is Simon angry about it?
  **a** No, he agrees with my decision.
  **b** No, he's agreeing with my decision.

**4** What does she do on the weekends?
  **a** She's usually gone shopping.
  **b** She usually goes shopping.

**5** Is Alex with you?
  **a** No, he's playing tennis with a friend.
  **b** No, he plays tennis with a friend.

**6** Does Alice have a part-time job?
  **a** Yes, she works in a café.
  **b** Yes, she's worked in a café.

**7** Is Erica still living in Spain?
  **a** No, she lives in Portugal now.
  **b** No, she's lived in Portugal now.

**8** When do you go to the gym?
  **a** I go before work.
  **b** I am going before work.

# 1D This app knows how you feel—from the look on your face.

# TEDTALKS

## AUTHENTIC LISTENING SKILLS

**1** Listen to Part 1 of the TED Talk and underline the words that are stressed. 🎧 **7**

> At Cambridge, thousands of miles away from home, I realized I was spending more hours with my laptop than I did with any other human.

**2** Listen again and complete the excerpt with the words you hear. Listen and check—are these content words stressed? 🎧 **8**

> I was _____, I was _____, and on some days I was actually _____, but all I had to communicate these _____ was this.

## WATCH ▶

**3** Look at the words and choose the correct emoji.

1 confused  ☺ ☹ ☺
2 angry  ☺ ☺ ☹
3 embarrassed  ☺ ☹ ☺
4 scared  ☹ ☺ ☺
5 delighted  ☺ ☹ ☺

**4** Choose the correct options to complete the sentences.

1 Rana says that our emotions influence…
   a what we learn.
   c everything about our
   b how we shop.    lives.

2 Fifteen years ago, Rana…
   a got married.
   c became a computer
   b went to live in England.    scientist.

3 Rana was frustrated because…
   a her laptop couldn't understand her feelings.
   b she spent a lot of time alone.
   c she felt homesick.

4 Action unit 12 is…
   a a facial muscle.   b a smile.   c an emotion.

5 A smirk and a smile…
   a look the same, but mean different things.
   b look different, but mean similar things.
   c look similar, but mean different things.

6 A computer learns to recognize expressions by…
   a looking at thousands of pictures.
   b learning about the characteristics of a face.
   c storing information about emotions.

**5** Match the paraphrases in bold with the words from Part 3 of the TED Talk. Then watch and check your answers.

| | |
|---|---|
| down the line | especially close to my heart |
| fighting a losing battle | golden opportunity |
| tracked your mood | visually impaired |
| want to share | |

Where is this data used today? I **would like to tell you about (1)** _____ some examples that are **very important to me (2)** _____.
Emotion-enabled wearable glasses can help individuals who are **not able to see very well**. **(3)** _____ read the faces of others…

What if your wristwatch **knew how you were feeling (4)** _____, or your car sensed that you're tired, or perhaps your fridge knows that you're stressed…

I think in five years **from now (5)** _____, all our devices are going to have an emotion chip…

As more and more of our lives become digital, we are **failing when (6)** _____ trying to curb our usage of devices in order to reclaim our emotions.

And by humanizing technology, we have this **important chance (7)** _____ to reimagine how we connect with machines…

## VOCABULARY IN CONTEXT

**6** Complete the sentences with these words.

| | | |
|---|---|---|
| characteristics | curiosity | gender |
| homesick | joy | wrinkles |

1 There are several _____ of a leader.
2 There were tears of _____ in her eyes as she held her grandson for the first time.
3 Talking to my parents on the phone makes me feel a little _____ .
4 Despite his age, he was very good-looking, with just a few _____ around his eyes.
5 A Why do you want to know?
   B Oh, just for my own _____ .
6 The competition is open to everyone, regardless of age or _____ .

# 1E The Feel-Good Factor

## SPEAKING

**1** Read and complete the conversation. Then listen and check your answers. 🎧 **9**

**Tom** I just saw *Scarlet's Destiny*.

**Paul** Oh, I haven't heard of that. **(1)** _____ of movie is it?

**Tom** It's a sci-fi movie. It has great special effects.

**Paul (2)** _____ come out?

**Tom** It was released about a week ago, I think.

**Paul (3)** _____ in it? Any well-known actors?

**Tom** Well, there's Jake Pomfroy, and Sara Linnett—she's really beautiful…

**Paul** I'm not sure I know who that is.
**(4)** _____ she been in?

**Tom** She was in that movie with Matt Grieve about Mars.

**Paul** Oh, yes, I remember the one.
So, **(5)** _____?

**Tom** It's about a woman who gets more intelligent every time she sleeps.

**Paul** Sounds interesting. **(6)** _____ set?

**Tom** In London, in 2070. I really loved the plot—a little weird, but fascinating.

**Paul** Oh, OK. So, **(7)** _____ it?

**Tom** Yeah, I would. There were some pretty good scenes in it and the ending was amazing.

**Paul** I'll give it a try!

**2** Listen to the questions in Activity 1 and underline the words that are stressed. Then listen again and practice. 🎧 **10**

**3** Put the words in the correct order to make questions. Then match the questions with the answers (a–g).

**1** did / come / when / out / it / ? ___

_____

**2** it / directed / who / ? ___

_____

**3** it / so / about / what's / ? ___

_____

**4** like / the / what's / acting / ? ___

_____

**5** recommend / would / it / you / ? ___

**6** set / it / where's / ? ___

_____

**7** kind / what / movie / it / of / is / ? ___

_____

**a** An action adventure.
**b** In New York.
**c** Some characters aren't well acted.
**d** It's about a battle to save the Earth.
**e** I'm not sure—it's not the best movie I've seen recently.
**f** Jack Peterson.
**g** Last month.

**4** Choose three of these movie genres and give your own answers to the questions in Activity 3 on a separate sheet of paper.

_____

| comedy | drama | horror | musical | sci-fi | thriller |

**5** Read the review and listen to the conversation that follows it. Then answer the question below. 🎧 **11**

Can sequels ever be a good thing? Although the quality of the second film in this superhero movie franchise is good, it's like a repeat of something that was magical the first time, but isn't quite as great anymore. *Cosmic Cops 2* has a fantastic plot and special effects, great characters, and excellent performances, but it just doesn't have the same impact as the first movie.

While they are protecting space and delivering vital top-secret supplies to a research facility, the team meets a space thief who steals the supplies and flies across the galaxy. They then chase after him. Add to this a subplot about an older officer returning to duty, and an accident that leaves the team stuck on an alien planet, and this is classic science-fiction.

Although we've seen it all before, the special effects, characters, and acting are all very high quality. The whole audience loved the movie's excitement and wonderful soundtrack.

**Question:** The woman expresses her opinion of the movie, *Cosmic Cops 2*. State her opinion and explain the reasons she gives for having that opinion.

# WRITING A review

**6** Put the parts of the movie review in the correct order.

_____ *The Pursuit of Happyness* is a **moving** film. Based on the real-life experiences of Chris Gardner, the movie explores the bond between a father and son who find themselves homeless. The two move from place to place, even spending one night in a subway bathroom. But despite such extreme hardships, Gardner continues to pursue his dream, eventually securing the job he really wants at a successful investment company.

_____ This is not a **feel-good** movie, but a real **tearjerker**, a touching portrayal of a true story. It might not be **action-packed** or make you smile, but it's a movie you won't quickly forget—definitely one to watch. Rating ****

_____ *The Pursuit of Happyness*

_____ However, though the story is very moving, it's also a bit depressing. We see Gardner face one problem after another in his struggle for financial stability. One thing I found myself wanting to know more about was what happened in the later part of Gardner's life. Although we find out he got the job, we never get to see the joy and success that come from his earlier struggles.

_____ In my opinion, it's the emotional connection between the two stars, Smith and his real-life son Jaden, that is the main strength of this movie. Jaden gives a brilliant performance as a child whose life and economic background are so very different from his own. The film is also a **thought-provoking** portrayal of homelessness and the problems faced by many in our society every day.

_____ 2006, Drama / **Biography**, 117 minutes Starring Will Smith, Jaden Smith, Thandie Newton

**7** Read the review again. Does the writer like the movie?

**8** Match the parts of the movie review in Activity 6 with these headings.

| | |
|---|---|
| a recommendation | a description of the plot |
| what the writer didn't like | title |
| what the writer liked | basic information |

1 _____     4 _____

2 _____     5 _____

3 _____     6 _____

**9** Complete the definitions with the words in bold in the review.

1 A _____ is a sad movie or story that makes you want to cry.

2 A _____ movie makes you feel happy.

3 A _____ is a book or movie about someone's life.

4 If something is _____, it makes you think a lot about a particular subject.

5 If a movie is _____, it is full of exciting events.

6 If a film is _____, it makes you feel emotional.

**10** Rewrite the sentences to add emphasis.

1 I really loved the ending.
The thing that _____
_____

2 I found the special effects a bit disappointing.
What _____
_____

3 I didn't like the soundtrack.
One thing that _____
_____

4 The portrayal of the prison wasn't very realistic.
It was _____
_____

5 I enjoyed the song and dance scenes the most.
What _____
_____

**11** Write a review of the last movie you saw. Include at least one sentence that starts with *One thing I didn't like / really loved…* Answer these questions:

- What type of movie is it?
- What's it about?
- Where / When is it set?
- Who's in it?
- What was good / bad?
- Would you recommend it?

| Tip box |
|---|
| • Include introductory sentences that give basic information about the movie. |
| • Provide a short description of the plot. |
| • Say the good and bad things about the movie. |
| • Give your opinion and emotional response to the movie. |
| • Include a sentence that tells the reader to watch it (or not). |

# Review

## ① Read the definitions and complete the words.

**1** not able to understand
c __ __ __ __ __ __ d

**2** frightened
s __ __ __ d

**3** feeling happy and calm
r __ __ __ __ __ d

**4** unhappy because you are not with other people
l __ __ __ __ y

**5** angry or impatient
a __ __ __ __ __ d

**6** worried and unable to relax
s __ __ __ __ __ __ d

**7** ashamed or shy
e __ __ __ __ __ __ __ __ __ d

**8** very happy
d __ __ __ __ __ __ d

## ② Choose the correct options to complete the text.

Where **(1)** *do you eat / are you eating* lunch? I usually
**(2)** *have gone / go* to the café on the main plaza. **(3)** *I try /
I've tried* the university cafeteria, but the food **(4)** *doesn't
taste / isn't tasting* as good. I **(5)** *have preferred / prefer* to eat
sandwiches at lunchtime, and the café **(6)** *is having /
has* much more choice. It also **(7)** *sells / has sold* really
delicious salads. However, it's much more expensive than
making them yourself, so this semester **(8)** *I've started /
I start* to bring my own food sometimes. **(9)** *I'm saving /
I have saved* for a trip to Brazil next summer, so **(10)** *I decide /
I've decided* to spend less.

## ③ Use the prompts to write questions in the simple past.

**1** What / they / decide / do?

_____

**2** How often / you / go / gym?

_____

**3** Whose / daughter / play / the piano?

_____

**4** How many / friends / she / invite?

_____

**5** What / he / ask / Elena?

_____

**6** What / make / you / feel / embarrassed?

_____

**7** How many / students / pass / test?

_____

## ④ Complete the email with these words.

| bored | confused | delighted | embarrassed |
|-------|----------|-----------|-------------|
| excited | interested | lonely | nervous |
| relaxed | worried | | |

Hi Amina,

Just thought I'd send you a quick message to tell you that I
got the job at the tourist office! I'm absolutely
**(1)** _____! I've been really
**(2)** _____ where I'm currently working
because there's not enough to do, and it also gets very
**(3)** _____ with no one to talk to all day.
I felt very **(4)** _____ when I went
into the interview, and I was **(5)** _____
that I wouldn't do my best, but the manager was very kind.
After a few minutes, I began to feel more
**(6)** _____ . He seemed really
**(7)** _____ in my past experience
and although I got a bit **(8)** _____ about
one of the questions, I generally gave good answers.
The only bad thing was that I completely forgot his
name when we were saying goodbye. I felt so
**(9)** _____! Anyway, never mind, it's all good
and I start next month, so I'm feeling very
**(10)** _____ about it!
Hope to see you soon,
Mei

## ⑤ Choose the correct options. Then listen and check your answers. 🎧 12

**1** What did he win in the competition?
  **a** He won a television. Lucky man!
  **b** Rami won. Lucky man!

**2** Who has the largest family?
  **a** Paul does. He has four brothers and two sisters.
  **b** Paul has four brothers and two sisters.

**3** What does she eat for lunch?
  **a** Amy usually eats a sandwich.
  **b** Amy does. She usually eats a sandwich.

**4** How much did they collect?
  **a** The teachers did. They were so generous.
  **b** Over $5,000. They were so generous.

## ⑥ Correct the sentences. Use the simple present, present continuous, or present perfect.

**1** He'll only be a minute—he just puts his coat on.

**2** My cellphone alarm rings. I'll turn it off.

**3** Carlos and Niko live in York since 2001.

**4** I've usually run in the park on Sundays.

**5** If water is freezing, it is turning to ice.

**6** We're knowing Kevin for about two years.

# 2 Enjoy the Ride

## 2A Getting from A to B

### VOCABULARY Travel

**1 Review** Choose the correct options to complete the sentences.

1 The *airport / fly* was crowded, and the line for security was really long.
2 I always enjoy *visiting / getting to* my family in Mexico during the summer.
3 Some *visits / tourists* are respectful travelers, and some are not.
4 The *plane / bus* station is in the city center—about 1,500 feet from the train station.
5 I prefer to stay in *hotels / stations* when I travel to new countries.
6 She *drives / flies* too fast, so she sometimes gets speeding tickets.
7 He's an experienced *travel / traveler*—he's been to over twenty countries.
8 I want to visit Jamaica for my next *vacation / visit*, but my sister wants to go to Brazil.

**2 Review** Read the clues and complete the words about travel. The first letter is given for you.

1 I'm afraid of flying, so I prefer to travel on this.
   t __ __ __ __
2 Planes arrive and depart from this place.
   a __ __ __ __ __ __
3 This person visits new places and goes sightseeing.
   t __ __ __ __ __ __
4 Buses arrive and depart from this place.
   s __ __ __ __ __ __
5 Many people stay here at night when they are traveling.
   h __ __ __ __
6 If you're going to take a car on vacation, you'll need to do this.
   d __ __ __ __
7 This is a digital file or printed piece of paper that you pay for and use to travel.
   t __ __ __ __ __
8 If it's too far to walk, I usually take one of these.
   t __ __ __

**3 Review** Listen to the sentences. Choose the correct options. 🎧 **13**

1 *train / plane*
2 *visitors / visits*
3 *traveler / traveling to*
4 *fly / drive*
5 *hotel / station*
6 *train / bus*

**4** Unscramble the letters to make words about travel.

1 t m c o u m e    c __ __ __ __ __ __ __
2 t u o r e    __ __ u __ __
3 e g o y v a    __ __ __ __ g __
4 c s u e i r    __ r __ __ __ __ __
5 o i t e e d i x p n
   __ x __ __ d __ __ __ __ n
6 d r e i    __ __ __ e
7 p c b a k c a i g n k
   __ __ c __ __ __ __ k __ __ g
8 g f i h l t    __ __ __ __ h __

**5** Complete the sentences with the correct forms of the words in Activity 4.

1 The ship made the _____ from London to New York in six days.
2 The car _____ through the jungle was long and uncomfortable.
3 My friends are going _____ this summer.
4 We really enjoyed the _____. It actually left on time!
5 I took a different _____ home from the restaurant and got lost.
6 I'd like to take a _____, but I often get seasick.
7 My dad usually _____ to work. The trip takes over an hour.
8 She went on an _____ to Kenya to study lions.

**6** Match these verbs with the nouns and phrases they collocate with.

**1** get to        **a** the train
**2** go for        **b** São Paulo
**3** catch        **c** from my house to school
**4** get           **d** a long ride in the car
**5** get to know   **e** the restaurant

**7** Complete the sentences with the correct forms of these words and phrases.

| get (x2) | get off (x2) | get to (x2) | get to know (x2) |
| --- | --- | --- | --- |

**1** I _____ the bus just in time—I almost missed my stop!
**2** I love _____ new cities and new people.
**3** What time should we _____ the airport before our flight?
**4** I _____ school late because my train was delayed.
**5** I'm always worried about _____ lost, so I carry my phone everywhere.
**6** _____ the road! There's a car coming!
**7** She _____ her way around by talking to the locals.
**8** How do I _____ from the port to the center of town?

**8** Complete the sentences with these words. There are two words you don't need.

| cruise | destination | excursion | expedition |
| --- | --- | --- | --- |
| flight | lift | ride | route |

**1** I'm planning to take a _____ to the Caribbean this summer if I save enough money.
**2** On Saturday, we're going on an _____ to a chocolate factory.
**3** We need to take another _____ to Mexico City. Ours has been canceled.
**4** Would you like to go for a bike _____ this weekend? We could go to Rock Creek Park.
**5** According to José, they should reach their _____ by about 5 pm tomorrow.
**6** We're going on an _____ into the Amazon for six weeks—we can't wait!

**9** **Extension** Match the words with a similar meaning.

**1** arrive       **a** leave
**2** depart      **b** visitor
**3** tourist      **c** journey
**4** excursion   **d** land
**5** route        **e** way
**6** voyage     **f** outing

**10** **Extension** Choose the correct options to complete the sentences.

**1** Hurry! The plane is about to *depart / arrive*, and the gate is a long *sight / way* from here!
**2** We're planning to *leave / stay* our hotel at noon and do some *sights / sightseeing* until dinnertime.
**3** It's time to *depart / board* the train. It's on platform 5.
**4** I don't *see / know* Chicago very well. I've lived here for a year, and I still get lost.
**5** Who are you going to *stay / keep* with while you're in Seoul?
**6** I'll meet you at the airport. What time does your plane *land / board*?

## LISTENING

**11** Match the two words of the compound nouns. Listen and check your answers. Then practice saying the words. 🎧 **14**

1 sky      **a** park
2 public      **b** tracks
3 building      **c** scraper
4 shopping      **d** top
5 railroad      **e** sites
6 amusement      **f** light
7 traffic      **g** transportation
8 roof      **h** mall

**12** Listen and choose the correct answers to the questions. 🎧 **15**

1 Do the man and the woman know each other?
   **a** Yes.
   **b** No.
   **c** It's not clear.

2 Why does the woman need to ask the man for directions?
   **a** She's lost her map of the city.
   **b** She doesn't know where she is.
   **c** She doesn't have her phone with her.

3 Does the man know where the Stratton Building is?
   **a** Yes, he gives the woman exact directions.
   **b** More or less, but he decides to check on his phone.
   **c** No, he has no idea. He needs to find out on his phone.

4 What word does the woman use meaning *annoy*?
   **a** bother
   **b** upset
   **c** irritate

5 How does the man think the woman should get there?
   **a** take the subway
   **b** walk
   **c** take a taxi

6 What should the woman do when she gets to Central Boulevard?
   **a** go straight
   **b** take a right
   **c** turn left

7 What does the woman need to walk through before she gets to the building?
   **a** an intersection
   **b** a park
   **c** a block

8 What does the man tell her that she can't miss?
   **a** the Stratton Building
   **b** lunch in the park
   **c** Central Boulevard

**13** Listen to the lecture. The speaker quotes the poet T. S. Eliot. What do you think Eliot meant? 🎧 **16**

   **a** Humans should focus more on living than on exploration.
   **b** Exploration gives us a better understanding of ourselves and our world.
   **c** We can learn the most valuable lessons from the very first explorers.
   **d** Exploration doesn't really answer any of our important questions.

**14** Listen again and choose the correct answers to the questions. 🎧 **16**

1 What does the speaker mean by "the final frontier"?
   **a** human exploration
   **b** the end of exploration
   **c** unexplored areas

2 What does she describe as "countless"?
   **a** planets
   **b** equipment
   **c** humans

3 Does the speaker agree that space is relatively unexplored?
   **a** No, she doesn't.
   **b** Yes, she does.
   **c** She isn't really sure.

4 What phrase does she use to describe our oceans?
   **a** a lot closer to home
   **b** the only final frontier
   **c** less than ten percent

5 According to the speaker, how much of the Earth is covered by oceans?
   **a** around 99%
   **b** less than 10%
   **c** more than 70%

6 How many people does the speaker say have traveled to the deepest parts of the oceans?
   **a** many
   **b** only a few
   **c** none

7 According to the speaker, what percentage of the living space on our planet is on land?
   **a** 10%
   **b** 70%
   **c** 1%

8 What does she say has yet to be discovered?
   **a** many kinds of sea life
   **b** all the oceans of the world
   **c** the deepest ocean

## GRAMMAR Adjectives ending in -ed and -ing

**15** Complete the definitions with these words.

| annoyed | bored | confusing | depressing |
|---|---|---|---|
| embarrassed | interesting | surprising | |

**1** _____ = keeping your attention because it is unusual or exciting

**2** _____ = not really interested in anything

**3** _____ = feeling shy or ashamed

**4** _____ = unexpected

**5** _____ = difficult to understand

**6** _____ = a little angry about something

**7** _____ = making you feel unhappy and disappointed

**16** Choose the correct participial adjectives to complete the sentences.

**1** The Great Pyramid of Giza was *amazing / amazed*. We weren't *disappointing / disappointed* when we finally visited it.

**2** It's *surprising / surprised* that the ancient city of Petra was built over 2,000 years ago, but was unknown to the West until 1812.

**3** We were all *confusing / confused* to hear the tour guide say that Venice is built on 118 islands.

**4** Pompeii was an ancient Roman city that was buried in ash after the *terrified / terrifying* eruption of Mount Vesuvius.

**5** No one could sleep last night because we were so *excited / exciting* about seeing the Taj Mahal.

**6** We spent a *relaxing / relaxed* afternoon on the banks of the Seine river.

**17** Complete the phrases with the correct participial adjectives formed from the verbs in parentheses.

**1** that _____ (depress) movie

**2** those _____ (exhaust) athletes

**3** a _____ (bore) flight that lasted six hours

**4** _____ (confuse) tourists who don't speak the language

**5** a _____ (frighten) accident involving a large truck

**6** _____ (annoy) travelers whose bags were lost

**7** an _____ (amaze) cruise in the Caribbean

**8** _____ (disappoint) passengers wanting to get home

**18** Choose the correct options to complete the text.

### Surprised students, surprising day

One day last week, teachers at Funston School told their **(1)** *bored / boring* students to go to the school gym for a meeting. The **(2)** *unexciting / unexcited* students thought that the **(3)** *boring / bored* prinicpal would give out awards for good grades as he did every month. But this time they were wrong. Instead, one hundred **(4)** *confuse / confused* students received a gift—new bikes!

The teachers and students were **(5)** *surprised / surprise* to learn that more than 2,000 generous football players from 80 high schools in Chicago each donated $1 to buy the bikes for the **(6)** *amazed / amazing* pupils at Funston School. It was all part of National Random Acts of Kindness Day.

The students thought it was **(7)** *amazing / amazed* that the players had given them such a great and completely **(8)** *unexpecting / unexpected* gift. Small acts of kindness—giving $1—can add up to a big surprise!

**19** Complete the article about Japanese customs with the correct forms of these words.

| confuse | embarrass | frighten | insult |
|---|---|---|---|
| relax | terrify | worry | |

Traveling to Japan might seem **(1)** _____ if you're not familiar with the customs before you go. But remember this list, and you can remain **(2)** _____ and enjoy your time in the country. Bowing is a way of showing respect. Don't be **(3)** _____ to bow when you meet people. It may sound **(4)** _____, but adding the suffix -*san* to someone's name is another way to show that you respect them. Making noise when you eat noodles shouldn't be **(5)** _____. Slurping shows that you are enjoying your meal. There's no need to leave a tip in a restaurant—in fact, it's kind of **(6)** _____ if you do! Be sure to take off your shoes at the entrance to a restaurant. Don't be **(7)** _____; no one will take them.

# 2B Urban Explorers

## VOCABULARY BUILDING Compound nouns

**1** Complete the sentences by making compound nouns with these words. There are two words you don't need.

| | | | | |
|---|---|---|---|---|
| back | center | horseback | line | park |
| public | sight | sky | tour | view |

**1** I'm going _____ packing with a couple of friends this summer.

**2** Using _____ transportation is much better for the environment than driving a car.

**3** The Burj Khalifa, in Dubai, is the tallest _____ scraper in the world.

**4** We did a walking _____ of Toronto. It was fascinating learning about the history of the city.

**5** Wouldn't it be amazing to go _____ riding on the beach?

**6** Passengers can relax by the pool after a full day of _____ seeing.

**7** There was a _____ point from the top of the castle. The scenery was breathtaking.

**8** Antonia and Rami went on an incredible zip-_____ tour of the forest canopy in Costa Rica.

## READING

**2** Read the article. Match the information (a–e) with the paragraphs (1–5).

**a** why sustainable tourism matters _____

**b** a positive, alternative form of tourism _____

**c** global tourism facts and statistics _____

**d** a model of sustainable tourism _____

**e** higher education and geotourism _____

**3** Read the text again and choose the correct options.

**1** How many people around the world does the tourist industry provide work for?
**a** 1.2 billion
**b** 300 million
**c** 1.5 trillion
**d** 1 in 11

**2** How much money does global tourism generate every year?
**a** $7 trillion
**b** $1.2 billion
**c** $1.8 billion
**d** $300 million

**3** What is the focus of sustainable tourism?
**a** developing roads, visitor centers, and hotels
**b** using natural and cultural resources
**c** changing a place so that tourists are more likely to visit
**d** protecting a place and its inhabitants

**4** Why is the Midlands Meander a good example of ecotourism?
**a** It appeals to people who aren't really interested in change.
**b** It includes preservation and educational programs.
**c** Visitors can go horseback riding among cattle or ride zip-lines through the forest.
**d** It attracts people who are interested in the arts and crafts of the region.

**5** Why is ecotourism important?
**a** Because you can now study for a degree in sustainable tourism at the University of Missouri.
**b** Because The UN General Assembly declared 2017 to be the International Year of Sustainable Tourism for Development.
**c** Because it helps develop cultural awareness and benefits local residents by using local workers, services, and products.
**d** Because students of ecotourism learn about community planning and environmental education.

**4** Read the article again. Are the sentences true (T) or false (F)?

**1** Global tourism generates $7 billion of global revenue annually. _____

**2** Ecotourists are interested in changing the places they visit. _____

**3** The Midlands Meander is a good example of traditional tourism. _____

**4** A degree in sustainable tourism includes classes on earth science and global studies. _____

**5** The United Nations believes that tourism helps break down barriers between people. _____

**6** More than 1.8 trillion people will travel to new places in 2030. _____

# Tourism That Helps

1  🎧 **17**  Would you like to go backpacking in Nepal? How about taking a cruise to Antarctica? Almost everyone loves to travel. In fact, the business of travel and tourism is considered the biggest industry in the world today. In terms of employment, the tourist industry currently provides work for almost 300 million people around the world—that's one in eleven jobs on the planet! In 2015, global tourism accounted for 1.2 billion international arrivals and billions of additional domestic visits. Overall, global tourism generates about $7 trillion of global revenue annually.

2  Over time, traditional tourism has had a significant impact on the planet. Successful tourism often requires the development of infrastructure, such as usable roads, visitor centers, and hotels. Such development, in turn, affects the natural and cultural resources of the destination visited. Fortunately, sustainable tourism, or *ecotourism*, is an alternative form of tourism that emphasizes the protection of a place and its inhabitants. Also known as *geotourism*, this exciting form of travel appeals to people who prefer to see the places they visit as they are, and aren't really interested in changing them.

3  The Midlands Meander, in KwaZulu-Natal, South Africa, is a good example of sustainable tourism. The organization began as part of a tourism route that attracted people interested in the arts and crafts of the region. Its mission has expanded to include educational programs and farm preservation. Visitors can ride zip-lines through the canopy of the Karkloof Forest, or go horseback riding among Nguni cattle, wildebeests, zebras, and buffalo, and know that they're supporting programs that help maintain the local farming culture and enrich the lives of the area's schoolchildren.

4  Sustainable tourism has become significant enough that you can now study for a university degree in it! The University of Missouri, in the United States, offers an undergraduate* degree in geotourism that includes courses in community planning, earth science, environmental education, geography, and global studies. Students in the program might study weather and climate, the economic aspects of tourism, or conservation issues and problems that occur in response to human use of the natural environment.

5  The United Nations General Assembly declared 2017 to be the International Year of Sustainable Tourism for Development. Why is sustainable tourism so important? As the UN states, tourism breaks down barriers between visitors and hosts. Sustainable tourism promotes cultural diversity and awareness, in some cases actually helping to revive* traditional activities and local customs. When done responsibly, ecotourism benefits local residents by using the local workforce, services, and products of the places being visited. Most importantly, because an estimated 1.8 billion international tourists will be visiting places across the globe in 2030, responsible, sustainable tourism is critical for the health of the planet and of the many wonderful and fascinating places people will travel to.

**undergraduate** *a college student who has not yet completed a degree*
**revive** *bring back*

# 2C Experiences

## GRAMMAR Narrative forms

**1** Listen and complete the sentences. 🎧 18

1  She _____ soccer practice _____.
2  He _____ on the weekends.
3  They _____ the dog _____ a loud crash.
4  I _____ my dad _____ I _____ in Tokyo.
5  Cars _____ as safe as they are today.
6  We _____ breakfast at the hotel because _____ too late.
7  _____ my email, Carol _____ her sister.

**2** Complete the chart with the correct forms of the verbs.

| Infinitive | Simple Past | Past Continuous | Past Perfect |
|---|---|---|---|
| go | | | |
| | ran | was/were running | |
| talk | | | |
| sit | | | had sat |
| | | was/were taking | |
| fly | | | |
| | | was/were catching | |

**3** Underline the past continuous verbs.

One day last week, I was reading a book and listening to the radio. I was enjoying some great classical music when suddenly, I heard an announcement. There was a huge thunderstorm coming our way! I hurried to close the windows, and called my sister Tami, who was riding her bike to volleyball practice. I told her about the storm, and she asked if our dad was driving home from work and could pick her up. So, I quickly called him to see if he could find Tami before the storm came. He'd left work already and was on his way home, so he said he'd pick her up in about five minutes. Once Tami was in the car with her bike in the back and they were driving home together, the storm hit. There was a lot of rain, thunder, and lightning—I was so glad they were safely on their way home.

**4** Underline the past perfect verbs.

When Omar was in high school, he studied math, physics, chemistry, and biology. In his last year, he got an opportunity to take a class at a local college. He was studying all the time, taking tests for his regular classes and at the college! Omar had always enjoyed biology and chemistry in school and wanted to learn more about biochemistry. He'd talked to some of his friends who had done courses at the college while they were still at school, and they all said that they'd learned a lot and had enjoyed it. Omar had been a little worried that his schedule might be too full, but he didn't really mind because he loved the college classes—they were so interesting and the professors were amazing. Omar especially loved being able to use the college library, and did all his homework there. He'd told so many of his friends about his great experience that they all wanted to take classes at the college, too.

**5** Choose the correct options to complete the questions and answers.

1  **A** What did you read when you were at the beach last summer?
   **B** I *read / had read* a book by Barbara Kingsolver.
2  **A** When did you listen to the latest podcast?
   **B** I listened to it while I *was walking / had walked* to school.
3  **A** How much money did he have when he went into town?
   **B** He *was having / had* $100.
4  **A** Did you *use / used* to see your grandparents a lot?
   **B** Yes, we *saw / used to saw* them every summer.
5  **A** Does Pete have a boat?
   **B** He *used to have / use to have* one, but then he *had sold / sold* it.
6  **A** *Were you trying / Had you tried* pineapple pizza before we went to Pizza Palace last night?
   **B** No, I *hadn't tried / wasn't trying* it before.
7  **A** How many times did you *take / taken* the test?
   **B** I *took / was taking* it twice before I finally passed.
8  **A** Did you like living in Los Angeles?
   **B** It was great! I *used to walk / use to walk* along the beach every day.

**6** Complete the second sentence so that it means the opposite of the first.

**1** When we went to Milan, we ate breakfast at the hotel every day.
When we went to Milan, _____ every day.

**2** My classmates were taking the test when I got to class.
My classmates _____ when I got to class.

**3** She made a lot of new friends when she studied in Colombia.
_____ when she studied in Colombia.

**4** I was looking for a book by Neil Gaiman.
_____ by Neil Gaiman.

**5** I'd eaten my lunch by the time Hiro arrived.
_____ by the time Hiro arrived.

**6** They were working in the garden when their neighbor came to say hello.
_____ when their neighbor came to say hello.

**7** I used to work at a bank.
_____

**8** Renting an apartment in the city used to be so expensive.
_____

**7** Choose the option (a or b) that is closest in meaning to the original sentence.

**1** Tennis practice had already started when Aliyah arrived.
**a** Tennis practice started. Then Aliyah got to tennis practice.
**b** Aliyah got to tennis practice. Then tennis practice started.

**2** Before I went to the movie theater, I dropped my little brother off at home.
**a** I dropped my little brother off at home and then I went to the movie theater.
**b** I went to the movie theater and then dropped my little brother off at home.

**3** Ming's favorite subject used to be geography.
**a** Today, Ming's favorite subject is geography.
**b** Today, Ming's favorite subject isn't geography.

**4** As they were walking up to the house, Hyun answered his phone.
**a** They walked up to the house. Then Hyun answered his phone.
**b** Hyun answered his phone at the same time as they were walking up to the house.

**5** After he went camping, he cleaned the tent.
**a** First he cleaned the tent. Then he went camping.
**b** First he went camping and then he cleaned the tent.

**6** She wasn't studying while she was at the library.
**a** At the library, she was doing something other than studying.
**b** She didn't use to study at the library.

**7** It started raining while we were having a picnic.
**a** We had finished our picnic before it started to rain.
**b** We didn't finish our picnic before it started to rain.

**8** Read and listen to the questions. Choose the correct answers. 🎧 **19**

**1** Had you studied another language before you took the English class?
**a** Yes, I'd studied Japanese.
**b** Yes, I'd studying French.

**2** Did Sally use to work at the hospital?
**a** No, she didn't use to work there.
**b** Yes, she use to working there on Mondays and Wednesdays.

**3** Did you like the play you went to see with Alicia?
**a** No, I was hating it!
**b** No, I hated it!

**4** Did you go to the gym while you were on vacation?
**a** Yes, I went every day except Tuesday.
**b** Yes, I had gone every day except Tuesday.

**5** Did Ms. Liston use to be a chemist?
**a** Yes, she used to work in a laboratory.
**b** Yes, she was worked in a laboratory.

**6** Had you told your parents about your grades before they saw the teacher?
**a** Yes, I had tell them last week.
**b** Yes, I'd told them on Thursday.

**7** Had you seen the Himalayas before we went there yesterday?
**a** Yes, I have seen them last year when I was in Nepal.
**b** Yes, I saw them last year when I was in Nepal.

## PRONUNCIATION  *Used to*

**9** Listen to the sentences and choose the pronunciation that you hear. 🎧 **20**

**1** /juzd/    /juzt/
**2** /juzd/    /juzt/
**3** /juzd/    /juzt/
**4** /juzd/    /juzt/
**5** /juzd/    /juzt/
**6** /juzd/    /juzt/

# 2D Happy Maps

# TEDTALKS

## AUTHENTIC LISTENING SKILLS

**1** Listen to the TED Talk excerpts. Choose the correct option to complete the sentences. 🎧 **21**

**1** I just remember a feeling of surprise; surprise at finding a street with no *cars / cause*.

**2** However, the app also assumes there are only a handful of directions to the *station / destination*.

**3** The result of that research has been the creation of new maps—maps where you *don't only find / don't find* the shortest path, the blue one, but also the most enjoyable path, the red one.

**4** Players are shown *pairs of urban scenes / persons on the scenes*, and they're asked to choose which one is more beautiful, quiet, and happy.

**5** Based on thousands of *user votes / usable votes*, then we are able to see where consensus emerges.

**6** They also *record / recalled* how some paths smelled and sounded.

**7** *More generally / Marginally*, my research, what it tries to do is avoid the danger of the single path, to avoid robbing people of fully experiencing the city in which they live.

**8** Walk the path full of *people you love / people who love* and not full of cars, and you have an entirely different path. It's that simple.

## WATCH ▶

**2** Choose the correct options.

**1** Why did Daniele feel shame when he discovered a different route to work?
   **a** He didn't realize his usual route to work was longer.
   **b** He had only thought about finding the shortest route.
   **c** He had used the wrong cellphone app to get to work.

**2** How did Daniele change after that experience?
   **a** He changed the focus of his research to create new maps.
   **b** He used a different app for finding a route.
   **c** He started to see the city differently.

**3** "Logic will get you from A to B. Imagination will take you everywhere." This means…
   **a** you should travel more if you want to be creative.
   **b** only logic can get you to where you need to go.
   **c** it's important to be creative as well as practical.

**4** Why did Daniele and his team build a new map of London?
   **a** They wanted to create a map of the city that was more enjoyable for people.
   **b** They wanted to make a lot of money from their app.
   **c** The maps of London were not easy to follow.

**5** Besides beauty and quiet, what else did they base the new map of London on?
   **a** tourist attractions
   **b** parks
   **c** smells, sounds, and memories

**6** Why does Daniele say that "routine is deadly"?
   **a** because you may get robbed if you always take the same path
   **b** because you might end up in heavy traffic
   **c** because it can make you lazy so you never experience life fully

**3** Put the events of Daniele's life in the correct order. Then watch the TED Talk again and check your answers.

   **a** Daniele did a PhD in London. ____
   **b** Daniele then joined Yahoo Labs. ____
   **c** He built a crowdsourcing platform with colleagues at Cambridge. ____
   **d** He changed the focus of his research to creating new city maps. ____
   **e** He moved to Boston and began cycling to work every day. ____
   **f** One day he took a new route to work. ____
   **g** The new bike route surprised him. ____
   **h** With his colleagues, he built a new map of London based on human emotions. ____

## VOCABULARY IN CONTEXT

**4** Choose the correct options to complete the text.

I live in Seattle and it's very rainy, so I usually **(1)** *team up with / come up with* my colleague Paulo who lives near me, to share a ride to work. Paulo's a little **(2)** *shy / angry* so he's always very quiet in the car. That's fine with me—I never feel like talking first thing in the morning! Last week, the weather was sunny and beautiful. There are only **(3)** *a lot of / a handful of* sunny days in April, so one day I decided to walk to work. The street I live on is **(4)** *lined by / joined by* trees. There were blossoms on them and the sun was shining—it was a beautiful day to walk.

When I got to work, I suddenly realized, to my **(5)** *curiosity / shame*, that I'd completely forgotten about Paulo! Later that morning, he came over to me and said, "**(6)** *Don't get me wrong / Don't talk to me*, Hana, I don't have a problem with you walking, but could you just let me know next time? I was waiting for you!"

# 2E You Can't Miss It

## SPEAKING

**1** Put the words in the correct order to make questions and sentences about directions. Then listen and check your answers. 🎧 22

**1** the / history museum / know / way / you / the / to / do / ?
_____

**2** all the way / you / the intersection / go / to / get / until / .
_____

**3** traffic / the / straight / at / light / go / .
_____

**4** first / 200 / take / after / traffic circle / yards, / the / off / exit / the / .
_____

**5** right / on / past / your / go / a bookshop / .
_____

**6** station / is / your / train / the / on / left / .
_____

**7** here / very / from / not / it's / far / .
_____

**8** more / mile / no / it's / than / away / a / .
_____

**2** In English, speakers stress key information to show it is important. Listen again and underline the key information / stressed words in the sentences in Activity 1. 🎧 22

**3** Look at the map and complete the conversation with the questions and directions (a–i).

**a** At the pier, turn right.
**b** Go straight all the way until you get to the clock tower.
**c** I'm trying to get to the train station.
**d** Do you know the way?
**e** Turn right at the clock tower and go straight on North Street for about five minutes,
**f** You can't miss it.
**g** at the first traffic light, turn left.
**h** It's pretty far away from here—about fifteen minutes' walk.
**i** so continue along the waterfront until you get to the pier on your left.

**A** Excuse me, can you help me? **(1)** _____.
**B** **(2)** _____.
**A** Oh, OK. **(3)** _____?
**B** OK, **(4)** _____.
**A** Right…
**B** **(5)** _____. Then, **(6)** _____. **(7)** _____.
**A** The clock tower, yes, OK.
**B** **(8)** _____, and the station is straight ahead of you. **(9)** _____.
**A** OK, great, thanks for your help.
**B** No problem.

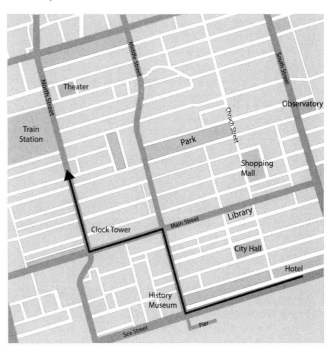

**4** Look at the map again. Give directions to a tourist. Make notes. Then listen to the model answers and compare your ideas. 🎧 23

Excuse me, do you know the way…
**a** from the hotel to the park?
**b** from the park to the shopping mall?
**c** from the shopping mall to the pier?

**5** Some friends are going on a day trip to the same city and plan to do three things during their visit. Make notes about the good and bad points of each activity, then decide which three things they should do and plan a route. Look at the map and the words below to help you with ideas. Remember to use the useful language. Then compare your notes with the sample answer of two people discussing the task. 🎧 **24**

- pier
- beach
- observatory
- theater
- shopping
- museum
- lunch
- dinner

## WRITING  A story

**6** Read the sentences with *just* and choose the correct options.

**1 a** Margarita just had left the airport when her phone rang.
  **b** Margarita had just left the airport when her phone rang.

**2 a** We had just booked our train tickets, and we were so excited!
  **b** We had booked our just train tickets, and we were so excited!

**3 a** The castle looked just as I'd imagined it would.
  **b** The castle looked as just I'd imagined it would.

**4 a** There wasn't much to just eat—a few bread rolls and one orange.
  **b** There wasn't much to eat—just a few bread rolls and one orange.

**5 a** They were just about to give up when, suddenly, a taxi appeared.
  **b** They just were about to give up when, suddenly, a taxi appeared.

**7** Read the stages of writing a story (a–e). Then match them with the correct section (1–5).

**a** Develop the main events. Say how you felt and what happened next.
**b** Bring the story to a close. Say what happened in the end and what you remember most.
**c** Make notes based on *Wh-* questions, like *What / Where / When / Why / Who…*
**d** Introduce the main events of the story. Say what happened.
**e** Set the scene. Let the reader know what the story is about and where it takes place.

**1** Planning ____
**2** Paragraph 1 ____
**3** Paragraph 2 ____
**4** Paragraph 3 ____
**5** Paragraph 4 ____

**8** Put the parts of the story in the correct order.

**a** An elderly couple sat next to me on the ferry. I left my seat to buy some coffee, and I was just about to pay, when, suddenly, I couldn't find my wallet. It had all my credit cards and cash, and now it was gone. Just then, I saw the old man who had been sitting beside me. He gave me my wallet! I burst into tears. Without realizing, I'd dropped it under my seat earlier. ____

**b** I just wanted two things from that trip: a little adventure and a lot of sunshine. Instead, I got a lot of adventure and only a little sunshine! ____

**c** I stayed on a small island that had no tourists, just local people. Greece is normally hot and dry, so I just packed T-shirts and shorts. Unfortunately, I didn't know that Greek winters are cold and rainy. I was freezing! One day, I decided to travel to another island. ____

**d** I went backpacking in Greece for a week last winter. None of my friends were free, so I traveled alone. ____

**9** Read the story again.  Then complete the summary with these words and phrases. There are two you don't need.

| a week | alone | adventure | bad weather | begins |
|---|---|---|---|---|
| concludes | found | lost | sunshine | with friends |

The writer traveled **(1)** _____ in Greece for
**(2)** _____ last winter. The first problem was
**(3)** _____. The second problem was a
**(4)** _____ wallet. Luckily, the wallet was
**(5)** _____. The writer
**(6)** _____ the story by saying the
trip had more **(7)** _____ than
**(8)** _____!

**10** Write a story that is 150–200 words. Begin with this sentence: *At first, we all thought the journey was fun.*

**Tip box**

- The story doesn't have to be true. You can make it up.
- Don't use the same story you wrote in Student Book, Unit 2.
- Write some notes to plan your story.
- Write at least four paragraphs.
- In Paragraph 1, set the scene for the story.
- In Paragraph 2, introduce the main events.
- In Paragraph 3, develop the main events. Explain how you felt.
- In Paragraph 4, bring the story to a close.
- Remember to use "just" and different adverbs.
- Have fun writing your story!

# Review

**1** Match the things (1–6) with the places (a–f) where you would find them.

**1** public transportation    **a** a shopping mall
**2** a lot of offices    **b** an amusement park
**3** a clothing store    **c** a rooftop
**4** a roller coaster    **d** a skyscraper
**5** an urban garden    **e** a subway station
**6** beautiful scenery    **f** a viewpoint

**2** Read. Are the sentences true (T) or false (F)? Correct the false sentences.

**1** A destination is the place where you begin your journey. _____

**2** An expedition is usually a short trip. _____

**3** If you commute, your journey to work often takes a long time. _____

**4** An excursion is usually a short trip for sightseeing or relaxing. _____

**5** If you give someone a ride, you take them somewhere. _____

**6** A cruise is a journey on a train. _____

**3** Complete the sentences with the correct forms of the words in bold.

**1** It's **interest** _____ that in Norway, you always eat with a knife and fork. (Even if you're eating a sandwich!)

**2** In Egypt, don't add salt to your food. (It's **annoyed** _____ for the host because it means you don't like their food.)

**3** In South Korea, it could be **terrified** _____ for someone if you write a family member's name in red ink. (It means that the person is dead.)

**4** In Russia, it's **confused** _____ to give someone you are in a relationship with yellow flowers. (It means that you want to break up with them!)

**5** In the Netherlands, your friend might be **worry** _____ if you give scissors or knives as gifts. (It's unlucky.)

**6** In Venezuela, it's **surprised** _____ to arrive on time for a party. (Guests who arrive on time seem too eager.)

**4** Are the words in bold correct or incorrect? Correct those that are incorrect.

**1** I **was fell** asleep in class yesterday. It was so **bored**.
_____

**2** Last week he **studied** at the library for eight hours every day. He was really **exhausting**.
_____

**3** **Has you ever being** on such an **excited** trip?
_____

**4** Leo **had came** home at midnight yesterday. His mother was very **worried**.
_____

**5** They **were shocking** when they heard the news.
_____

**6** Mr. Hernandez just **had told** Karina that she didn't win the award. It's such **disappointed** news.
_____

**7** He hadn't **telling** me his secret until today. It's **amazed** that he's going to Peru for the summer!
_____

**5** Choose the correct options to complete the sentences.

**1** _____ it a disappointing movie?
   **a** Was
   **b** Was being
   **c** Did be
   **d** Had been

**2** I _____ my neighbor to look after my house while I _____ away on vacation.
   **a** asking, am
   **b** was asked, was
   **c** asked, was
   **d** ask, had been

**3** Were they _____ to the party when they _____, Meg?
   **a** drive, were calling
   **b** drove, called
   **c** been driving, had called
   **d** driving, called

**4** It _____ a difficult test, but Sivan _____ most of the answers.
   **a** had been, was knowing
   **b** was, knew
   **c** was, had know
   **d** had been, known

**5** Renting an apartment in the city didn't _____ to cost so much.
   **a** used
   **b** use
   **c** had been
   **d** being

**6** I had _____ seen the Grand Canyon _____, so my friends and I decided to go.
   **a** never, before
   **b** before, yet
   **c** for, ever
   **d** ever, before

**7** _____ you _____ taken the bus to school before today?
   **a** Has, never
   **b** Have, since
   **c** Had, for
   **d** Had, ever

# 3 Active Lives

## 3A Pushing the Limits

### VOCABULARY Sports

**1** **Review** Read the clues and complete the words about sports. The first letter is given for you.

1 This sport is played with a bat and a ball and each team has nine players.    b __ __ __ __ __ __ __
2 This popular Olympic sport happens in a pool.
    s __ __ __ __ __ __ __ __
3 People do this sport in the snow and it is popular in cold countries.    s __ __ __ __ __
4 This sport can be done on a track or outside over long distances.    r __ __ __ __ __ __
5 This sport is played on a field and is popular around the world.    s __ __ __ __ __
6 People use a mat to do this activity, which is good for the mind and body.    y __ __ __

**2** **Review** Complete the chart with these words.

| baseball | basketball | boxing | ice hockey | ice skating |
|----------|-----------|--------|-----------|-------------|
| soccer | surfing | tennis | volleyball | yoga |

| Team sports | Individual sports |
|-------------|-------------------|
|  |  |
|  |  |
|  |  |

**3** **Review** Put the words in the correct order to make sentences.

1 baseball / favorite / my / least / sport / is / .
_____
2 can / dangerous / boxing / be / sport / a / very / .
_____
3 more / countries / than / soccer / played / is / in / 200 / .
_____
4 good / heart / running / for / your / is / .
_____
5 swimming / popular / is / Australia / a / in / sport / .
_____
6 doing / makes / feel / yoga / calm / you / .
_____

**4** Match the sports (1–6) with the equipment (a–f).

| 1 | tennis | **a** | hoop |
|---|--------|-------|------|
| 2 | basketball | **b** | boat |
| 3 | diving | **c** | club |
| 4 | sailing | **d** | board |
| 5 | golf | **e** | helmet |
| 6 | cycling | **f** | racket |

**5** Unscramble the letters to make places where people do sports.

1 k r n i        __ __ n __
2 t o r c u      __ __ __ r __
3 d e i f l      f __ __ __ __
4 r c a k t      __ r __ __ __
5 n m t u o i n a   m __ __ __ __ a __ __
6 o l p o        __ __ o __

**6** Read the paragraph and choose the correct options.

Last weekend, I went to watch my first professional basketball game. I loved it! Even though our seats were far from the **(1)** _____ , we still had a good view. The home team was from New York, and their **(2)** _____ were from Boston. There were over 17,000 **(3)** _____ in the stadium, and it was exciting to watch with so many people.
At one point in the game, the **(4)** _____ of the team from Boston got really angry with the **(5)** _____ about a call he thought was unfair. He was told to be quiet or leave the stadium! It was a very close game. The final **(6)** _____ was 100-96, and the team from New York **(7)** _____ .

| 1 | **a** rink | **b** court | **c** equipment |
|---|-----------|------------|-----------------|
| 2 | **a** spectators | **b** opponents | **c** coaches |
| 3 | **a** opponents | **b** players | **c** spectators |
| 4 | **a** opponent | **b** referee | **c** coach |
| 5 | **a** referee | **b** coach | **c** player |
| 6 | **a** score | **b** win | **c** count |
| 7 | **a** played | **b** won | **c** beat |

**7** Complete the sentences with the correct sports. The first letter is given for you.

1 My favorite sport to watch is d_____, but I'm always worried the athlete will hit the board.
2 G_____ can be done by both men and women and takes incredible strength and skill.
3 The boys take k_____ lessons on Saturdays to learn discipline and self-defense.
4 S_____ can be quite dangerous if the sea is very rough.
5 Ropes and holds are used for c_____.
6 Players are allowed to bounce the ball in b_____.

**8** Choose the correct options to complete the sentences.

1 Today, I'm trying to *achieve* / *represent* my personal best in the 100m race.
2 Her goal is to *score* / *beat* the current champion and become the best boxer in the country.
3 The ultimate goal of the team is to *score* / *win* as many medals as possible for their country.
4 It's important to *achieve* / *encourage* everyone to participate in sports.
5 To be a professional athlete, you have to *train* / *represent* almost every day.
6 He *scored* / *achieved* the winning goal in the match against Germany.
7 It's an incredible honor to *achieve* / *represent* your country in the Olympics.

**9 Extension** Complete the sentences with the correct forms of *play*, *do*, or *go*.

1 I like most sports, but I absolutely love _____ basketball.
2 I have a stressful job, so I relax by _____ yoga.
3 When it's hot outside, we _____ swimming in the lake near our house.
4 I _____ running four days a week, even if I'm tired!
5 He likes to _____ tennis with friends on the weekends.
6 Jerome gets plenty of exercise because he _____ gymnastics every week.
7 Every winter, my family _____ skiing in Colorado.

**10 Extension** Choose the correct options to complete the sentences.

1 The girls like to go *horseback riding* / *yoga* when we're on vacation.
2 In the winter, tourists can go *ice skating* / *jogging* on a rink in Hyde Park.
3 Racquetball is *done* / *played* in an indoor court surrounded by walls.
4 Do you want to go *diving* / *snowboarding* on the mountain tomorrow?
5 People play *soccer* / *hockey* with a puck and a stick.
6 Would you like to play a game of *table tennis* / *skateboarding*?
7 A flat board with a sail is used for *snowboarding* / *windsurfing*.

# LISTENING

**11** Listen to the conversation and choose the correct options. 🎧 **25**

1 What, in general, are they talking about?
  **a** fitness and physical activity
  **b** favorite games and interests
  **c** healthy food and drinks

2 What does the woman say she is the first to do?
  **a** criticize people
  **b** encourage people
  **c** discourage people

3 Why is the man feeling unhappy?
  **a** He doesn't have any interests.
  **b** He doesn't have many friends.
  **c** He doesn't think he's in good shape.

4 What does he eat when he plays computer games?
  **a** salad
  **b** snacks
  **c** a picnic

5 How does the young man first react to the idea of a hike?
  **a** He's enthusiastic.
  **b** He's confused.
  **c** He's unsure.

6 What does the young woman mean when she says, "…there's no time like the present"?
  **a** The time for action is now.
  **b** It's a little late to take action.
  **c** The present situation is not good.

7 What is the young man afraid that he's turning into?
  **a** a jealous, angry person
  **b** a mean, unfriendly person
  **c** a lazy, unhealthy person

8 What is the best description of the woman's attitude toward the man?
  **a** She's really frustrated.
  **b** She's very supportive.
  **c** She's slightly critical.

**12** Listen to the two speakers. Choose the best title for both descriptions. 🎧 **26**
  **a** Biker Dogs!
  **b** Let's catch a wave!
  **c** Skateboards rule!
  **d** Extreme dogs!

**13** Listen to the first speaker again and choose the correct options. 🎧 **26**

1 What word does the woman use meaning "dog"?
  **a** puppy
  **b** pooch
  **c** mutt

2 What do some dogs do "…a thousand feet in the air"?
  **a** surf
  **b** paddle
  **c** cruise

3 What kind of dog is Bandit?
  **a** a breed
  **b** a terrier
  **c** a bulldog

4 What did Bandit learn to do first?
  **a** ride motorcycles
  **b** surf waves
  **c** steal food

**14** Listen to the second speaker again and choose the correct options. 🎧 **26**

1 What makes Tillman a natural skateboarder?
  **a** his attitude
  **b** his body
  **c** his owner

2 What did Tillman first learn to do on his skateboard?
  **a** fall off
  **b** push it
  **c** roll along

3 What do you think "mad" means when the owner says "mad skater skills"?
  **a** extremely good
  **b** very angry
  **c** pretty bad

4 What is Tillman's owner most proud of?
  **a** Tillman's skating skills
  **b** Tillman's lack of fear
  **c** Tillman's effect on people

# GRAMMAR Simple past and present perfect

**15** Read the sentences and complete the chart.

1 Have you ever refereed a basketball game?
2 He stayed in shape during the winter by jogging.
3 My cousin has done gymnastics for five years.
4 My favorite football team has already won twice.
5 No one has broken the world record since 2015.
6 Our best player injured herself when she tried to score.
7 The players encouraged the team captain to run faster.
8 They canceled the match because it rained.

| Simple past | Present perfect |
|---|---|
|  |  |
|  |  |
|  |  |
|  |  |

**16** Choose the correct options to complete the sentences.

1 When I was younger, I *enjoyed / enjoy / have enjoyed* building sculptures out of things I *found / finded / have find* around the house.
2 Most kids *have did / has done / did* karate or *rode / has ridden / have rode* their bikes, but I just *wanted / have want / have wanted* to make things.
3 One summer, I *have built / build / built* some shelves to hold my comic books.
4 Another time, I *design / designed / have designed* and *make / made / have made* a table for my parents.
5 My friends *have not understood / didn't understand / not understand* that I *have prefer / preferred / have preferred* creating new things, not playing soccer.
6 A few years ago, I *enter / entered / have entered* one of my sculptures in a competition and I *have win / have won / won*!

**17** Complete the sentences with the present perfect forms of the verbs in parentheses.

1 Paola and Mai _____ (be) friends since they were small children.
2 They _____ (live) next door to each other for fifteen years.
3 Mai _____ (not know) anyone as long as she _____ (know) Paola.
4 Paola _____ (always want) to learn how to play the guitar.
5 She _____ (not practice) as much as her teacher recommended, so she _____ (not improve) very much.
6 Mai _____ (decide) that she wants to go to the same college as Paola.
7 But Paola _____ (not think) about going to college yet.
8 Her parents _____ (tell) her that she needs to be more serious.

**18** Choose the correct options to complete the sentences.

1 If you *have decided / decided* you want to get in shape, you really should see your doctor to find out if you're healthy enough for exercise.
2 Our friends *joined / have joined* a running club last year and now they run three times a week.
3 She *never skipped / has never skipped* breakfast since the doctor advised her not to.
4 Jack *has now recovered / now recovered* and is exercising again.
5 He *began / has begun* a meditation class last week as a way to deal with stress.
6 My father *only ate / has only eaten* healthy food since he was in the hospital.

**19** Read the article. Complete the sentences with the simple past or present perfect forms of the verbs in parentheses.

Extreme sports are sports that people consider risky. They usually involve speed, height, and/or extreme physical activity. Here are some examples from around the world:

- **Badwater ultramarathon** For several years, athletes **(1)** _____ (participate) in this race each summer in the hottest place in North America: Death Valley, California. Last year, the athletes **(2)** _____ (run) 135 miles, starting at 280 feet below sea level and ending in the mountains at 8,300 feet.
- **Wingsuit flying world championship** For this competition, athletes wear a jumpsuit that has extra cloth between their arms and legs so they can glide long distances. People **(3)** _____ (call) it "horizontal skydiving" because the athletes often travel long distances. In 2016, in Zhangjiajie, China, the athletes **(4)** _____ (jump) from Tienmen Mountain in Hunan Province and **(5)** _____ (travel) almost a mile to the goal. The winner **(6)** _____ (complete) the race in 23.41 seconds.
- **Street luge skateboarders** These extreme-sports athletes **(7)** _____ (always want) to go faster and faster. In 2014, the twelfth annual competition **(8)** _____ (be) in Brazil, which has the fastest downhill skateboarding track in the world. The world record for street luge, set in 2008, is 97.81 miles per hour!

# 3B Extreme Sports

## VOCABULARY BUILDING Phrasal verbs

**1** Complete the sentences with the correct forms of these phrasal verbs.

| give up | join in | keep up | knock out |
|---------|---------|---------|-----------|
| take on | take up | warm up | work out |

1 It's important to _____ before you start running, or you could pull a muscle.
2 I'm trying to _____, but you run too fast!
3 I usually either swim or _____ for about an hour after school.
4 She had to _____ running after that problem with her ankle.
5 Which team do you think will _____ Brazil in the semi-final?
6 When you feel more confident, you can _____ for the rest of the game.
7 I was so disappointed when Murray was _____ of the tournament.
8 I'm thinking of _____ karate. I need more exercise, and I like learning new things.

## READING

**2** Read the text and choose the correct options.

1 What does Steph Davis experience before jumping off a cliff?
   a risk and danger
   b pleasure and peace
   c fear and excitement

2 Which of these sports is often considered risky or extreme?
   a swimming
   b rock climbing
   c running

3 What do researchers believe some extreme-sports athletes are attracted to?
   a taking risks
   b racing down steep slopes
   c dopamine

4 What do some people believe about extreme-sports athletes?
   a They're reckless adventurers.
   b They're not interested in low-risk sports.
   c They don't need to practice.

5 What is one explanation behind the appeal of extreme sports?
   a Some people like to push their own limits.
   b Athletes need something to do in the summer.
   c Some athletes are scared of competition.

**3** Choose two possible explanations the writer gives for why people take up dangerous activities.

a People like the feeling of being frightened.
b People who enjoy taking risks may share an adventure gene.
c Many people think yoga and running are boring.
d Some people enjoy the burst of dopamine that comes with extreme activities.
e Some athletes don't really care about the consequences.

**4** Choose two points that the writer makes about extreme-sports athletes.

a Many extreme-sports athletes are very well-prepared for what they do.
b Unlike traditional athletes, extreme-sports athletes care about the consequences of what they do.
c Both traditional and extreme-sports athletes prepare carefully for their sports.
d Many extreme-sports athletes have high levels of self-awareness.
e Like traditional athletes, extreme-sports athletes enjoy doing things that feel good.

**5** Match the two parts of the sentences.

1 According to recent research, _____
2 Sports, such as surfing and skiing, _____
3 The "adventure gene" _____
4 Many extreme-sports athletes are _____
5 There seem to be _____

a may involve risks and even danger!
b some people may be genetically predisposed to taking risks.
c a number of reasons why people enjoy extreme sports.
d well-prepared, highly-skilled, and aware of what they're doing.
e may influence how some people process dopamine.

# Why take the risk?

🎧 **27** Just before jumping off a thousand-foot cliff, professional climber, BASE jumper, and wingsuiter Steph Davis admits to experiencing fear and excitement. That's not surprising, since wingsuiting is an extremely risky sport that has claimed the lives of several wingsuiters, including Steph's husband. So why does she do it? Why, in spite of the danger, would Steph want to jump at all, let alone almost every day of the year?

Steph isn't alone in her search for thrills*, and hers isn't the only risky or extreme sport. Surfing, rock climbing, diving from great heights, and even skiing or snowboarding all involve risks and sometimes real danger. Recently, scientists have studied people who pursue these, and other potentially dangerous sports, to learn more about what makes certain individuals take up activities that other people prefer to avoid.

Research suggests that some people attracted to extreme sports may be genetically predisposed* to risky behaviors. According to Cynthia Thomson, a researcher at the University of British Columbia, it's possible that extreme-sports athletes, along with people who enjoy taking risks, share an "adventure gene." This genetic variation may influence how some people process dopamine. Dopamine is a substance that's partially responsible for the feeling of excitement a person experiences when skiing down a steep slope, surfing a giant wave, or even racing down a hill on a bicycle. People with the adventure gene may "need to seek out intense situations to bring up their dopamine levels,"

according to Thomson. That burst* of dopamine might make the individual want to repeat the behavior because it feels so good.

But there's more to extreme sports than dopamine. Researchers compared participants* in low-risk sports, such as yoga and running, to fans of high-risk activities. They wondered whether, as some people believe, thrill-seekers are reckless* adventurers who don't care about the consequences of what they do. What they found is that many extreme-sports athletes are actually very skilled at what they do, train hard, and are responsible and well-prepared when practicing their sport. Eric Brymer is a researcher from Queenstown University of Technology in Brisbane, Australia, who has been studying extreme-sports athletes for years. In his opinion, extreme-sports athletes are "actually extremely well-prepared, careful, intelligent, and thoughtful athletes with high levels of self-awareness and a deep knowledge of the environment and of the activity."

In the end, it seems that there are a number of explanations behind the appeal of extreme sports. For some, it might be the dopamine. Others might be interested in pushing their own limits. One thing is clear, though—extreme-sports athletes like to play hard! As Daron Rahlves, a top downhill-ski racer who spends the summer racing in motocross competitions, puts it: "I'm in it for the challenge, my heart thumping as I finish, the feeling of being alive… I definitely get scared on some of the courses. It just makes me fight more."

**thrill** *a strong feeling of excitement and pleasure*
**predisposed** *likely to behave in a particular way*
**burst** *a sudden outpouring*

**participant** *someone who is involved in an activity*
**reckless** *dangerous and not caring about what might happen*

# 3C Have you ever...?

## GRAMMAR Present perfect and present perfect continuous

**1** Listen and complete the sentences. 🎧 **28**

1 How long _____ the piano?
2 I _____ Tina to tell her about the party.
3 _____ to put new batteries in the remote control. It _____ doesn't work.
4 _____ on the phone _____ 45 minutes.
5 How often _____ to the library this week?
6 _____ since five o'clock this morning.
7 He _____ the physics test _____ .

**2** Complete the chart.

| Infinitive | Present perfect | Present perfect continuous |
|---|---|---|
| take | | |
| | | have / has been choosing |
| | | have / has been representing |
| try | | |
| encourage | | |
| | | have / has been winning |
| feel | | |

**3** Choose the correct options to complete the sentences.

1 We've been going to that school _____ 2016.
   a since        c already
   b for          d ever

2 She's lived in Guadalajara _____ two years.
   a since        c already
   b for          d ever

3 Have you started making the sauce _____ ?
   a ever
   b yet
   c just
   d since

4 I've _____ made a sauce with garlic and mushrooms before.
   a for
   b yet
   c ever
   d never

5 He's _____ listened to the new album five times.
   a already
   b ever
   c since
   d yet

6 Has she _____ met your friend Mia?
   a since
   b yet
   c ever
   d for

7 She's _____ met Mia. They were both at the party.
   a ever
   b already
   c since
   d yet

8 He's _____ started taking driving lessons.
   a ever
   b yet
   c just
   d for

**4** Match the questions and answers.

1 How many cookies has Meg eaten? _____
2 How long have you been going to the gym? _____
3 How many Harry Potter books have you read? _____
4 How many times have you been to the hospital for this problem? _____
5 How often does your family go to the theater? _____
6 How long has she been a hairdresser? _____

a At least four, I think.
b I think she's already had three.
c I've read the first five. I love them!
d Oh, for about two years.
e Since she was 21.
f We've been going once or twice a month for the past year.

**5** Your roommate is asking what chores you've done in the apartment. Answer the questions using the prompts.

**1** Have you changed the light bulb yet?
   _No, I still haven't changed it._ (no / still)

**2** Have you washed the frying pan?
   _____ (no / yet)

**3** Did you turn on the oven for dinner?
   _____ (yes / already)

**4** Have you locked the door yet?
   _____ (yes / just)

**5** Have you put the towels in the washing machine?
   _____ (no / still)

**6** Have you put the ice cream in the freezer?
   _____ (yes / already)

**6** Read the sentences and choose the options with similar meanings.

**1** I've already been to the gallery to see the new show.
   **a** I saw the new show at the gallery.
   **b** I didn't see the new show at the gallery.

**2** They've been watching TV for three hours. It's seven o'clock now.
   **a** They started watching TV at four o'clock.
   **b** They are not watching TV now.

**3** Dylan has just finished his second driving lesson.
   **a** Dylan took two driving lessons.
   **b** Dylan has never taken a driving lesson.

**4** We hadn't bought tickets before we went to the train station.
   **a** We had tickets before we got to the train station.
   **b** We didn't have tickets before we got to the train station.

**5** I'd told her to set her alarm, but Natalie was still late for class.
   **a** Natalie was late for class, even though I told her to set her alarm.
   **b** I hadn't been telling Natalie to set her alarm, and she was late for class.

**6** They've learned about the geography of Morocco, and now they want to learn about its culture.
   **a** They've learned about Moroccan culture and geography.
   **b** They learned about Moroccan geography, and they want to learn about its culture.

**7** Write a question for each answer using the present perfect or present perfect continuous.

**1** _Have they ever been to South America?_
   No, they've never been to South America.

**2** _____
   No, I've never seen such beautiful scenery.

**3** _____
   I've been working on that math question for fifteen minutes.

**4** _____
   No, he hasn't eaten dinner yet.

**5** _____
   I've taken the train to school four times this week.

**6** _____
   No, I've never taken the bus to the airport.

**7** _____
   She's been reading that novel for a week.

**8** Choose the correct options to complete the sentences.

**1** Teresa *has been* / *has been going* to Lisbon four times. The last time she went, she stayed for five days.
**2** How much luggage has she *brought* / *bringing* with her?
**3** I have *disliked* / *been disliking* eggs since I was a child.
**4** Have you finished your homework *still* / *yet*?
**5** Xavier *has been* / *has gone* to Miami. He'll be back home next week.
**6** I've *just* / *ever* returned from Manila. I'm still tired from the flight.
**7** You've *deserved* / *been deserving* a promotion for more than six months.
**8** We have *never* / *ever* been to that restaurant.

## PRONUNCIATION *For*

**9** Listen to the sentences and choose the pronunciation that you hear. 🎧 **29**

**1** /fɔr/     /fər/
**2** /fɔr/     /fər/
**3** /fɔr/     /fər/
**4** /fɔr/     /fər/
**5** /fɔr/     /fər/
**6** /fɔr/     /fər/

# 3D How I Swam the North Pole

## AUTHENTIC LISTENING SKILLS

**1** Complete the text with the signposts. Then listen to the TED Talk excerpts and check your answers. 🎧 **30**

> And he came up to me and he said,
> And I thought,
> And on day four,
> And then, after a year of training,

**(1)** _____ I felt ready. I felt confident that I could actually do this swim. So, myself and the five members of the team, we hitched a ride on an icebreaker which was going to the North Pole.

**(2)** _____ we decided to just do a quick five-minute test swim. I had never swum in water of minus 1.7 degrees before, because it's just impossible to train in those type of conditions. So, we stopped the ship, as you do. We all got down onto the ice and I then got into my swimming costume and I dived into the sea.

I have never in my life felt anything like that moment. I could barely breathe. I was gasping for air...

**(3)** _____ in two days' time, I was going to do this swim across the North Pole. I was going to try and do a twenty-minute swim, for one kilometer across the North Pole. There is no possibility that this was going to happen...

And my close friend David, he saw the way I was thinking.

**(4)** _____ "Lewis, I've known you since you were eighteen years old. I've known you, and I know, Lewis, deep down, right deep down here, that you are going to make this swim. I so believe in you, Lewis."

## WATCH ▶

**2** Watch the TED Talk and complete the chart. Write no more than two words and/or a number for each answer.

| **(1)** _____ before | Two years before | **(4)** _____ before | **(6)** _____ later |
|---|---|---|---|
| Pugh went to the Arctic for **(2)** _____ time | **(3)** _____ percent of the Arctic Sea ice cover melted away. | Pugh did a **(5)** _____ -minute test swim. | Pugh could feel his hands again. |

**3** Watch Part 3 of the TED Talk and choose the correct options.

**1** Pugh says it took years of training, planning, and _____ to do the North Pole swim.
   **a** bravery
   **b** money
   **c** preparation

**2** A couple of hours before his swim, he was feeling _____.
   **a** frightened and emotional
   **b** proud and excited
   **c** happy and relaxed

**3** Pugh says the swim was _____.
   **a** painful
   **b** worth it
   **c** fun

**4** He thinks that _____ must play its part regarding climate change.
   **a** every country
   **b** Britain, America, and Japan
   **c** the same ship

**5** He also thinks that even _____ understand climate change.
   **a** swimmers like himself
   **b** rich politicians
   **c** children in poor countries

**6** Pugh believes that people need to _____.
   **a** believe in themselves
   **b** spend money to make a difference
   **c** walk more often

**7** Finally, he says we should ask ourselves, _____
   **a** "What is a sustainable world?"
   **b** "What type of world do we want to live in?"
   **c** "Where in the world do we want to live?"

## VOCABULARY IN CONTEXT

**4** Choose the correct options to complete the sentences.

**1** The water was so cold that I couldn't go in and I *barely / easily / really* got wet.

**2** She twisted her ankle and within a few minutes it was *grown / expanded / swollen*.

**3** Sharks don't live in *fresh water / sea water / salt water*, so I prefer swimming in rivers.

**4** His face was painted white and he was wearing this brightly colored clown *equipment / costume / uniform*.

**5** I went up to my sister just before the race, smiled and said *"I believe in you, Sis." / "Don't get me wrong, Sis."*

**6** What decisions are we going to make today to *ensure / deny / say* that something is done about climate change?

# 3E School Sports

## WRITING An opinion essay

**1** Read the sentences and complete the chart.

1 I don't think that swimming pools should be free.
2 I've written a short history of the Olympic Games.
3 In my view, schools should make PE mandatory.
4 Many parks in the UK now have outdoor gyms.
5 Next year, I want to run the New York Marathon!
6 Of course, there's too much advertising in sports.
7 Personally, I think that Lewis Pugh is an inspiration.
8 The World Cup takes place every four years.

| Expressing an opinion | Making a general statement |
|---|---|
| | |
| | |
| | |

**2** Match the two parts of the sentences.

1 In my opinion, cyclists who bike in traffic should have to pass a test
2 I don't think that sports should be taken so seriously
3 I strongly believe that some professional athletes are paid too much money
4 There is no question that we should have better protective clothing in contact sports

a and this sends the wrong message to young people.
b to make sure they understand the rules of the road.
c because some players risk serious injury.
d as their true purpose is just for enjoyment.

**3** Complete the opinion essay with the correct sentences (a–f).

Anyone interested in trying a new sport has a lot of choices these days. Of course, people prefer to do sports they know they'll enjoy, and that's a very important factor.
**(1)** _____ It's true that most sports are good for us, but in my view, team sports offer additional benefits. They teach us useful lessons both on and off the field. **(2)** _____ In order to be successful, team members have to communicate with each other quickly and clearly.
**(3)** _____ I strongly believe that team sports improve our ability to understand expectations and to respect others. **(4)** _____ There is no question that they are better at collaborating and working towards a common goal.

**(5)** _____ It's true that there's the convenience of training in your own time. In addition, some people are more suited to working alone.

**(6)** _____ In my opinion, sharing

responsibility for success or failure helps us to become better human beings.

a Of course, individual sports have advantages, too.
b Secondly, team sports help us to develop healthy relationships.
c Overall, however, I believe that team sports bring more value to our lives.
d Firstly, I would say that we learn to communicate better when we play team sports.
e Personally, I think that team sports are much better than individual sports.
f Finally, people who play team sports are better at working together.

**4** Read the essay again. Choose the correct options to complete the sentences.

1 The writer first expresses her opinion in the *first sentence* / *third sentence*.
2 She believes that team sports offer more *players* / *benefits* than other sports.
3 In her view, *team sports* / *individual sports* improve our communication skills.
4 She thinks that team sports help us to have *good* / *more* relationships.
5 People who play team sports are also good at *winning* / *working* together.
6 The writer mentions some of the *good* / *bad* points about individual sports.
7 She ends the essay with *an opinion* / *a statement* about sharing responsibility.

**5** What is your opinion of the following statement?

Some people feel the Olympic Games should not be continued because too many athletes cheat.

**Use specific reasons and examples to support your answer.**

| Tip box |
|---|
| • Spend a few minutes planning your main points. |
| • Introduce the topic. |
| • State your opinion in the introduction. |
| • In the second paragraph, develop your ideas. |
| • Provide examples to support your opinion. |
| • Use linking words and phrases (e.g. "However," "In addition"). |
| • In the third paragraph, consider some opposing views. |
| • Sum up your main idea in the conclusion. |
| • Restate your opinion at the end. |
| • Check your spelling and punctuation. |

# SPEAKING

**6** Complete the useful phrases with the missing words. Then decide if the phrase is for agreeing (A) or disagreeing (D).

1 I _____ what you're saying, but… ____
2 He's _____ a good point. ____
3 I _____ what you mean, it's just… ____
4 You're _____ wrong there. ____
5 _____, but… ____
6 I'm _____ sure I agree. ____
7 He's _____ about that. ____
8 That's _____. ____
9 That's a _____ point. ____
10 I _____ agree with you. ____
11 Maybe, _____… ____
12 I _____ up to a point, but… ____

**7** Listen to the sentences in Activity 6 and decide if the missing word is higher or lower in pitch than the words near it. Draw an arrow ↗ or ↘ to mark the pitch. 🎧 **31**

**8** Match the sentences (1–6) from Speaker 1 with the replies (a–f) from Speaker 2. Then match the responses (i–vi) from Speaker 3. Then listen to check your answers. 🎧 **32**

Speaker 1:

1 The government should spend more on sports education in schools.
2 Sports teach everyone about the value of hard work and determination.
3 I think we should have access to a wider variety of sports.
4 I believe sports give young people much better role models than the media or politics do.
5 I think big sports competitions stop people from focusing on the real problems with the country.
6 Athletes are excellent role models for young people.

Speaker 2:

a **That's a good point.** Not everyone likes soccer or swimming.
b **She's got a good point.** They often ignore the serious issues with the economy or infrastructure.
c **Maybe, but** in my opinion there's way too much corruption in sports.
d **I'm not sure I agree.** I think there's too much pressure in sports now.
e **I totally agree with you.** Young people are the future of the country.
f **I agree up to a point, but** the best athletes earn so much that it creates unrealistic expectations!

Speaker 3:

i **He's right about that.** Look at the problems FIFA had with fraud.
ii **I see what you're saying, but** in my opinion, schools need more money for teachers.
iii **I understand what you mean, it's just** that other sports can be expensive. Cheap ones like those are more accessible.
iv **That's true.** Every year, you hear about more new athletes taking risks with steroids.
v **You're not wrong there.** Some of the salaries football players get are unbelievable.
vi **Yes, but** the competitions bring lots of investments, which create jobs and help businesses.

**9** How would you respond to these opinions in discussions? Write your ideas and then listen to compare them with the sample answers. 🎧 **33**

1 **A** I don't think football players should be paid more money than other athletes.
   **B** _____

2 **A** There should be more mixed competitions with men and women playing against each other.
   **B** _____

3 **A** I don't believe that the government promotes enough alternative sports.
   **B** _____

4 **A** It seems strange to me that there's so much focus on sports, but not as much on culture.
   **B** _____

5 **A** There are just too many sports on TV these days.
   **B** _____

**10** Read and discuss. Make notes on your ideas for each question. Then listen to the sample answer and compare your ideas. 🎧 **34**

We've been talking about issues in sports. Now, I'd like to discuss some more general questions relating to this topic. First, let's consider how sports affect people's lives.

- Do you think there should be more space to do sports in cities?
- How much influence do you think athletes have as role models for young people?

Finally let's think about the role of funding.

- What do you think of the funding of sports by the government?

# Review

**1** Delete the word or phrase that does <u>not</u> collocate with the verb.

1 beat + *an opponent / a record / a limit*
2 encourage + *a friend / your best / your teammate*
3 achieve + *a goal / exercise / an ambition*
4 score + *your opponent / a goal / a point*
5 represent + *your team / your nation / your goal*
6 train + *hard / for years / a win*

**2** Put the words in the correct order to make sentences and questions.

1 she / running / to / stay / only / goes / in shape / .

_____

2 try / limits / my / I / push / to / own / .

_____

3 hard / they / trained / race / before / the / .

_____

4 represent / school / our / who / going / to / is / ?

_____

5 won / medals / has / he / gold / many / gymnastics / for / how / ?

_____

6 coach / our / us / to / encouraged / a team / as / work / .

_____

**3** Complete the information about world records with the correct forms of the verbs in parentheses.

1 Chris Walton _____ (hold) the world record for the longest fingernails since 2011. She _____ (not cut) her fingernails for two decades.
2 In 2014, twenty chefs _____ (make) the world's largest dish of fried rice in Turkey. The dish _____ (weigh) over 3,000 kg!
3 The record for the largest wedding party _____ (belong) to a Sri Lankan couple since 2013. Their wedding party _____ (consist) of 126 bridesmaids, 25 best men, 20 page boys, and 23 flower girls.
4 Since 2007, the New York restaurant Serendipity 3 _____ (be) the record holder for the world's most expensive dessert. Their frozen hot chocolate costs $25,000!
5 Japanese fashion designer Kazuhiro Watanabe _____ (hold) the world record for the tallest Mohawk hairdo since 2011. His mohawk is almost four feet tall!
6 Two American men _____ (win) the world record for the longest handshake in 2008. They _____ (shake) hands for 9 hours 30 minutes.

**4** Choose the correct options to complete the sentences.

1 Chen *took / has been taking* three science classes last term.
2 *They've been making / They've been made* bread with their grandmother since they were young children.
3 She was checking the ads in the newspaper when she finally found what she *had been looking / looked* for.
4 Leila *had laughing / had been laughing* loudly when the teacher entered the classroom.
5 She *hadn't ever repaired / hadn't repaired* her computer before her essay was due.
6 I *confirmed / had been confirming* the exchange rate and then I bought some perfume at the duty-free shop.

**5** Put the words in the correct order to make sentences.

1 sick / I've / since / been / Saturday / last / .

_____

2 on / Adir / an / trying / has / shoes / for / been / hour / .

_____

3 wanted / has / in / live / never / to / Canada / she / .

_____

4 for / I've / Darren / known / years / three / .

_____

5 new / they / yet / met / their / haven't / teacher / .

_____

6 been / has / all / studying / Dinah / day / .

_____

7 moved / Lin and Sarah / Seattle / have / to / already / .

_____

# 4 Food

## 4A Learning to Cook

### VOCABULARY Describing food

**1 Review** Unscramble the letters to make words about food.

1 e c k i h c n    c _ _ _ _ _ _
2 a p t a s    _ _ s _ _ _
3 p s r n a w    p _ _ w _ _ _
4 e e f c f o    c _ _ _ _ _
5 l a p e p    _ _ _ _ _ e
6 l m o e n    l _ _ _ _
7 r c r y u    _ _ _ _ y
8 t m o a o t    _ _ _ a _ _

**2 Review** What flavor are these foods? Complete the chart. Then add two more foods to each column.

| cake | curry | chilli powder | chocolate |
| French fries | ice cream | potato chips | strawberry |

| Sweet | Spicy | Salty |
|-------|-------|-------|
|       |       |       |
|       |       |       |
|       |       |       |
|       |       |       |

**3** Match the opposites.

1 tasty    a healthy
2 junk    b fresh
3 processed    c meat-eater
4 raw    d mild
5 vegetarian    e disgusting
6 strong    f cooked

**4** Choose the correct options to complete the sentences.

1 Good sushi is always *fresh / sweet*.
2 I can't eat *wheat / junk food*, so I don't usually eat pasta.
3 Thank you for a *well-balanced / delicious* meal. I loved it!
4 *Raw / Processed* vegetables have a lot of vitamins.
5 Could we go somewhere that is *natural / suitable* for vegetarians?
6 Fast food isn't always *junk / natural* food these days. There are more fast-food places with healthy options.

**5** Unscramble the letters to make adjectives that describe food.

1 c k o d o e    c _ _ k _ _ _
2 s e f r h    _ _ _ s h
3 l e b o i d    b _ _ l _ _
4 f e i r d    _ r _ _ _ _
5 a s t y t    _ _ _ _ _ y
6 d e m s a t e    s t _ _ _ _ _ _
7 l a t u n r a    n _ _ _ _ r _ _

**6** Complete the sentences with the words from Activity 5.

1 _____ food can be fried, boiled, or steamed.
2 _____ foods are not processed and they are often good for you.
3 I don't like _____ potatoes. They don't have much flavor.
4 In Vietnam, I picked _____ mangos and oranges for breakfast every day.
5 _____ chicken isn't very healthy, but it's OK to eat it once in a while.
6 I had such a _____ dinner last night. It was delicious!
7 _____ vegetables contain many vitamins.

**7** Read and complete the text with one word in each blank.

My father used to eat a lot of **(1)** _____ meals that weren't good for him, and he especially loved **(2)** _____ food, like potato chips and chocolate bars. Then his doctor told him that he needed to change his diet to keep his heart healthy. So he started eating more **(3)** _____ vegetables that had lots of vitamins. He also started eating **(4)** _____ fruit and eggs for breakfast and drinking less coffee. Now, the doctor says his heart is much **(5)** _____, and my dad says the new foods he eats **(6)** _____ delicious!

**8 Extension** Match the words with their definitions.

1 appetizer
2 grill
3 stir-fry
4 main course
5 diet
6 appetite
7 tasteless

a cook using direct heat
b the biggest part of your meal
c the first thing you eat at a restaurant
d the type of foods that you usually eat
e the feeling of wanting to eat
f having no flavor
g cook by quickly moving around in hot oil

**9 Extension** These sentences are incorrect. Correct them so that they are true.

1 Eating well-balanced meals is part of an unhealthy diet.
*Eating well-balanced meals is part of a healthy diet* .

2 An appetizer is the last thing you eat when you are having dinner.

_____

3 A main course is usually a small dish.

_____

4 Vegetarians mainly eat meat.

_____

5 Steaming fish is less healthy than frying it.

_____

6 A cake is a type of appetizer.

_____

**10 Extension** Complete the chart with these words.

| apple pie | bread and butter | chocolate cake |
| ice cream | mashed potatoes | pasta |
| roast chicken | salad | soup |
| steak | | |

| Appetizer | Main Course | Dessert |
|-----------|-------------|---------|
|           |             |         |
|           |             |         |
|           |             |         |
|           |             |         |

## LISTENING

**11** Listen to the speaker. Then complete the text with these words. There are two words you don't need. 🎧 35

| bakers | celebrating | century | edible |
| gingerbread | horrible | oven-baked | spice |
| sugar | sweet-tasting | wicked | |

Have you ever tasted delicious, **(1)** _____ gingerbread cookies? Or have you ever seen, eaten, or even made a **(2)** _____ house? In many countries, gingerbread is an important part of **(3)** _____ winter holidays. You can thank a **(4)** _____ witch for gingerbread houses. Gingerbread has been around since at least the eleventh **(5)** _____. But, in 1812, the brothers Grimm published *Hansel and Gretel*, featuring a witch who lives in a house made of **(6)** _____. The witch used her **(7)** _____ house to attract unsuspecting children. Luckily for Hansel and Gretel, they were clever enough to escape from the witch. After the success of the story, miniature **(8)** _____ homes became popular. The witch's candy-covered home has inspired **(9)** _____ ever since.

**12** Listen to the recipe for gingerbread. Put the instructions in the correct order. 🎧 36

    **a** refrigerate the dough for three hours ____

    **b** add the spices—cinnamon, ginger, and allspice—to the mixture ____

    **c** bake the cookies at 375 degrees for seven minutes ____

    **d** mix the butter, sugar, an egg, and syrup ____

    **e** complete the dough by mixing in four cups of flour ____

    **f** use a cookie cutter to shape your cookies ____

    **g** let the cookies cool before you decorate with icing ____

    **h** roll out the dough on a floured surface ____

**13** Listen to the speaker and choose the best title for the talk. 🎧 37

    **a** Antarctic Expedition
    **b** Food for Thought
    **c** Breaking Bread Together
    **d** Everybody Loves Candy

**14** Listen to the speaker again and choose the correct options. 🎧 37

    **1** What does the speaker say has always been a part of our human story?
        **a** eating candy
        **b** baking bread
        **c** sharing food

    **2** What was important about the loaf of bread that was discovered?
        **a** It could easily be divided.
        **b** It was found in Italy.
        **c** It had a circular shape.

    **3** What does the speaker say that breaking bread symbolizes?
        **a** children imitating adults
        **b** strengthening relationships
        **c** causing disagreements

    **4** What does the speaker say many people associate with food?
        **a** laughter
        **b** candy
        **c** love

    **5** Why do people in some cultures leave food at graves?
        **a** to show they remember the person
        **b** to forget all the bad things about the person
        **c** to ask the loved one to give them help

    **6** What was the name of the Antarctic expedition in 1902?
        **a** The Discovery Expedition
        **b** The Scott Expedition
        **c** The Midwinter Expedition

    **7** What were the men of the expedition celebrating?
        **a** the cold and the darkness
        **b** the longest night of the year
        **c** the Antarctic regions

## GRAMMAR Future plans, intentions, and arrangements

**15** Choose the correct options to complete the sentences.

    **1** I *'ll probably / might probably* meet some friends for coffee after work.

    **2** I *'m bringing / bring* information about a new restaurant that *opening / opens* next month.

    **3** We *may decide / are going to decide* to have dinner there with our friends in a few weeks.

    **4** We *check / 're going to check* the menu to make sure there's something everyone can eat.

    **5** I'm sure we *'re finding / 'll find* something that everyone will enjoy.

    **6** After we've checked the menu, we *'re going to make / 'll going to make* a decision.

    **7** Later, I *'ll email / 'm emailing* the others to let them know when and where we *'re meeting / meet*.

    **8** I think everyone *will be / is being* pleased with our decision.

    **9** We *possibly invite / might invite* our teacher, too.

**16** Choose the correct options to make the sentences negative.

    **1** If humans ever travel to Mars, they're going to find plants that can be used for food.
        If humans ever travel to Mars, they *aren't going to find / not going to find* plants that can be used for food.

    **2** Humans will probably grow food the same way they did on Earth.
        Humans probably *won't not grow / won't grow* food the same way they did on Earth.

    **3** They may be able to raise animals the way they did on Earth.
        They *may not be / not may be* able to raise animals the way they did on Earth.

    **4** They'll probably have to develop new ways to grow food.
        They *probably might not have to / probably won't have to* develop new ways to grow food.

**5** They're bringing food with them on their spacecraft.
They *don't bring / aren't bringing* food with them on their spacecraft.

**6** Humans will grow food crops outdoors.
Humans *won't grow / willn't grow* food crops outdoors.

**7** The way crops are grown on Mars will work on Earth.
The way crops are grown on Mars *aren't going to work / isn't going to work* on Earth.

**8** If scientists discover a way to feed humans on Mars, we'll go there.
If scientists *won't discover / don't discover* a way to feed humans on Mars, we *won't go / don't go* there.

**17** Read the sentences and decide which is correct. If both are correct, choose "both."

**1 a** Our coffee break starts at 2:30.
 **b** Our coffee break will start at 2:30.
 **c** both

**2 a** Hani is going to teaching me how to make Somali food.
 **b** Hani is going to teach me how to make Somali food.
 **c** both

**3 a** We will eats something when we get to the park.
 **b** We will eat something when we get to the park.
 **c** both

**4 a** Mei meet her friend at the pizza place near the river.
 **b** Mei is meeting her friend at the pizza place near the river.
 **c** both

**5 a** Travis might practice baking cakes next weekend.
 **b** Travis may practice baking cakes next weekend.
 **c** both

**6 a** Is Leon starting a food blog?
 **b** Will Leon starting a food blog?
 **c** both

**7 a** Abdul will spend next semester studying food science.
 **b** Abdul will to spend next semester studying food science.
 **c** both

**8 a** Alejandro is going to text his parents about the new restaurant.
 **b** Alejandro might to text his parents about the new restaurant.
 **c** both

**18** Complete the sentences with the simple present or *going to* form of the verbs in parentheses.

**1** Sophia _____ (work) part-time at a restaurant this semester.

**2** When you _____ (see) Juan tomorrow, tell him that I've made a cake.

**3** Giorgio _____ (plan) to attend a cooking school next summer.

**4** I think Asha _____ (make) us a salad for lunch.

**5** I _____ (steam) some broccoli for the stir-fry.

**6** Malcolm and Shani _____ (bake) a birthday cake for their friend.

**7** The supermarket is closed now, but it _____ (open) at 8 am tomorrow morning.

**8** Dana _____ (come up with) with a menu that everyone will love.

**19** Are these sentences correct or incorrect? Correct those that are incorrect.

**1** We'll have a party at school and eat food from different cultures.

**2** Everyone preparing a dish that is popular in their own country.

**3** Chen is going bring his favorite Chinese dish.

**4** Marisol will cooking a Mexican dish that's very spicy.

**5** Khalid doesn't cook and so he'll ask his mother to prepare falafel for everyone.

**6** Kasia may to make a special dessert—if she can remember where the recipe is.

**7** If he can find the right ingredients, Milan will to make fish stew.

**8** When we will have everything in the cafeteria, it will smell so good.

**9** Everyone is going to have a great time together!

Notes: _____

_____

_____

_____

_____

_____

_____

_____

_____

_____

_____

_____

_____

# 4B Superfood

## VOCABULARY BUILDING Compound adjectives

**1** Match the words to make compound adjectives.

| **1** | | | **2** | | |
|---|---|---|---|---|---|
| **a** | deep- | baked | **a** | well- | cooked |
| **b** | oven- | dried | **b** | old- | finished |
| **c** | home- | fried | **c** | good- | fashioned |
| **d** | sweet- | made | **d** | over- | known |
| **e** | sun- | tasting | **e** | half- | looking |

## READING

**2** Read the text and match the summaries (a–f) with the paragraphs (1–5) next to each statement.

**a** the real cost of avocados _____
**b** superfoods and natural resources _____
**c** the consequences of quinoa's popularity _____
**d** a description of superfoods _____
**e** a description of quinoa _____
**f** the limitations of superfoods _____

**3** Read the statements. Are the sentences true (T), false (F), or is the information not given (NG)?

**1** Superfoods are packed with benefits that aren't always available in other foods. _____
**2** Quinoa can be cooked like rice. _____
**3** Quinoa has only recently become known in South America. _____
**4** Because quinoa is so rich in nutrients, it's a good substitute for meat. _____
**5** Like quinoa, avocados have very specific requirements for growth. _____
**6** Superfoods are good for us, and they're also good for the environment. _____

**4** Choose the correct options to complete the sentences.

**1** Avocados, like quinoa, blueberries, almonds, and salmon, are considered a _____.
   **a** grain
   **b** seed
   **c** superfood

**2** These types of food are thought to be rich in nutrients and low in _____.
   **a** diets
   **b** calories
   **c** resources

**3** Quinoa is an ancient _____ that, until recently, was unknown outside South America.
   **a** grain
   **b** fiber
   **c** nutrient

**4** The _____ of the quinoa plant can be cooked and eaten.
   **a** flower
   **b** seeds
   **c** production

**5** A consequence of quinoa's popularity is a change in the _____ of people who've traditionally grown it.
   **a** price
   **b** popularity
   **c** diet

**6** Rice and noodles are less _____ than quinoa.
   **a** tasty
   **b** nutritious
   **c** popular

**7** The _____ of a kilo of avocados takes more than 800 liters of water!
   **a** resources
   **b** advantage
   **c** production

# The Quinoa Conundrum*

1  🎧 38  Do you love avocados? Do you adore almonds? These familiar foods have, among others, recently become known as "superfoods." What makes a food "super"? So-called superfoods are a special category of foods that are considered nutrient-rich, low in calories, and packed with health benefits not always found in other foods. Almonds, avocados, blueberries, and salmon are among the most commonly known superfoods.

2  There are also a number of less familiar foods that fall into the category of superfoods. Among these is an ancient grain called quinoa. Quinoa is a flowering plant that, until very recently, was known and used only in the Andean highlands of South America. The seeds of the quinoa plant can be cooked like rice and other grains, and are unusually well-balanced—the tiny grain is rich in fiber*, amino acids*, vitamins, minerals, and other important nutrients. Although quinoa has been eaten in South America for thousands of years (the ancient Incas referred to it as "the mother grain"), it's only recently become known to the rest of the world as a superfood.

3  One result of the sudden and tremendous popularity of quinoa is a change in the diets of people who've traditionally grown and eaten it. Because their crops are now more valuable and they have more money to spend, some quinoa growers prefer to eat less quinoa and more of the non-traditional and often less nutritious foods that were previously unavailable to them, such as rice or noodles, and even candy and fizzy drinks.

Other quinoa farmers can no longer afford to eat the newly expensive grain they grow and have to find alternative foods to eat.

4  Another issue related to the popularity of this superfood is the availability of resources needed to grow it. As prices for quinoa continue to rise, so do prices for the land on which it's grown. And because the quinoa plant has very specific requirements, there's only so much available land on which to successfully farm it. The same is true for avocados. Avocados are another ancient Latin American food that has become wildly popular after being labeled a superfood. Avocados require water, and lots of it! It takes more than 800 liters* of water to produce a kilo* of avocados. That's like filling a bathtub with water for each avocado you eat! In the state of California, half a billion kilos of avocados are grown annually, and that means billions of liters of water for their production. But California sometimes experiences extended periods of drought*, making the cost of water, like the cost of land, rise dramatically. This makes water-hungry avocados expensive to buy and sometimes too expensive to grow.

5  Are superfoods good for your health, but bad for the planet? As is the case with almost anything we eat or use, sustainability is always an issue. It's becoming clear that we won't always be able to have everything we'd like to eat, at any time of year, wherever we are. Even superfoods come at a cost.

**conundrum** *a question that has no real answer*
**fiber** *a substance in plants that helps food pass through the body*
**amino acids** *acids that occur in living things and that sometimes form proteins*

**liter** *about a quarter of a gallon*
**kilo** *about 2.2 pounds*
**drought** *a long period of time during which there is very little or no rain*

# 4C  Will you… ?

## GRAMMAR  Making predictions

**1** Underline the sentences that make predictions about future plans, intentions, and arrangements.

Camila grew up in a small town. Her family had lived there for many years. She loved walking to school with her sisters and cousins, and stopping by her grandparents' house on the way home. When she was in high school, her aunt asked Camila what she wanted to do in the future. Camila said, "I'm going to go to college. I'll probably study biology. I might have to do more training, but then I'm going to be a doctor." Her aunt replied, "That sounds great, Camila! You may have to work very hard if that's your ambition. I wanted to be a doctor when I was younger, but I didn't have enough money for college. I had to work after school. I'm sure you will do well if you study a lot and ask for help when you need it."

**2** Choose the correct options to complete the sentences.

1 Amy *will meet / meet* us for a picnic after she *finishes / is going to finish* work.
2 I *'ll / might* probably buy some cheese for my omelet.
3 As soon as she *will get / gets* more business, her store *will be / be* successful.
4 I *won't / willn't* order a cupcake if I have a big lunch.
5 Makoto *going to / may* graduate early if his grades *are / will be* good enough.
6 When I *won't ask / ask* my parents if I can go on the trip, *I'll / I'm* also ask if I can borrow some money.
7 I'm sure Celina will *be taking / be taken* her brother to the barbecue because her dad *won't / isn't* be able to look after him.
8 She's *will / going to* study in Colombia next year so that she'll *have spoken / spoken* a lot of Spanish before graduating.

**3** Complete the sentences about future plans, intentions, and arrangements.

| does | going to | is | 'll | might | she'll | will | won't |
|------|----------|----|----|-------|--------|------|-------|

1 What time _____ the concert start?
2 This book is so great—I know you _____ want to read it.
3 He really wants to get his own apartment. I think he _____ move back to his parents' house after graduation.
4 What time _____ Paolo's graduation party?
5 Carlos _____ order mashed potatoes with his steak.
6 I imagine Tetsu _____ want to take a shower after jogging in the park.
7 They're _____ be ready to leave at seven thirty.
8 I don't know if _____ have enough time to help me study.

**4** Choose the sentence in each pair that is more certain.

1 a We might walk to the post office this afternoon if it doesn't rain.
  b I'm going to order a green tea when we get to the café.
2 a We're going to my parents' house on Monday for my dad's birthday.
  b They may go for a pizza if they haven't already eaten lunch.
3 a We're leaving at six o'clock tomorrow morning.
  b If you arrive by five o'clock, we might have enough time to go out for dinner.
4 a I think she'll be home by 3:30.
  b He won't go to work tomorrow because it's a holiday.
5 a We'll probably take the train to the game.
  b Khalid isn't going to study for the exam this afternoon.
6 a I imagine he'll be disappointed if he doesn't win.
  b Isha will be studying tonight because she has a test tomorrow.
7 a Perhaps we can talk to our coach next week.
  b By the end of the summer, Aurelia will have played soccer for three months.

**5** Rewrite each sentence to make it positive.

**1** My uncle won't plant more flowers this spring.

_____

**2** Mara isn't going to buy balloons for Jed's birthday.

_____

**3** I'm not going to listen to the program.

_____

**4** We won't have learned about Ancient Rome by the end of this semester.

_____

**5** We won't be eating dinner when you arrive.

_____

**6** My parents won't buy me a new car after graduation.

_____

**6** Put the words in the correct order to make sentences and questions.

**1** clap / the / bad, / if / the / play / is / won't / audience / .

_____

**2** Tanzania / January / be / to / in / flying / they'll / .

_____

**3** going / US / I'm / not / to / next / study / in / the / year / .

_____

**4** a / you / for / when / year / will / have / here / worked / ?

_____

**5** assignments / collecting / the / Ms. Shultz / be / in / class / won't / .

_____

**6** party / the / by the time / downloaded / the / songs / she'll / have / we / get / to / .

_____

**7** Match the two parts of the sentences.

**1** Are you going _____
**2** They'll be _____
**3** I expect _____
**4** I'm going to _____
**5** I think if we all recycle more, there _____
**6** I'm going to stay up late tonight, so I'll _____
**7** When will you _____
**a** 'll be less litter around campus.
**b** have bought the books you need?
**c** probably be tired tomorrow.
**d** seeing the movie with Daniel's cousins.
**e** to read the book before you see the movie?
**f** watch that documentary about chefs tonight.
**g** to decorate the classroom for our teacher's last day.

**8** Read and listen to the questions. Choose the correct options. 🎧 **39**

**1** Will you invite Zhen to your party?
   **a** No, I won't possibly invite her.
   **b** No, I don't think I'll invite her to my party.
**2** Will the hockey players be wearing their red or white uniforms?
   **a** They will have worn the red ones.
   **b** They're going to wear the red ones.
**3** Will Mr. Jackson be hiring more people to work at the library?
   **a** Yes, he will hiring more people.
   **b** No, he won't.
**4** Will you have listened to the jazz album before your performance?
   **a** Yes, I'll have listened to it before my performance.
   **b** No, I won't be listened to it before my performance.
**5** When is the violin concert?
   **a** It will have been playing on Sunday.
   **b** It's on Sunday.
**6** As soon as you get home, will you turn on the oven?
   **a** No problem. I'll turn it on as soon as I get home.
   **b** Sure. I turn it on as soon as I will get home.
**7** What did you think about the play you saw last night?
   **a** It's great. You're going to love it!
   **b** It'll be great. You won't like it.
**8** Will he have gotten his driver's license by June?
   **a** Yes, he's planning to get it at the end of April.
   **b** Yes, he'll get it last month.

## PRONUNCIATION  Sentence stress with the future continuous and future perfect

**9** Listen to the sentences. Underline at least two words that are stressed in each sentence. Then practice saying the sentences. 🎧 **40**

**1** Anna won't be eating seafood.
**2** The chef will be preparing something special.
**3** They won't have arrived in Shanghai yet.
**4** He'll have left by the time you get there.
**5** What will you be doing tomorrow?
**6** She won't have finished her work.

# 4D Why I'm a Weekday Vegetarian

## TEDTALKS

## AUTHENTIC LISTENING SKILLS

**1** Listen to the TED Talk excerpts. Choose the type of pause the speaker uses in each one. 🎧 **41**

**1** So really, any of these angles should have been enough to convince me to go vegetarian. *adverbial time phrase / end of a sentence / commas*

**2** On the weekend, your choice. *adverbial time phrase / between a long subject and verb / before an important phrase*

**3** After all, cutting five days a week is cutting 70 percent of your meat intake. *commas / before an important phrase / between a long subject and verb*

**4** My footprint's smaller, I'm lessening pollution, I feel better about the animals, I'm even saving money. *commas / before an important phrase / adverbial time phrase*

**5** After all, if all of us ate half as much meat, it would be like half of us were vegetarians. *end of a sentence / commas / before an important phrase*

## WATCH ▶

**2** Choose five reasons Graham Hill gives for becoming a vegetarian.

**a** Eating too much red meat is unhealthy.
**b** It's easy to become a vegetarian even if you enjoy meat.
**c** Raising animals for meat causes environmental damage.
**d** Raising cows for beef uses 100 times the water that vegetables use.
**e** Giving up meat is an easy way to lose a lot of weight.
**f** The conditions in factory farms are cruel.
**g** Steak doesn't taste as good as it used to.
**h** The emissions caused by meat production are higher than all transport combined.

**3** Read the questions and choose the best summaries of Graham Hill's answers.

**1** Graham Hill asked himself: "Knowing what I know, why am I not a vegetarian?"
He answered:
**a** "I had all the facts, but I still kept eating meat."
**b** "I had no idea how bad meat was."
**c** "Meat isn't as bad as people say."

**2** Graham Hill asked himself: "So why was I stalling?"
He answered:
**a** "I realized there was no way to change my taste buds."
**b** "I realized I was only given two options—give up meat entirely or not at all."
**c** "I realized I never really wanted to eat vegetarian food."

**3** Graham Hill asked himself: "Might there be a third solution?"
He answered:
**a** "Not yet. I'm still thinking about this."
**b** "Simple. Just stop eating meat altogether."
**c** "Absolutely. I stopped eating meat on weekdays."

**4** Graham Hill asked the audience: "What's stopping you from giving weekday veg a shot?"
He answered:
**a** "If everyone did their part, it would make a big difference."
**b** "If only half of you did this, it wouldn't have an effect."
**c** "Half of you should become vegetarian, and the other half should eat meat."

## VOCABULARY IN CONTEXT

**4** Choose the correct options to complete the sentences.

**1** Eating too much red meat may be a
_____ to your health.
**a** damage    **b** risk    **c** conflict

**2** My grandmother lives in the country and
_____ chickens on her farm.
**a** grows    **b** lifts    **c** raises

**3** Eating a lot of meat also causes environmental
_____ .
**a** conflict    **b** damage    **c** shame

**4** If you haven't _____ a solution by now, you never will.
**a** come up with      **c** caught up with
**b** teamed up with

**5** My love for animals was _____ my love for fried chicken.
**a** teamed up with      **c** in agreement with
**b** in conflict with

**6** The amount of greenhouse gas created by meat production is greater than for all forms of transportation
_____ .
**a** surrounded      **c** combined
**b** joined

# 4E Future Plans

## SPEAKING

**1** Look at the photos and match the two parts of the sentences. Then listen and check your answers. 🎧 42

Gena

Tom

Stefan

**Gena**
1 I'm thinking of…
2 I'm interested in…
3 I'm hoping to…

**Tom**
4 I'm looking forward to…
5 I'd really like to…
6 I'm aiming to…

**Stefan**
7 I think I might…
8 I expect to…

a be famous.
b becoming a vegetarian.
c work on the farm next month instead of going on a vacation.
d helping people.
e become a farmer like my dad and grandpa.
f have read several Shakespeare plays by the end of the semester.
g studying theater in college.
h volunteer for a charity.

**2** Complete the conversation with the phrases (1–8) from Activity 1. Then listen and check your answers. 🎧 43

A Hey, what's going on with you this summer? Are you going to be around?

B I'm not sure, actually. **(1)** _____ try to find a job. It'll be a long summer without any money.

C Yeah, **(2)** _____ be here. My parents are working, so I don't think we're going on vacation or anything.

A Well, **(3)** _____ going to the coast for a week or two, just camping and having a relaxing time. Are you interested in coming along?

B Hmm, I'm not sure. In the long term, **(4)** _____ study tourism in college, so I think finding a job would be a good idea for me this summer, to give me some practical experience. **(5)** _____ have something worked out by next month, so if I don't, can I let you know then?

A Sure. **(6)** _____ hang out with you this summer so let me know whether you can make it. How about you, Maria? Are you up for it?

C Yeah, **(7)** _____ spending some time by the sea. I love the beach! What are you planning to do while you're there?

A Well, **(8)** _____ learning to surf, so I guess I'll spend a lot of time doing that.

C Oh, really? Me, too! We could practice together.

A That sounds awesome. What do you think, Sal, still can't tempt you to a couple of weeks on the beach?

B Well, maybe. But only if I can't find a job, otherwise I can always come for a day or two. But do you know anyone who's looking for a . . . ?

**3** Think about your hopes and goals for the topics below and write a list. Make notes and then compare your ideas with the sample answers. 🎧 44

**Think about:**

a school and study
b hobbies and interests
c friends and relationships

*I expect to go to college…*

**4** Answer the question below. Make notes on a separate sheet of paper and give reasons for your ideas. Then listen to the sample answer and compare it with your ideas. 🎧 45

What type of job do you imagine yourself doing in the future?

# WRITING  A social media update

**5** Complete the chart with these examples of tips for writing social media updates.

We enjoyed a fabulous feast.

~~We were furious because the bus left early.~~

Having a wonderful time.

In the next few days, we're hoping to do more sightseeing.

It's amazing here!

This morning, I had the best melon I've ever tasted.

| Tip | Example |
|-----|---------|
| Leave out the subject in sentences. | |
| Use exclamation points. | |
| Use descriptive vocabulary. | |
| Use emotionally powerful words. | *We were furious because the bus left early.* |
| Talk about recent events. | |
| Talk about future plans and hopes. | |

**6** Complete the tips (1–6) with the reasons for doing them (a–f).

**1** It's OK to leave out the subject in some sentences _____

**2** It's good to use exclamation marks _____

**3** Using descriptive vocabulary is recommended _____

**4** Emotionally powerful words improve the post _____

**5** It's a good idea to talk about recent events _____

**6** Try to mention some future plans and hopes _____

**a** because they give the reader a very clear sense of how the writer is feeling.

**b** because this gives readers an idea of what they will find in your next update.

**c** because they help the reader to recognize surprising or unusual events.

**d** because readers are interested in what's happening currently.

**e** because this helps informal posts to sound more like a diary entry or a postcard.

**f** because it makes the writing much more interesting for the reader.

**7** Complete the social media update with these words.

| camping | delicious | magnificent | meat dishes |
| on the way here | planning | terrified | traditional |

South Africa is truly amazing! Left Cape Town yesterday and drove to our camp at Storms River. Oh, **(1)** _____, we stopped to see the wildlife at a national park. The elephants were beautiful, I mean, really **(2)** _____! Some people were frightened when we suddenly saw a lion… it was so close! To be honest, I was pretty **(3)** _____, but later I was glad I'd seen it. The scenery around here is astonishing. We're staying in comfortable but very basic huts (don't like **(4)** _____!). Last night, we went to a **(5)** _____ restaurant for dinner. The local seafood was absolutely incredible, but I didn't try any of the **(6)** _____. Never expected to find crocodile, zebra, and ostrich on a dinner menu, but others in the group said they were **(7)** _____.

For the rest of this week, we'll be hiking along the river and through the forest. Can't wait to see the waterfall. I'm **(8)** _____ to go bungee jumping tomorrow, have never done it before! I'll post a photo. ☺

**8** Read the social media update again. Choose the seven things that the writer did.

**1** left the subject out of some sentences

**2** said how many other people are on the trip

**3** used exclamation points

**4** mentioned the cost of the trip

**5** included descriptive vocabulary

**6** talked about some of the food on the trip

**7** described the weather

**8** used emotionally powerful words

**9** complained about some of the activities

**10** talked about recent events

**11** explained what they're doing next week

**12** mentioned future plans and hopes

**9** Write at least 250 words on the topic below. Include any relevant examples from your knowledge or experience.

These days, more and more people do not have enough money to buy food. Many supermarkets throw away food items they have not sold. Governments should force all supermarkets to donate food rather than waste it.

What are the advantages and disadvantages of this?

# Review

① Match the words with a similar meaning.

| | | | |
|---|---|---|---|
| **1** | tasty | **a** | uncooked |
| **2** | healthy | **b** | delicious |
| **3** | disgusting | **c** | well-balanced |
| **4** | raw | **d** | terrible |
| **5** | junk | **e** | unnatural |
| **6** | processed | **f** | unhealthy |

② Complete the second sentence so that it means the same as the first. Use no more than three words.

**1** I haven't eaten processed food in a long time.

It's been a long time _____ processed food.

**2** Don't eat so much unhealthy stuff like chocolate and potato chips!

Don't eat so much _____ food!

**3** Fried chicken is popular because of the ease of cooking it.

Fried chicken is popular because _____ to cook.

**4** If you don't boil rice long enough, it will be hard.

Rice will be hard if you don't _____ long enough.

**5** The food at camp is too unhealthy to eat.

The food at camp isn't _____ to eat.

**6** I prefer being a vegetarian to eating meat.

I'd rather be a vegetarian than a _____.

③ Put the words in the correct order to make sentences and questions.

**1** arrive / the food / will / in time / for us / to eat / ?

_____

**2** making / the chef / is / week / risotto / next / .

_____

**3** find out / about / the daily specials / how / the customers / will / ?

_____

**4** be / for / everyone / tomorrow / to / get together / might / the best time / .

_____

**5** carefully / the ingredients / measure / I / will / very / .

_____

**6** are / the inspectors / for / going to / ask / more information / .

_____

**7** help / tomorrow / my cousin / at their café / might / his parents / .

_____

**8** cold / soon / get / going to / if / we / the soup / is / don't eat / .

_____

④ Complete the conversations about predictions, plans, intentions, and arrangements.

**1 A** Is Hugo driving to Chicago on Tuesday?
**B** Yes, he _____.

**2 A** What's wrong?
**B** You're driving too fast! You're _____ get a speeding ticket.

**3 A** Is she stopping at the clinic on the way home?
**B** I don't remember if she's _____ stop at the clinic.

**4 A** Will students register for courses online next year?
**B** No, students _____ be registering online next year.

**5 A** Daria is eating so much chocolate.
**B** I think she _____ have a stomach ache tonight.

**6 A** What time do you want to leave for the movie theater?
**B** Well, the movie _____ at nine o'clock. So let's leave by eight-thirty.

⑤ Are the words in bold correct or incorrect? Correct those that are incorrect.

**1** I expect that **you'll** want to take a lot of pictures of the beautiful mountains.

**2** We don't have time to stop for lunch. You're **will be** hungry when we get to the beach.

**3** We're going into town for the game tonight. We **possibly** try the new Vietnamese restaurant.

**4 A** How long are you **going to staying** in Mexico?
**B** I'll be there for a week.

**5** Until I **will graduate**, I'll live with my parents.

**6** By the end of the summer, Ben **will have gone** camping with his friends three times.

**7** I **think I won't** pass my exam today.

# 5 Work

## 5A New Ways of Working

### VOCABULARY Describing work

**1 Review** What type of jobs are these? Complete the chart.

| accountant | chief executive | firefighter | lawyer |
|---|---|---|---|
| paramedic | police officer | salesperson | store manager |

| Emergency services | Desk jobs | Retail |
|---|---|---|
| | | |

**2 Review** Listen and complete the words for jobs. The first letters are given for you. 🎧 46

1 n __ __ __ __
2 t __ __ __ __ __ __
3 l __ __ __ __ __
4 c __ __ __
5 a __ __ __ __ __ __ __ __ __
6 a __ __ __ __ __ __ __

**3 Review** Which people often work together? Match the jobs.

| 1 doctor | **a** police officer |
|---|---|
| 2 lawyer | **b** paramedic |
| 3 firefighter | **c** waiter/waitress |
| 4 salesperson | **d** manager |
| 5 office worker | **e** nurse |
| 6 chef | **f** store manager |

**4** Match the two parts of the sentences.

1 After he lost his job, _____
2 Being a chief executive is well paid, _____
3 I love being a writer _____
4 The newspaper industry is changing _____
5 Acting is competitive because _____
6 I am very busy at home, _____

**a** but it is also very demanding.
**b** because I can be creative.
**c** he was out of work for six months.
**d** so I'd prefer a part-time job.
**e** so many people want to do it.
**f** because people often get their news online.

**5** Choose the correct options to complete the sentences.

1 If you don't have many qualifications, your *career prospects / part-time work* are limited.
2 My job as a doctor is rewarding, but it's also *demanding / well-paid*.
3 Her job is *creative / flexible*. She can work whatever hours she wants.
4 I've been *working on / working for* a new design for six months.
5 He has been in the film *career / industry* for over twenty years.
6 Being a paramedic is *stressful / competitive*. I have to make life-or-death decisions every day.
7 She enjoys being a lawyer, but she's looking for something more *demanding / creative*, like writing or designing.

**6** Match the words and phrases with a similar meaning.

| 1 stressful | **a** unemployed |
|---|---|
| 2 industry | **b** with a good salary |
| 3 out of work | **c** business |
| 4 job | **d** work |
| 5 well-paid | **e** responsible for |
| 6 in charge of | **f** demanding |

**7** Complete the sentences with *in*, *for*, or *on*.

1 I work _____ my parents at their ice-cream shop every summer.

2 The architect has been working _____ a new building in the city center.

3 I've been working _____ my new book for months, but I have writer's block!

4 He's been working _____ the publishing industry for years. He's a great editor.

5 She doesn't like her job as a lawyer, but she does it _____ the money.

6 My friend was working _____ an exciting project when she lost her job.

7 I used to work _____ the office five days a week, but now I work from home on Tuesdays.

**8** Put the words in the correct order to make sentences.

1 being / I / of / a / like / charge / in / team / large / .
_____

2 out / work / he / been / has / of / three / months / for / .
_____

3 big / for / me / working / projects / is / on / stressful / .
_____

4 writer / such / a / is / being / creative / a / job / .
_____

5 with / job / for / I / looking / career / am / a / prospects / .
_____

6 wants / work / the / in / entertainment / she / industry / to / .
_____

7 aren't / jobs, / so / many / competitive / very / it's / there / .
_____

**9** **Extension** Complete the sentences with the correct forms of *find*, *need*, or *quit*.

1 I have to _____ a job soon—I really need the money.

2 She finally _____ her job as a doctor after seven years.

3 My friend _____ her job as a salesperson by looking at the store's website.

4 Do you know anyone who _____ a part-time job? We're hiring at our restaurant.

5 I don't do this job because I _____ it. I do it because I love it!

6 Why did you _____ your job? Was it too stressful?

**10** **Extension** Read the statements. Are the sentences true (T) or false (F)? Correct the false statements.

1 A rewarding job makes you feel like you are doing something important and useful. _____

2 An open position is a job that is no longer available for someone to do. _____

3 A challenging job is a job that doesn't require much effort. _____

4 If you resign, you quit your job. _____

5 A supervisor is in charge of other members of staff. _____

6 A person who is retired is at the beginning of their career. _____

7 A trainee is a person who is learning to do a job. _____

## LISTENING

**11** Listen and complete the sentences. 🎧 47

1 You _____ look for a job that gives you a feeling of satisfaction.

2 The referee at a soccer match _____ enforce the rules.

3 The dog trainer _____ stop the dog from biting people.

4 Police _____ drive faster than the speed limit when they _____ .

5 I _____ understand how some people _____ work such long hours.

6 He _____ apply for the job. His father owns the company.

**12** Listen to the speaker. Are the sentences true (T) or false (F)? 🎧 **48**

**1** Cesar Millan is a dog trainer. _____
**2** Millan couldn't tell Kisses and Kitten apart. _____
**3** The dog was the color of cotton candy. _____
**4** The name of Millan's TV show is *The Whisperer*. _____
**5** A "whisperer" can talk to animals. _____
**6** Millan tries to fix behavioral challenges. _____
**7** Millan thinks dogs often behave badly. _____
**8** Millan trains both the dog and the owner. _____

**13** Listen and choose the correct options. 🎧 **49**

**1** What breed is the pink dog?
  **a** Kisses
  **b** Maltese
  **c** Millan

**2** Was Kisses' problem very unusual?
  **a** Yes, it was a first for Millan.
  **b** No, not for young, female dogs.
  **c** No, it happens with all dogs.

**3** What word does the speaker use to mean *a learned response*?
  **a** a routine
  **b** a pattern
  **c** a habit

**4** What does Millan always try to do for his audience?
  **a** teach a lesson
  **b** answer questions
  **c** fix their problems

**5** How does Millan change dogs' behavior?
  **a** He teaches their owners to punish them more.
  **b** He rewards the owners when they succeed.
  **c** He teaches them new responses to situations.

**6** How would you describe Millan's training method?
  **a** patience and punishment
  **b** repetition and rewards
  **c** respect and patience

**7** What is another word for *reward* that the speaker uses?
  **a** a sweet
  **b** a cookie
  **c** a treat

**14** Listen and choose the correct options. 🎧 **50**

**1** What two animals are mentioned as "service animals"?
  **a** dogs and sheep
  **b** elephants and dogs
  **c** monkeys and dogs

**2** What do service animals do?
  **a** control other farm animals
  **b** assist blind and deaf people
  **c** provide transportation

**3** What was Gavin the dog's previous job?
  **a** working for the military
  **b** working for the police
  **c** controlling other animals

**4** What was Gavin's biggest problem?
  **a** He was afraid of other dogs.
  **b** He was a workaholic.
  **c** He needed a new job.

**5** What did Millan do for Gavin?
  **a** He taught him to be calm and relax.
  **b** He gave him a new purpose in life.
  **c** He helped him to start a new family.

**6** What was Gavin's first new job?
  **a** protecting a mother dog and her puppies
  **b** adopting a new human family
  **c** learning not to fear loud sounds

**7** What is the joke in the last sentence?
  **a** a dog chewing on shoes and couches
  **b** a dog taking a human for a walk
  **c** a dog chasing a Frisbee or ball

## GRAMMAR Verb patterns: verb + -ing or infinitive with to

**15** Complete the chart with these sentences.

He's the kind of person who doesn't like disappointing people.

I think the owner is planning to hire more people.

I've promised to talk to the bank about a business loan.

Remember to check your spelling before you submit the application form.

She'll go on searching for a job until she finds something.

We agreed to continue the discussion tomorrow.

We only hire people who don't mind accepting challenges.

Why don't you try looking on the company website?

| Verb + -ing | Infinitive with to |
|---|---|
|  |  |
|  |  |
|  |  |
|  |  |
|  |  |
|  |  |

**16** Choose the correct options to complete the sentences.

**1** I'm planning *looking / to look* for a part-time job when I can finally drive.

**2** I'd consider *to work / working* at a shopping mall.

**3** I've spent hours *to apply / applying* for jobs online and *asking / to ask* my friends if they know of any.

**4** I haven't managed *to get / getting* any interviews so far.

**5** I hope *finding / to find* a job sometime soon because I really need the money.

**6** My friends invited me *to travel / traveling* across Spain with them and I want *going / to go*.

**7** We want *flying / to fly* to Barcelona and visit some friends there.

**8** I'll keep *looking / to look* for a job until I find one that I really like.

**17** Complete the sentences with the correct forms of the verbs in parentheses.

**1** Office workers often have to get used to _____ (spend) all day in front of their computers.

**2** But many of them don't mind _____ (sit) at their desks, _____ (send) emails, and _____ (talk) on the phone.

**3** Some people even manage _____ (go) outside during their lunch break.

**4** They'd like _____ (spend) more time outdoors, but they can't.

**5** People who work outside often dislike _____ (work) in the winter.

**6** Some of them hope _____ (find) office jobs so they can be more comfortable.

**7** But then they realize that they would miss _____ (be) in the fresh air.

**18** Complete the sentences with the correct forms of these verbs.

| be | give | miss | solve | talk | tell | work |
|---|---|---|---|---|---|---|

**1** Would you mind _____ me directions to City Hall?

**2** I can't afford _____ another day of work.

**3** We all pretended _____ really busy when the boss walked in.

**4** Please stop _____ me how to do my job!

**5** How did you end up _____ here?

**6** Thankfully, we managed _____ the problem.

**7** Do you enjoy _____ to new people?

**19** Find and correct the mistakes. There is one in each sentence.

**1** Our hard-working and creative employees have learned producing smartphone apps more efficiently.

**2** Neither of my parents likes to working long hours.

**3** I don't want be in charge of people who don't do their jobs well.

**4** Most college graduates expect finding well-paid jobs.

**5** I agreed attending the training course because we want the company to remain competitive.

**6** Have you considered to research jobs in the tech industries?

**7** Customers often go on to complaining even when you've told them there's nothing you can do.

# 5B An Unusual Job

## VOCABULARY BUILDING Ways of seeing

**1** Choose the correct options to complete the sentences.

1 I hadn't seen Javier for years—I hardly *recognized / identified* him.

2 Over a two-month period, researchers *observed / spotted* schoolchildren in three different countries.

3 I didn't have time to read the report in detail—I only *glanced / caught* at it.

4 Has the driver of the vehicle been *noticed / identified* yet?

5 Ava's leaving work early—I just *observed / spotted* her getting into her car.

6 We suddenly *noticed / recognized* that the door had been left open.

## READING

**2** Read the text and choose the correct options to answer the questions.

1 How did Krithi Karanth first become interested in wildlife conservation?
   a She saw a tiger in the wild when she was three years old.
   b Her father started taking her to work with him when she was very young.
   c She grew up on the Indian subcontinent.
   d She went on an expedition to track tigers.

2 According to paragraph 2, why are conflicts between people and wildlife in India inevitable?
   a Much of the wildlife in India lives in protected national parks.
   b Conservation workers and local communities disagree about preserving wildlife.
   c People and wildlife must share limited space along park borders and edges.
   d Wildlife conservation efforts are directed mostly toward tigers and elephants.

3 According to paragraph 3, approximately how many of the households surveyed by Krithi Karanth were affected by conflicts with wild animals?
   a about 80%          c 2,000
   b all of them         d 15%

4 How does the Wild Seve project help villagers affected by conflicts with wild animals?
   a They leave a voice message with details about the incident.
   b They teach local people to use cellphones to report conflicts with wildlife.
   c They compensate Indian citizens for losses caused by protected wildlife.
   d They help the Indian government track animals.

5 Why is it helpful to be flexible in order to work as a wildlife conservation scientist?
   a Wildlife conservation scientists aren't very well-paid.
   b Wildlife conservation scientists must sleep outside.
   c A wildlife conservation scientist must learn to use sophisticated technology.
   d A wildlife conservation scientist must be happy to work both in an office and outdoors.

**3** Read the statements. Are the sentences true (T), false (F), or is the information not given (NG)?

1 Krithi Karanth spotted her first leopard when she was only a year old. _____

2 People and wildlife are in conflict in India because space for both is shrinking. _____

3 Roughly 65% of households surveyed by Krithi Karanth lost valuable animals as a result of conflicts with wildlife. _____

4 The Indian government is looking for ways to move elephants that are involved in conflicts with villagers. _____

5 Elephants in India do more damage than feral pigs. _____

6 A wildlife biologist must know how to use technology and how to survive in the field. _____

**4** Choose the correct options to complete the sentences.

1 Krithi Karanth first _____ a leopard in the wild at the age of two.
   a held            c observed
   b rescued         d photographed

2 Krithi and other researchers are _____ for ways to help humans and animals avoid conflict.
   a listening       c looking
   b noticing        d recognizing

3 Researchers _____ to identify households that had suffered losses as a result of conflicts with wildlife.
   a were allowed    c were able
   b didn't need     d don't have

4 The Wild Seve project teaches people _____ situations in which villagers and wildlife come into conflict.
   a to compensate   c to encourage
   b to report       d to call

5 Krithi's daughter _____ her first leopard in the wild at the age of four.
   a spotted         c caught
   b described       d helped

# A Wild Job

**1** 🎧 **51** Her father, one of India's most well-known conservationists and tiger experts, started taking her into the jungle with him when she was just a year old. She spotted her first leopard in the wild at the age of two. By the time she was eight, she was going along on expeditions to track tigers. Today, conservation scientist Krithi Karanth works to help some of the world's most familiar species, including tigers and Asian elephants, to coexist* with the approximately one billion people who live on the Indian subcontinent.

**2** Much of India's wildlife lives in protected national parks. Because humans and wildlife must share space along park edges and borders, conflicts are inevitable*. As Krithi says, "Spaces for wildlife are shrinking, and therefore you are putting people in closer contact with wildlife." Krithi, a National Geographic Explorer, is looking for ways to address conflicts between wildlife conservation efforts and local communities that are affected by wild animals, particularly tigers and elephants.

**3** As part of that effort, Krithi and other researchers initially surveyed nearly 2,000 households within 10 kilometers (about 6.2 miles) of a nature reserve. They found that roughly 65% of those households had suffered crop losses due to feral* pigs and elephants, while another 15% lost livestock* to tigers, leopards, foxes, and wild dogs. Krithi also found cases of human injury or death caused by the animals the reserves are meant to protect.

**4** While the Indian government compensates* Indian citizens for losses caused by protected wildlife, the process can be complicated for farmers and compensation is sometimes not enough. As a result, according to one of Krithi's colleagues: "the level of distrust between conservation officers and local villagers is extremely high." Wild Seve, an action-based research project that Krithi helped create, is hoping to help. The Wild Seve project teaches farmers and local people to use cellphone technology to report and hopefully resolve conflicts with wildlife. After a wildlife encounter, villagers are encouraged to call a toll-free phone number and are prompted to leave a voice message with details about the incident. Field staff from Wild Seve then visit the site, view and document the damage, file a claim on behalf of the farmer, and track the claim until the farmer is compensated.

**5** A wildlife conservation scientist must be flexible enough to work long hours both in the field and in a lab or office. He or she must be comfortable with sophisticated technology and with sleeping in a tent or on the ground. It's not an extremely well-paid job and it's very demanding, but it can be a deeply satisfying career for someone who loves wildlife and the outdoors. Krithi is passing her passion for wildlife on to her own child, who glimpsed* her first leopard at the age of four. "We were with my parents, and all three generations of us sat in absolute silence, taking in the moment, watching this amazing leopard. There are not enough words to describe that memory."

**coexist** *to live together*
**inevitable** *sure to happen*
**feral** *describing a farm animal or pet that has become wild*

**livestock** *farm animals such as cows and pigs*
**compensate** *to give money in return for something*
**glimpse** *to see something for a very short time*

# 5C Advice

## GRAMMAR Present and past modals

**1** Listen and complete the sentences. 🎧 52

1 My parents are working, so I _____ dinner for my little brother.
2 They _____ their friends while they're having breakfast.
3 Our team really _____ this game.
4 They _____ three more points to win.
5 We _____ Julia to come to the concert with us.
6 I _____ the dog for a walk before I go out.
7 You _____ her some flowers when you visit.

**2** Complete the chart with these sentences.

Do you think she'll be able to help with the project?
I think you should ask him for help with your resume.
Ron couldn't take a day off because he didn't have enough vacation time.
I could pay for lunch if you like.
She isn't allowed to use the phone at work.
Should I ask her for an interview?
You shouldn't eat lunch at your desk.
Can you send an application after the closing date?
You should come to the office party.

| Ability or possibility | Advice | Prohibition |
|---|---|---|
|  |  |  |
|  |  |  |
|  |  |  |
|  |  |  |
|  |  |  |
|  |  |  |
|  |  |  |
|  |  |  |

**3** Do these sentences refer to permission (P), no ability/possibility (NA/P), or deduction/speculation (D/S)?

1 Are you allowed to drive your parents' car? _____
2 I couldn't send the email before I left—there wasn't enough time. _____
3 She really likes science. She may decide to study biology in college. _____
4 Sorry, but I wasn't able to talk to José because he was in a meeting. _____
5 The train leaves at six o'clock. We might want to eat dinner at five thirty. _____
6 They aren't able to deal with this today. It'll have to wait until tomorrow. _____
7 They must have won the contract—they look so happy! _____
8 You can come with us if you drive. _____

**4** Put the words in the correct order to make pieces of advice.

1 read / should / before / the / you / chapter / class / .
_____
2 aren't / you / eat / in / allowed / to / class / .
_____
3 the teacher / you / class / listen / in / talks / when / should / .
_____
4 understand / ask / you / need to / don't / the teacher / for / help / if / you / something / .
_____
5 may / classmates / to / you / with / your / study / want / .
_____
6 in / miss / semester / you / can't / classes / more / than / three / a / .
_____
7 you / in / chat / with / friends / shouldn't / class / your / .
_____
8 three / books / you / can / check out / each / from / the library / week / .
_____

**5** Rewrite the sentences in the present tense.

**1** We weren't allowed to talk in class unless the teacher asked us to.
*We aren't allowed to talk in class unless the teacher asks us to.*

**2** We couldn't miss more than three classes during the semester.

_____

_____

**3** He didn't have to tell his teacher if he wasn't going to be in class.

_____

_____

**4** They could talk to their friends after class.

_____

_____

**5** I needed to borrow the car to drive to work.

_____

_____

**6** Tomas had to finish the report before 5 pm.

_____

_____

**7** I couldn't go to Bangkok with Mikasa.

_____

_____

**8** She had to work, so she couldn't to go to the museum with us.

_____

_____

**6** Complete the sentences with these modals. Read the hints in parentheses.

| can | can't | isn't allowed to | might |
|-----|-------|------------------|-------|
| need to | should | shouldn't | |

**1** We _____ clean our apartment before the party. (obligation)

**2** You _____ bother watching that show—it was really boring. (advice)

**3** She completed the training, so now she _____ use the new equipment. (permission)

**4** If Raul has enough vacation time, he _____ be able to travel to Sri Lanka next year. (speculation)

**5** He hasn't passed his driving test, so he _____ drive on the highway. (prohibition)

**6** You _____ hear Sam play the drums—he's really good! (advice)

**7** We _____ forget our tickets when we leave for the airport. (prohibition)

**7** Choose the correct options to complete the sentences.

**1** Do you think I ought *to catch* / *catch* an earlier train?
**2** Can we *to take* / *take* the test on Monday?
**3** Are advanced students allowed *to skip* / *skip* a class?
**4** You must *to hand in* / *hand in* your projects by Tuesday.
**5** Our team might *to win* / *win* the championship.
**6** You should *to study* / *study* at a school in Mexico and learn Spanish.
**7** Those flowers don't look good. Do you think we should *to throw* / *throw* them out?
**8** I asked Kari, but she wasn't able *to help* / *help*.

**8** Match the two parts of the conversations.

**1** I'm hungry. _____
**2** Can you come with us to the festival tomorrow? _____
**3** Does Manuel know about the party? _____
**4** Is Yen doing well at school? _____
**5** I need to lose a little weight. _____
**6** Do you think I should apologize to my sister? _____
**7** What are you doing tomorrow? _____
**8** Ooh, that salad looks delicious! _____

**a** I'm not sure. We may go to the festival at the park.
**b** No, and you can't tell him—it's a surprise!
**c** No, I can't. I have to work.
**d** Yes, really well—she must be studying a lot.
**e** Yes. You should call her right away.
**f** You can't eat it now—it's for the party.
**g** You should join a gym.
**h** You should try this melon—it's really fresh!

# 5D Why the Best Hire Might Not Have the Perfect Resume

## TEDTALKS

## AUTHENTIC LISTENING SKILLS

**1** Listen to the TED Talk excerpts. Choose the type of contrast the speaker uses in each one. 🎧 **53**

**1** We call A "the Silver Spoon," the one who clearly had advantages and was destined for success. And we call B "the Scrapper," the one who had to fight against tremendous odds to get to the same point.
*contrasting words / repeating structures*

**2** A series of odd jobs may indicate inconsistency, lack of focus, unpredictability. Or, it may signal a committed struggle against obstacles.
*repeating structures / replacing with opposites*

**3** Getting into and graduating from an elite university take a lot of hard work and sacrifice. But if your whole life has been engineered toward success, how will you handle the tough times?
*contrasting words / replacing with opposites*

**4** One person I hired felt that because he attended an elite university, there were certain assignments that were beneath him, like temporarily doing manual labor to better understand an operation. Eventually, he quit. But, on the flip side, what happens when your whole life is destined for failure and you actually succeed? *contrasting words / repeating structures*

**5** They don't think they are who they are in spite of adversity, they know they are who they are because of adversity. *contrasting words / repeating structures*

## WATCH ▶

**2** Watch Part 2 of the TED Talk and choose the correct answers to the questions.

**1** What does Regina Hartley do when a resume reads "like a patchwork quilt"?
**a** She stops and considers the person.
**b** She throws it away.
**c** She thinks about her own life story.

**2** Hartley feels that a Scrapper deserves an interview because
**a** he/she may be unpredictable.
**b** he/she may have struggled against obstacles.
**c** he/she may have a lack of focus.

**3** Hartley believes that graduating from an elite university
**a** does not guarantee you can handle tough times.
**b** means that your life is engineered towards success.
**c** means that you are destined for failure.

**4** How did the person she hired, who'd attended an elite university, feel when he was asked to do manual labor?
**a** He thought it was a good learning opportunity.
**b** He wanted to learn more about the operation.
**c** He felt he was too intelligent for it.

**5** Why does she urge the audience to interview the Scrapper?
**a** She was one herself and overcame obstacles.
**b** She finds their stories interesting.
**c** She wants to give them a chance in life.

**6** What did Hartley say that successful business people had in common?
**a** Many of them went to elite business schools.
**b** Many of them had early hardships in life.
**c** Some of them were adopted.

**7** According to Hartley, what type of resume did Steve Jobs have?
**a** a resume that most people wish they had
**b** the resume of the Silver Spoon
**c** the patchwork quilt resume of a Scrapper

**3** Watch Part 3 of the TED Talk. Match the entrepreneurial traits with the consequences.

**1** dyslexia _____
**2** believing that you have control over yourself _____
**3** a sense of humor _____
**4** good relationships _____
**a** becoming a better listener and learning to pay greater attention to detail
**b** getting you through tough times and changing your perspective
**c** having people mentor and encourage you helps you overcome adversity
**d** never giving up because challenges give you a sense of purpose

## VOCABULARY IN CONTEXT

**4** Complete the sentences with these words and phrases.

| a piece of cake | assignment | count on |
|---|---|---|
| term | tough | turn out |

**1** Job interviews are _____ for me. I never know what to say.
**2** Her first _____ was to write a report.
**3** Did your presentation _____ well?
**4** If you need help with that project, you can _____ me. I'm here for you.
**5** The staff invented the _____, "bulldog," for their boss. He wasn't a nice person.
**6** For some people, getting a job is _____. They just have good interview skills.

# 5E Going for the Job

## SPEAKING

**1** Put the words in the correct order to make sentences and questions. Then listen and check your answers. 🎧 54

1  was / I'd / creative person / I / a / say / pretty / .

   _____

2  work / I'm / to / long / willing / hours / .

   _____

3  people / to / at / pretty / talking / good / I'm / .

   _____

4  restaurant / I've / of / experience / a lot / had / .

   _____

5  English / working / I'm / my / on / .

   _____

6  wanted / always / work / outdoors / to / I've / .

   _____

7  think / job / me / I / this / new / would / skills / give / .

   _____

8  what / job / the / involve / does / ?

   _____

9  would / just / have to / I / was / if / wear / wondering / I / a uniform / .

   _____

10 to / we / wear / allowed / jewelry / are / ?

   _____

**2** Complete the interview with phrases and questions from Activity 1. Then listen and check your answers. 🎧 55

**Interviewer**  Hi, Tomas. Thank you very much for coming in.

**Tomas**  It's good to meet you.

**I**  What attracted you to work for Market Finance?

**T**  Well, **(1)** _____ work at a financial company and I've been very interested in the company for a long time—it has an excellent reputation.

**I**  Great. And why do you think you're right for this job?

**T**  Well, I like to think I'm not afraid to work hard, and this is an entry-level position, so **(2)** _____ the opportunity to understand a lot of new things, and **(3)** _____ learning new skills.

**I**  Now, as I'm sure you're aware, the job is very demanding.

**T**  Yes, **(4)** _____ enthusiastic person and able to deal with difficult situations and new challenges.

**I**  I see.

**T**  And **(5)** _____ work long hours when necessary to get the work done.

**I**  OK, so, that all sounds very good. And what are your main strengths?

**T**  Well, **(6)** _____ with people; I used to be a waiter working at a busy restaurant in the tourist part of town. And my English is pretty good.

**I**  Yes, your English is very good!

**T**  And, as I mentioned, I learn new things quickly and I'm well organized.

**I**  And what about negatives? What do you need to improve?

**T**  Well, I know I can sometimes be a perfectionist, like when I was designing the school magazine, I spent too long on the design work, so **(7)** _____ my time management skills.

**I**  So, do you have any questions you'd like to ask?

**T**  Err, I do have a couple. **(8)** _____ wear a suit to the office every day?

**I**  Generally, yes, we expect everyone to wear business attire.

**T**  Right. And just one other thing, **(9)** _____ take work home if we want to get ahead with something?

**I**  No, that's against company policy. Company information needs to stay in the office and all your work should be completed within working hours.

**3** Prepare your own interview questions and answers for a job that you would like to get. Then compare your ideas with the sample interview above.

**4** Make notes on your answers to the questions below. Remember to use the useful language. Then listen to the sample answer and compare your ideas. 🎧 56

- *Why are you learning English?*
- *Do you think it will be useful for your future career?*

## PRONUNCIATION Showing confidence

Remember to speak slowly and use an even tone to sound confident in conversations.

**5** Listen to the sentences and decide whether the speakers are confident (C) or not confident (NC). 🎧 57

| 1 _____ | 3 _____ | 5 _____ | 7 _____ |
| 2 _____ | 4 _____ | 6 _____ | 8 _____ |

# WRITING  A cover letter

**6** Read the sentences from a cover letter and choose the correct functions.

**1** I am writing to apply for the job of part-time assistant at the veterinary clinic.
   **a** giving the reason for wanting the job
   **b** clearly stating the reason for writing
   **c** giving details of relevant experience

**2** Last summer, I volunteered at the local animal shelter.
   **a** giving details of relevant experience
   **b** providing school qualifications
   **c** providing information on availability

**3** I am a responsible person and absolutely dedicated to the care of animals.
   **a** asking for information about the job
   **b** giving information on education
   **c** describing relevant personal qualities

**4** I would value this experience as I plan to study Veterinary Medicine in college.
   **a** giving information about availability
   **b** describing formal qualifications
   **c** giving the reason for wanting the job

**5** I look forward to hearing from you soon.
   **a** describing past experience
   **b** asking politely for a reply
   **c** giving the reason for writing

**7** Label the parts of the cover letter.

| | |
|---|---|
| asking about the job | formal greeting |
| full mailing address | information about availability |
| personal qualities | polite ending |
| reason for writing | relevant experience |
| requesting a reply | today's date |

**(1)** _____ 818 Doris Avenue
2059 North Sydney

**(2)** _____ June 4, 2018

**(3)** _____ To Whom It May Concern:

**(4)** _____ I am writing to apply for the role of waiter at Squash Juice Bar, which I saw advertised on your website. I feel I would be a very good candidate for this job.

**(5)** _____ While I do not have the direct experience of working at a juice bar, I was a waiter for two months last summer at The Bay Leaf in town.

**(6)** _____ I would say I was a fast learner who enjoys working in a team. In addition, I have received very positive feedback from my former manager and customers at The Bay Leaf.

**(7)** _____ I was just wondering if I would have to work every weekend or just some weekends?

**(8)** _____ I would be free to begin after June 25th and am available until mid-September. I hope that you will consider me for the job.

**(9)** _____ I look forward to hearing from you soon.

**(10)** _____ Sincerely,
Luis Campo

**8** Read the letter again. Are the statements true (T) or false (F)?

**1** Luis knows the person he is writing to. _____
**2** He saw the job on the Squash Juice Bar website. _____
**3** Luis doesn't have any experience as a waiter. _____
**4** He mentions relevant points about his personality. _____
**5** One of his qualities is teamwork. _____
**6** He includes a question about the salary. _____
**7** He is not available to begin work until mid-May. _____
**8** He ends the letter appropriately. _____

**9** Underline six mistakes in this cover letter. How would you correct them?

11 Lindsay Street
Edinburgh
EH23 6BD
June 2018

Hi Mr. Yoon,

I'm writing to apply for the job of part-time assistant at the veterinary clinic, which I saw advertised online.

I have some relevant experience. Last summer, I volunteered at the local animal shelter where I learned a lot about managing animals.

It's obvious that I am the perfect candidate for this job. Also, I would say that I was a very responsible person, dedicated to the care of animals.

I finish school in June and will be free until September. Drop me a line with some more details about the job.

Thanks,

Agustina Garcia

**10** Follow the instructions.

• This is part of a letter you received from a Polish friend:

> I just spotted a cool summer job. It's in Chicago, based at O'Hare Airport. I'm excited because I really want to work in the tourism industry! The job involves meeting and greeting passengers, checking their documents, that kind of thing. Do you think I should apply?

• Write a letter (about 100 words) giving your friend advice about what to include in their cover letter.

# Review

**1** Match the opposites.

| | | | |
|---|---|---|---|
| **1** | temporary | **a** | relaxing |
| **2** | part-time | **b** | employed |
| **3** | out of work | **c** | low-paid |
| **4** | demanding | **d** | permanent |
| **5** | well-paid | **e** | easy |
| **6** | challenging | **f** | full-time |

**2** Listen to the sentences and choose the most appropriate adjective. 🎧 **58**

**1** *demanding / competitive / flexible*
**2** *creative / competitive / well-paid*
**3** *creative / flexible / stressful*
**4** *creative / stressful / competitive*
**5** *well-paid / permanent / creative*
**6** *flexible / stressful / well-paid*

**3** Complete the sentences with the correct forms of these verbs.

| count | give | help | lock | quit | take | work |
|---|---|---|---|---|---|---|

**1** My cousin doesn't regret _____ her job at the newspaper. It was very stressful.

**2** I told them that I'd miss _____ with such great people.

**3** If you forget _____ your time sheet to payroll, then you won't get paid.

**4** Do you remember _____ the front door when you left last night?

**5** My boss asked someone else _____ that difficult customer.

**6** Did Juan decide _____ the job at the café or is he working somewhere else?

**7** We didn't finish _____ all the stock last night, so we'll have to do it tonight.

**4** Find and correct the mistakes in the words in bold. Two sentences are correct.

**1** You **can't to forget taking** your medicine before you go to bed.

**2** She **should try studying** with friends.

**3** He **might to remember calling** Tom if he writes himself a note.

**4** They **shouldn't continuing taking** pictures once the play starts.

**5** When I was younger, I **wasn't allowed stop to have** piano lessons.

**6** She **might regret skipping** breakfast.

**5** Choose the correct options to complete the sentences.

**1** You can _____ me anything. I won't be angry.
  **a** ask
  **b** to ask
  **c** asking
  **d** had asked

**2** Scientists _____ tell us a lot about climate change.
  **a** should
  **b** isn't able to
  **c** can
  **d** should to

**3** You might _____ that new exhibition at the art gallery.
  **a** like
  **b** to like
  **c** liking
  **d** had liked

**4** Natalie _____ come on vacation with us last year.
  **a** may
  **b** couldn't
  **c** wasn't able
  **d** didn't need

**5** You _____ study in India. It would be such an interesting experience.
  **a** are able
  **b** might to
  **c** ought
  **d** should

**6** You should _____ at least two new languages.
  **a** learn
  **b** to learn
  **c** learning
  **d** have learned

**7** _____ I ask you about your job?
  **a** Should to
  **b** Be able to
  **c** Ought
  **d** Can

**8** I couldn't _____ for the job.
  **a** apply
  **b** to apply
  **c** applying
  **d** applied

# 6 Superhuman

## 6A Amazing Bodies

### VOCABULARY The human body

**1 Review** Unscramble the letters to make the names of parts of the body.

1 w b e o l     __ __ __ __ w
2 r a t h o t     t h __ __ __ __
3 e e n k     __ __ __ __
4 s o n e     __ __ __ __
5 f i r n e g     __ __ __ __ __ __
6 t o s a c h m     __ t __ __ __ c h
7 t s c e h     __ __ __ __ t
8 h d n a     __ __ __ __

**2 Review** Put the parts of the body in order from the highest in the body (1) to the lowest (7).

| chest | foot | head | knee | neck | shoulder | stomach |
|-------|------|------|------|------|----------|---------|

1 _____
2 _____
3 _____
4 _____
5 _____
6 _____
7 _____

**3 Review** Complete the words about health. The first letter is given for you.

1 Feeling sick because of the way a boat is moving.

s __ __ __ __ __ __

2 A very common viral infection.  c __ __ __
3 It's important for your health that this isn't too high or too low.  t __ __ __ __ __ __ __ __ __ __
4 If you fall and hurt a bone, it might be. . .

b __ __ __ __ __

5 A feeling that you have in a part of your body when you are sick or hurt.  p __ __ __
6 A person who comes to a doctor for help.

p __ __ __ __ __ __

**4** Match the parts of the body with the descriptions.

1 heart
2 skeleton
3 blood vessel
4 brain
5 skin
6 lungs

a supports the body
b moves blood around the body
c carries blood to different parts of the body
d protects the body from the environment
e allow air into and out of the body
f controls the body

**5** Unscramble the letters to make words about the digestive system.

1 f d o o     __ __ __ __
2 e b c t a r a i     __ a __ __ __ __ __ __
3 n t i e r n t s u     __ __ __ r __ __ __ __ __
4 b a s o r b     __ __ __ __ __ b
5 g d i s i t n o e     __ __ g __ __ __ __ __ __
6 g u t o n e     __ __ __ __ u e

**6** Complete the sentences with the correct form of the words from Activity 5.

1 Nutrients are _____ into the blood and carried around the body.
2 The _____ is covered in thousands of taste buds.
3 _____ is the process of changing food into nutrients for our bodies.
4 The body uses _____ for energy and to repair cells.
5 Some foods have a lot more _____ than others.
6 Your stomach is full of _____—some are healthy and some are not.

**7** Listen and complete the advice from a doctor. 🎧 **59**

You're feeling sick because of problems in your
**(1)** _____. You're eating too many
processed things. It's important to eat a variety
of **(2)** _____ that are full of
**(3)** _____ . Your organs and
**(4)** _____ need these to stay healthy.
You should also eat more yogurt to get plenty of good
**(5)** _____ into your stomach. When you do
this, your **(6)** _____ will improve and you'll
feel much better, too.

**8** Choose the correct options to complete the sentences.

1 Everyone has red and white blood *cells / vessels* in their body.
2 The lungs help bring *oxygen / nutrients* into the body.
3 The tongue is important for a person's sense of *touch / taste*.
4 Babies' bones don't *beat / break* quite as easily as adults'.
5 There are over 200 bones in a human *skeleton / digestive system*.
6 *Muscles / Cells* are tissues in the body that help you move.
7 If you find it difficult to *break / breathe*, you should see a doctor immediately.

**9** **Extension** Are these things internal (inside the body) or external (outside)? Complete the chart.

| eyebrow | fingernail | intestines | liver | ribs |
| skin | spine | vein | wrist | |

| Internal | External |
|----------|----------|
|          |          |
|          |          |
|          |          |
|          |          |

**10** **Extension** Choose the word that is <u>not</u> related to each of the five senses.

1 taste      *tongue / flavor / vein*
2 touch      *tendon / skin / nerves*
3 smell      *nose / ribs / food*
4 hearing    *ear / blood / sound*
5 sight      *bacteria / eyes / brain*

## LISTENING

**11** Listen to the voicemail and choose the correct options. 🎧 **60**

1 Why did Dr. Jacobs leave Kevin a message?
   **a** He wants Kevin to take some tests.
   **b** He has the results of Kevin's tests.
   **c** He wants Kevin to call for his test results.
   **d** The results of the tests weren't clear.

2 Dr. Jacobs said that Kevin has a _____ infection.
   **a** backbone
   **b** breathing
   **c** bone
   **d** bacterial

3 How does the doctor describe the problem?
   **a** some need to worry
   **b** pretty bad news
   **c** nothing serious
   **d** causing other problems

4 What does the doctor want Kevin to do?
   **a** go to his pharmacy as soon as possible
   **b** drink water when he's in the sun
   **c** call now to make an appointment
   **d** stop taking the tablets when he feels better

5 What does the doctor want Kevin to follow very carefully?
   **a** any other problems he has
   **b** the prescription instructions
   **c** when his next appointment is
   **d** what the name of the tablets is

6 When does the doctor want Kevin to make a follow-up appointment?
   **a** when the prescription is finished
   **b** if he starts feeling better
   **c** if he doesn't take all his tablets
   **d** if he's still feeling unwell

**12** Listen and choose the correct options to answer the questions. 🎧 **61**

**1** How do you think James felt when the little girl stared?
  **a** He was upset.
  **b** He didn't like the joke she told.
  **c** He wasn't worried. He's used to it.

**2** What other way of saying "to joke" does James use?
  **a** to kid around
  **b** to clown around
  **c** to fool around

**3** What is very important to James?
  **a** eating your vegetables
  **b** having a sense of humor
  **c** going to the beach

**4** Why does James make jokes about himself?
  **a** because he accepts who he is
  **b** because it helps other people
  **c** because people think he's strange

**5** How does James describe the fact that he doesn't have arms?
  **a** a physical problem
  **b** a physical challenge
  **c** a physical accident

**6** What happened when James was two and a half years old?
  **a** He lost his arms.
  **b** He moved to India.
  **c** He was adopted.

**7** How many brothers and sisters does James have?
  **a** eleven
  **b** eight
  **c** one

**13** Listen and choose the best title for the talk. 🎧 **62**

  **a** Not Normal, But OK
  **b** No Arms, Amazing Feet
  **c** Hard to Deal With

**14** Listen again and choose the correct options to answer the questions. 🎧 **62**

**1** What does James _not_ mention doing?
  **a** brushing his teeth
  **b** texting
  **c** getting dressed

**2** What comes naturally to James?
  **a** using his feet like hands
  **b** answering lots of questions
  **c** asking for help sometimes

**3** Which statement is true?
  **a** He never needs help.
  **b** He sometimes needs help.
  **c** He doesn't like help.

**4** What does James think is very important?
  **a** to be helpful
  **b** to be adaptable
  **c** to be acceptable

**5** What is hard for James to deal with?
  **a** teachers who don't know him
  **b** getting to know people
  **c** people who judge him

**6** What is James's message for all of us?
  **a** explain yourself
  **b** accept yourself
  **c** admire yourself

## GRAMMAR  Zero and first conditional

**15** Read the sentences and put them in the correct column in the chart.

Call your doctor if the pain is really bad.
Drinking tea with honey may help if you have a sore throat.
I can make you a sandwich if you're hungry when you arrive.
If you have a high temperature, you shouldn't go to school.
If you see Elena, tell her I'm not feeling well.
If your clothes no longer fit, it's time to go on a diet!
Your bones will get weak if you don't drink enough milk.

| Zero conditional | First conditional |
|---|---|
| | |

**16** Choose the correct options to complete the zero conditional sentences.

**1** If you *wash / to wash / washed* your hands frequently, you *is reduced / reduce / reducing* the chance of infection.

**2** You *should to treat / should treated / should treat* the infection right away if you *are recognizing / recognize / recognized* the symptoms.

**3** If you *receiving / to receive / receive* the correct treatment, you *recovering / recover / recovered* very quickly.

**4** *Go / Gone / Will go* to bed if you *will feel / feel / feeling* really sick.

**5** If the wound *isn't / won't / not been* clean, *don't apply / doesn't apply / won't apply* a bandage.

**6** A headache usually *goes / is going / go* away if you *taken / took / take* an aspirin.

**7** He *should seen / should to see / should see* a doctor if his temperature *be / being / is* very high.

**17** Complete the first conditional sentences with the correct form of the verbs in parentheses.

**1** If you don't wash your hands, you _____ (catch) my cold.

**2** You _____ (feel) much healthier if you drink plenty of water every day.

**3** Germs will enter your body if you _____ (touch) your nose and eyes.

**4** If she bites her nails, she _____ (introduce) germs into her mouth.

**5** Your immune system _____ (improve) significantly if you eat more vegetables.

**6** If people don't get a flu shot, they _____ (not be) protected for a year.

**7** If your headache gets really bad, _____ (relax) in a quiet, dark room.

**18** Choose the correct options to complete the sentences.

**1** You will get better quickly if your doctor *will treat / treats / should treat* your illness.

**2** If the germ gets into your body, it *will destroy / is destroying / will destroys* cells.

**3** You *injured / 'll injure / 'll injured* yourself if you aren't careful!

**4** If you want to reduce his temperature, *give / may give / gives* him an aspirin.

**5** If we avoid areas with lots of mosquitoes, we probably *not catch / aren't catching / won't catch* malaria.

**6** You'll damage your lungs if you *breathed / breathe / will breathe* in poisonous chemicals.

**7** *May wear / Will wear / Wear* insect repellent if you want to prevent mosquito bites.

**8** Scientists will find a cure for cancer if they *will continue / continue / continued* doing research.

**19** Complete the first conditional sentences with the correct form of the verbs in parentheses.

**1** If you _____ (increase) how much you exercise, you _____ (begin) to lose weight.

**2** You probably _____ (not get) injured if you _____ (warm up) before you exercise.

**3** If you _____ (end up) up in the hospital, the staff _____ (take) good care of you.

**4** The nurse _____ (contact) you if she _____ (observe) any changes.

**5** You _____ (not get) dehydrated if you _____ (remember) to drink water.

**6** Your condition _____ (not improve) unless you _____ (follow) your doctor's instructions.

# 6B  More Than Human?

## READING

**1** Match the headings (a–f) with the paragraphs (1–5) in the text. There is one heading you don't need.

a  "Aha!" moment _____

b  A young inventor's beginnings _____

c  Easton goes to NASA _____

d  A very personal goal _____

e  Easton's $80,000 hand _____

f  Changing an industry _____

**2** Match the two parts of the sentences.

1  Easton taught himself to code _____

2  Easton had an "Aha!" moment _____

3  While developing a prosthetic limb, _____

4  If everything goes as planned, _____

5  One of Easton's personal goals _____

a  when he met a girl with a prosthetic arm at a local science fair.

b  in order to continue improving his invention.

c  is to help a student at his school walk for graduation.

d  NASA's Robonaut will become a member of the space crew.

e  Easton saw an opportunity to change an industry.

**3** Complete the definitions with these words. There are two words you don't need.

| bone | brain | crew | functional | headset |
|------|-------|------|-----------|---------|
| muscle | skeleton | skin | sophisticated | tubing |

1  The _____ is the natural outer covering of a body.

2  The _____ is the organ of the body that controls thoughts and feelings.

3  A _____ is one of the hard pieces that form the structure of a person's body.

4  _____ describes a machine or system that works in a clever way.

5  The _____ is the structure that supports the body of a person or animal.

6  A _____ is one of many pieces of body tissue that can produce movement.

7  A _____ is a piece of equipment that you wear over your ears with a part that you can speak into.

8  _____ describes something that is designed to be good at doing a particular job.

## VOCABULARY BUILDING  Verbs describing ability

**4** Complete the sentences with the correct forms of these verbs.

| allow | enable | help | let | prevent | save | stop |
|-------|--------|------|-----|---------|------|------|

1  I can lend you a map if you like—that will _____ you from buying one.

2  This piece of equipment _____ you to make several recordings at the same time.

3  I wrote down the names of all the characters to _____ myself from getting confused.

4  If you wear safety glasses, you'll _____ an eye injury.

5  It makes things easier and _____ me concentrate on what's important.

6  If that box is too heavy for you, then I'll _____ you carry it upstairs.

7  Extremely sensitive fingertips _____ the robotic hand to pick up tiny objects.

# Easton LaChappelle: Inventor

1  🎧 **63**  Since he was a small child, Easton LaChappelle has been taking things apart and putting them back together again. At the age of fourteen, Easton made his first robotic hand from plastic Lego™ bricks, fishing line, and electrical wiring. But that wasn't good enough for Easton. In order to continue improving his invention, Easton taught himself to code*. He learned how to use a 3-D printer and work with complicated electronics and wireless communication technology. By the time he was sixteen, Easton had created a more sophisticated and much stronger robotic arm. It could throw balls, shake hands, and do many of the things that humans do.

2  Easton entered his robotic arm into a local science fair in Colorado. While there, he met a seven-year-old girl with a prosthetic* arm and hand. Easton learned that the prosthetic limb* had cost over $80,000, despite the fact that it had very limited functionality. He realized that the girl would need several prosthetics during her life, and thought of the enormous expense she and her family would face. Easton calls that meeting his "Aha!" moment. As he later explained, "This turned something that started from boredom into something that could change people's lives."

3  Easton then became interested in developing fully functional prosthetic limbs that people could afford.

He began experimenting with 3-D printers, silicone (for skin), motors, and advanced technology, all in his bedroom! He found ways of using cheaper technology that functioned just as well as much more expensive equipment. "I really saw an opportunity to change this industry by creating a prosthetic that was under a thousand dollars."

4  The latest version of Easton's prosthetic limb uses a wireless headset that works with ten different channels of the brain. The technology is so effective that it caught the attention of NASA, where Easton is now working as an intern on the Robonaut, a robot that copies human movements and performs tasks and duties too dangerous for astronauts. If everything goes as planned, NASA hopes that the Robonaut will eventually become a working member of the space crew.

5  Along with several friends, Easton has also started a company called "Unlimited Tomorrow." One of their projects involves designing and developing exoskeletons* that will allow paraplegics* to walk again. This is a personal goal for Easton, who knows of a young man at his school who became a paraplegic as the result of an accident. Easton would like to help him achieve something that seems simple to most of us. "My goal is to create an exoskeleton pair of legs for him so he can actually walk for graduation."

**code** *to write computer programs*
**prosthetic** *used to replace a missing body part*
**limb** *a leg or arm of a person or animal*

**exoskeleton** *a piece of equipment like an "external skeleton" that a paraplegic can wear to help them move*
**paraplegic** *a person who cannot move the lower part of their body*

# 6C If

## GRAMMAR Second conditional

**1** Put *if* and commas in the correct places in the sentences. Not all the sentences need commas.

1 _____ I would be really disappointed _____ I didn't pass.
2 _____ we won the game _____ we would be the champions.
3 _____ I improved my English _____ I could get a job in London.
4 _____ I could answer questions in class _____ I did the homework.
5 _____ I'd know what to do _____ I listened to his advice.
6 _____ They would fly to Tamil Nadu _____ they had enough money.
7 _____ Maria took a vacation _____ she might feel more relaxed.

**2** Read the sentences and complete the answers to the questions.

1 If dogs could talk, I think they'd have a lot to say.
Are dogs able to talk?
_____, they _____.
2 Pranav would buy his mother that scarf if she liked bright colors.
Why isn't Pranav going to buy his mother that scarf?
Because she _____.
3 If Maddie liked fish, Zach would recommend that new restaurant.
Does Maddie like fish?
_____, she _____.
4 Alani and Marcus could take an Italian class together if Alani liked learning languages.
Why aren't Marcus and Alani going to learn Italian together?
Because _____.
5 Lilya said, "I wish I could climb Mount Everest."
Is Lilya able to climb Mount Everest?
_____, she _____.

6 Dev could go to the theater with me if he didn't have to work.
Does Dev have to work?
_____, he _____.
Can Dev go to the theater?
_____, he _____.
7 I'd invite Anna to come with us if she liked baseball.
Does Anna like baseball?
_____, she _____.
8 If Natalia didn't have a cold, she would play tennis with us tomorrow.
Does Natalia have a cold?
_____, she _____.
Is Natalia going to play tennis tomorrow?
_____, she _____.

**3** Choose the correct options to complete the sentences.

1 If I had all the money in the world, *I'd / I will* buy you a horse.
2 If the day *had / has* thirty hours, we *would / had* be able to get everything done.
3 I wish I *had / have* a brother.
4 If you *were / could* here, *I'd / I'm* take you to my favorite restaurant.
5 Emmet *would be / had* less stressed if he *made / makes* a list of what he needs to do.
6 If only I *could / can* wake up to this view every morning.
7 I *would / would be* offer you a drink if we *had / has had* any clean cups.
8 If there *were / could* life on far-away planets, I *would / were* like to live on one.

**4** Complete the second sentence so that it means the same as the first. Use no more than three words in each space.

1 I'd leave now and visit you if I didn't have class.
I _____ to leave now and visit you because I _____.
2 If you drove a sports car, you'd get to school in three minutes.
You _____ a sports car, so it takes you _____ three minutes to get to school.
3 If only I had long, blonde hair.
I _____ long, blonde hair.

**4** I would live in the palace if my mother were the queen.

My mother _____ the queen and I

_____ in the palace.

**5** I wish I could graduate tomorrow.

I'm _____ to graduate tomorrow, but

I want to.

**6** If she had more spare time, she'd write to him every week.

She _____ enough spare time, so she

_____ to him every week.

**5** Are the words in bold correct or incorrect? Correct those that are incorrect.

**1** He'd be exhausted if he **would ran** the Boston

Marathon. _____

**2** If only I didn't **had** to tell you this. _____

**3** You could win the competition if you **practiced** every

day. _____

**4** She **call** an ambulance if it was an emergency.

_____

**5** If only **could I write** fantastic novels like J. K. Rowling's.

_____

**6** If you ate beans and salad for lunch, you **would have**

more energy in the afternoon. _____

**7** **I'll** wash my hands if I had soap. _____

**6** Put the words in the correct order to make sentences.

**1** in shape / I / be / chocolate / if / I / would / less / ate / .

_____

**2** if / you / only / now / I / talk / could / to / right / .

_____

**3** would / if / the / , / Akira / pharmacy / pick up / her /

were / open / medicine / .

_____

**4** Oslo / I / lived / in / wish / I / .

_____

**5** if / they'd / didn't / worried / she / be / call / day / every / .

_____

**6** I'd / if / I / teeth / had / brush / toothbrush / , / a / my / .

_____

**7** wish / I / didn't / to / I / go / have / bed / to / !

_____

**7** Read and listen to the questions. Choose the correct answers. 🎧 **64**

**1** Do you want to come shopping with us?

**a** I'd come if I had more time.

**b** I'll come if I had more time.

**2** Did you hear that Sally isn't moving to Greece now?

**a** Yes. I'd be sad if she will move there.

**b** Yes. I'd be sad if she moved there.

**3** What do you think about playing tennis after school?

**a** I would have a sore throat if I'm playing.

**b** If I didn't have a sore throat, I'd play.

**4** Do you exercise every day?

**a** No, I don't. But if I made time to, I'd feel better.

**b** Yes, I do. If I made time to, I'd feel better.

**5** Have you tried that new Mexican restaurant?

**a** No, I haven't. I'd try it if I liked spicy food.

**b** Yes, I have! I'd try it if I liked spicy food.

**6** Do you have a photograph of your grandfather?

**a** No, I don't. I'd be putting it on my wall when I have one.

**b** No, I don't. If I had one, I'd put it on my wall.

**7** Do you ever go to the science museum?

**a** Yes, I do sometimes. I wish I had a membership there.

**b** No, I don't. I'll go if I would have a membership there.

## PRONUNCIATION *I wish* and *If only*

Remember that *wish* and *if only* can be used to express present regrets.

**8** Listen and underline the stressed words in the sentences. Then practice saying the sentences. 🎧 **65**

**1** I wish I didn't have a headache.

**2** If only I knew what to say.

**3** I wish I could dance.

**4** If only I hadn't broken my leg.

**5** I wish I did more exercise.

**6** If only I could find better food.

**7** I wish I had more time.

**8** If only I hadn't lost my phone.

# 6D Deep Sea Diving… in a Wheelchair

## TEDTALKS

## AUTHENTIC LISTENING SKILLS

**1** Listen to the TED Talk excerpt. Underline four phrases that help structure the argument. 🎧 66

It is the most amazing experience, beyond most other things I've experienced in life. I literally have the freedom to move in 360 degrees of space and an ecstatic experience of joy and freedom. And the incredibly unexpected thing is that other people seem to see and feel that too. Their eyes literally light up and they say things like, "I want one of those," or "If you can do that, I can do anything." And I'm thinking, it's because in that moment of them seeing an object they have no frame of reference for, or so transcends the frames of reference they have with the wheelchair, they have to think in a completely new way. And I think that moment of completely new thought perhaps creates a freedom that spreads to the rest of other people's lives. For me, this means that they're seeing the value of difference, the joy it brings when, instead of focusing on loss or limitation, we see and discover the power and joy of seeing the world from exciting new perspectives.

## WATCH ▶

**2** Limitations prevent us from doing things. Freedoms allow us to do them. Decide if these words and phrases are examples of limitations or freedoms. Then watch the TED Talk to check your answers.

| doing something unexpected | fear |
| feeling joy | having a new toy |
| pity | preconceptions |
| restrictions | taking a journey |

| Limitations | Freedoms |
| --- | --- |
|  |  |
|  |  |
|  |  |

**3** Watch Part 1 of the TED Talk. Complete the sentences with a word or short phrase.

**1** Sue says the wheelchair has bought her _____.

**2** An extended _____ changed the way she could access the world.

**3** When Sue first started using the wheelchair, it was like having an enormous _____.

**4** She felt that being out _____ in the wheelchair was exhilarating.

**5** But people's _____ towards her was completely different when she was in a wheelchair.

**6** Sue felt invisible. She felt as if people couldn't _____ her anymore.

**7** Sue felt she had been _____ on a core level because of responses to the wheelchair.

**8** Sue knew that she had to reclaim her _____.

**4** Watch Parts 2 and 3 of the TED Talk. Match the details of Sue Austin's journey with their explanations.

**1** 2005 _____
**2** "I wonder what'll happen if I put the two together?" _____
**3** Seven years _____
**4** 360 degrees _____
**5** "I want one of those." _____
**6** nobody has seen an underwater wheelchair before _____

**a** how long the journey with the underwater wheelchair has lasted so far
**b** Sue's freedom of movement underwater
**c** the reason why people have to think in a completely new way
**d** what people say when they see Sue dive in her wheelchair
**e** what Sue thought about diving while being in a wheelchair
**f** when Sue began to dive

## VOCABULARY IN CONTEXT

**5** Choose the correct options to complete the sentences.

**1** If I could _____ the accounts, I could tell you how much money was spent.
**a** extend      **b** access      **c** enter

**2** The _____ of someone deep-sea diving in a wheelchair is pretty unusual.
**a** outcome      **b** risk      **c** concept

**3** My son's eyes _____ when I told him we were going rock climbing. It's his favorite activity.
**a** lit up      **b** started crying      **c** looked sad

**4** We plan to _____ the range of products for sale in our larger stores.
**a** access      **b** extend      **c** allow

**5** People with _____ creativity have the power to change the way we see the world.
**a** tough      **b** tremendous      **c** clear

**6** The best _____ would be for our team to win the tournament.
**a** outcome      **b** experiences      **c** assignment

# 6E Photos

## SPEAKING

**1** Match the two parts of the sentences. Then listen to the description of the photo and check your answers. 🎧 **67**

| | |
|---|---|
| **1** This photo shows | **a** very happy. |
| **2** It's obviously an | **b** the teacher. |
| **3** It looks like | **c** they're painting pictures. |
| **4** The children seem | **d** a messy lesson, because of the aprons. |
| **5** It looks as if | **e** art lesson. |
| **6** It must be | **f** a lot of different paints. |
| **7** Behind the tables, | **g** blackboard. |
| **8** She looks like | **h** an elementary-school class. |
| **9** In the background, there's a | **i** some children in a classroom. |
| **10** On the table, there are | **j** you can see a woman. |

**2** Underline the stressed words in the numbered phrases in Activity 1. Then listen again and check your answers. 🎧 **67**

**3** Listen to someone describing a photo and draw what you hear. 🎧 **68**

**4** Look at these two photos from the Student Book and think about how you can describe them. Make notes about your ideas on a separate sheet of paper. Then listen to the sample answers and compare your ideas. 🎧 **69**

# WRITING An informal email describing people

**5** Read the phrases used in informal emails and complete the chart.

---
Give my love to your family.
How are things?
It was great to get your news!
Please write soon.
Say hi to everyone for me.
Sorry I haven't written for a while.
Speak to you soon!
Thanks so much for your email.

---

| Ways of starting an informal email | Ways of ending an informal email |
|---|---|
| | |
| | |
| | |

**6** Complete the sentences with these words or phrases. There are two you don't need.

---
| | | | |
|---|---|---|---|
| a bunch of stuff | ages | BTW | in a rush |
| LOL | my place | my stuff | sad |
| say hi to | thrilled | | |

---

1 Sorry I haven't written for _____.
2 I have _____ to tell you!
3 I had a pizza party at _____ last night.
4 I have so much to do. I'm always _____.
5 I was totally _____ to get your last email!
6 _____, do you ever see Zhang these days?
7 Well, _____ the guys for me.
8 I don't know how I'm going to carry _____ to the airport!

**7** Complete the informal email with the correct phrases (a–h).

**From:** khalid-90@emailz.ae
**To:** Takumi_K@gotmail.com.jp
**Subject:** Inspirational people

Hi Takumi,

**(1)** _____. It sounds like your family reunion is going really well! **(2)** _____ , and I especially enjoyed reading your description of your grandfather. Actually, it made me think about my own grandfather, **(3)** _____. Should I tell you about him?

**(4)** _____. When we were kids, we didn't live near him, but he called us every weekend. It sounds like a small thing, but

he always asked me questions, too. He also asked for my opinion on things! It made me feel special that an adult was interested in what I thought. Once a month, he came to visit us, or we went to visit him. **(5)** _____! He used to take us to the beach and we'd play there all day.

Then, when I was ten, he moved very close to us and we saw him every day. He taught me to play tennis, **(6)** _____ and advice about everything. BTW, he could speak four different languages. Imagine that! My grandfather wasn't famous or anything, **(7)** _____.

Anyway, I'm thrilled we've shared stories about our grandfathers—I hope we can inspire others the way they inspired us! ☺

**(8)** _____,

Khalid

**a** All the best
**b** and he gave me a lot of encouragement
**c** and how much he's inspired me
**d** but he was the kindest person I ever met
**e** First of all, he's probably the person I admire the most
**f** I was excited to hear all the news
**g** Thanks for your great email
**h** Those were the best times

**8** Read the email in Activity 7 again. Then write *Takumi* or *Khalid* to complete the summary.

**(1)** _____ is replying to an email from **(2)** _____ . **(3)** _____ has told **(4)** _____ about his family reunion. **(5)** _____ really enjoyed **(6)** _____'s description of his grandfather. In fact, it gave **(7)** _____ the idea to describe his own grandfather to **(8)** _____. **(9)** _____ explains how his grandfather made him feel and how kind he was. He hopes that he and **(10)** _____ can one day inspire other people in the same way.

**9** Follow the instructions.

> Your family has moved from Peru to Los Angeles in the US. You have become good friends with your new next-door neighbor, who is your age and makes very popular video blogs. You want to tell your cousin Julio, back in Peru how amazing this person is.

Write an email to Julio in 150–200 words. You should:
- ask Julio for news and how he is.
- describe your new neighbor.
- explain why this person is amazing.

# Review

## 1 Put the words in the correct order to make sentences.

1 needed / by / all / oxygen / major / organs / the / is / .

_____

2 the / computer / a / like / body / the / controls / brain / is / that / .

_____

3 protects / skin / the / body / dangerous / from / bacteria / .

_____

4 the / heart / blood / through / moves / body / the / .

_____

5 vessels / oxygen / to / brain / the / blood / carry / .

_____

6 skeleton / bones / made / of / is / the / set / a / of / .

_____

7 cell / job / has / each / different / a / .

_____

8 are / muscles / used / move / of / parts / body / the / to / .

_____

## 2 Match these verbs with the nouns and phrases they collocate with.

| | | | |
|---|---|---|---|
| 1 | absorb | a | an infection |
| 2 | break | b | nutrients |
| 3 | digest | c | a bone |
| 4 | have | d | blood |
| 5 | breathe | e | food |
| 6 | carry | f | air |

## 3 Complete the sentences with the correct forms of the verbs in parentheses.

1 You should see your doctor if you _____ (have) a very high temperature.

2 If traditional headache medicines _____ (not work), I sometimes try alternatives.

3 If you _____ (not drink) enough water, you may get dehydrated.

4 If you _____ (put) a cool cloth on your forehead, your headache might go away.

5 Some people _____ (not trust) alternative treatments unless their doctors say they're okay.

6 You _____ (start) to see the benefits if you do yoga every day.

7 You may be able to prevent health problems if you _____ (exercise) regularly.

8 _____ (see) your doctor if you have headaches several times a week.

## 4 Correct the mistake in each sentence.

1 If you eat more protein, it help your muscles grow.

2 If you will exercise a lot, you need to eat more so your body has the energy it needs.

3 If you will want your muscles to grow, drink a protein drink before you work out.

4 If you will be serious about building muscle, you should lift weights every other day.

5 If you eat a small meal every three hours, your body build muscle throughout the day.

6 Your body will build muscle as you sleep if you will eat certain foods before bed.

## 5 Complete the conversations with the correct forms of the verbs in parentheses. Use the second conditional.

1 A Do you comb your hair every day?

   B Yes, I do. I _____ (be) embarrassed if I _____ (forget) to comb it.

2 A We always have to wait in such a long line at the cafeteria.

   B I know. If only we _____ (can skip) it!

3 A Do you swim every day?

   B No, I don't. But I think I _____ (be) in better shape if I _____ (do) some regular exercise.

4 A Have you heard of Shakespeare's A Midsummer Night's Dream?

   B No, I haven't.

   A Well, if you _____ (study) drama at school, you _____ (know) all about this play.

5 A I need a bookshelf!

   B I agree. Your books _____ (not be) all over the floor if you _____ (have) some shelves.

6 A What do you want to do today?

   B Well, if the weather _____ (be) warmer, we _____ (can go) go to the beach.

7 A I don't understand what Mr. Spicuzza was talking about in class today.

   B If you _____ (listen) more carefully, you _____ (know) what he was talking about.

8 A Have you ever felt nervous before a big presentation?

   B No, I haven't. But if I _____ (feel) nervous, I _____ (breathe) slowly for a minute or two.

# 7 Shopping Around

## 7A Money and Me

**VOCABULARY** Money and shopping

**1 Review** Are these words connected with the beginning or the end of a product's life? Complete the chart.

| advertise | create | design | grow |
|---|---|---|---|
| manufacture | recycle | throw away | |

| Beginning | End |
|---|---|
| | |
| | |

**2 Review** Choose the correct words to complete the sentences.

1 This shirt doesn't feel nice against my skin. The *material / design* is rough.
2 I can't decide which dress to buy. There are too many *designs / options*.
3 People don't know how wonderful this new product is. We need to *produce / advertise* it better.
4 One reason computers are expensive is because they are difficult to *manufacture / sell*.
5 It's hard to *choice / pick* one of those perfumes—they all smell really nice.
6 *Producing / Recycling* plastic bags helps the environment and decreases waste.
7 In some cities, restaurants are *growing / recycling* vegetables on their rooftops.

**3 Review** Read and choose the correct options to complete the email.

Hi Saul,

We're having a wonderful time in New York City. The shopping is fantastic! There are signs everywhere that are **(1)** _____ new products. Today, I bought a new jacket. The **(2)** _____ is so soft and warm. There were a lot of **(3)** _____, so it was hard to choose. The man who **(4)** _____ me the jacket is a great fashion designer. He uses **(5)** _____ buttons and beautiful fabrics. He **(6)** _____ all the jackets in the store, but they're **(7)** _____ in a factory nearby. I love my new jacket and will never **(8)** _____! Can't wait to show you—see you soon!

Love,

Kayo

1 a advertising     c producing
   b recycling      d manufacturing
2 a option        c design
   b material       d recycling
3 a options       c produces
   b picks         d advertisements
4 a designed     c sold
   b advertised    d recycled
5 a advertised    c produced
   b picked       d recycled
6 a designs       c picks
   b recycles      d grows
7 a recycled      c advertised
   b manufactured   d sold
8 a throw it up     c throw it down
   b throw it away   d throw it in

**4 Complete the phrases about shopping and money.**

1 shopping a __ __ __ __ __
2 on s __ __ __
3 give money a __ __ __
4 be in d __ __ __
5 d __ __ __ __ __ to charity
6 take something b __ __ __
7 get a r __ __ __ __ __
8 s __ __ __ __ money on

**5** Complete the sentences with *more*, *back*, *off*, or *for*.

**1** He really wants that watch, but he doesn't have enough to pay _____ it.

**2** I don't have my wallet right now—can I pay you _____ later?

**3** Paying _____ doesn't always mean better quality.

**4** How are you going to pay _____ that—credit card or cash?

**5** Don't pay _____ for a t-shirt just because it's made by a famous designer.

**6** We need to pay _____ the debt before we can buy a new car.

**7** I'm hoping to get a job this summer to help pay _____ the vacation in Japan.

**8** Maria bought lunch for me, so I need to pay her _____.

**6** Choose the correct words to complete the sentences.

**1** I don't need any help, thanks. I'm just *browsing* / *shopping*.

**2** My new phone stopped working after one week! I'm taking it back to get a *return* / *refund*.

**3** If you need to *borrow* / *lend* some money this month, I can help.

**4** Aroon's new coat was a really good value—it was cheap, but the *bargain* / *quality* is pretty good.

**5** If people recognize the *bargain* / *brand*, they might be more likely to buy the product.

**6** Sometimes I buy winter clothes during the summer when they're *on* / *in* sale.

**7** Her goal is to find a job where she *lends* / *earns* a lot, so that she can travel.

**8** That jacket looked almost the same as the cheaper one, but it had a different *logo* / *company*.

**7** Match the words and phrases.

**1** afford to         **a** something back
**2** take             **b** around
**3** shop             **c** someone money
**4** lend             **d** buy something
**5** waste money      **e** away
**6** give something   **f** on something

**8** Listen and choose the correct options. 🎧 **70**

**1** *pay for* / *pay off*
**2** *bargain* / *donation*
**3** *brand* / *browse*
**4** *logo* / *lend*
**5** *brand* / *company*
**6** *sold in* / *sold out*
**7** *shop around* / *shop out*

**9** **Extension** Complete the sentences with the correct forms of these words.

| consumer | interest | loan | owe | return | seller |
|---|---|---|---|---|---|

**1** If you change your mind about the suit, you can always _____ it to one of our stores.

**2** My parents gave me a _____ to buy my car, so I need to start paying them back.

**3** Don't borrow money from the bank, they charge far too much _____.

**4** She still _____ me some money that I lent her last year!

**5** Online shopping gives _____ far more choice about where to buy.

**6** I bought the rug online and the _____ was very efficient. I'd buy from him again.

**10** **Extension** Choose the correct words to complete the sentences.

**1** I always do my grocery shopping *online* / *browsing*.

**2** They'd like to move but they need to find a *seller* / *buyer* for their house.

**3** Could your parents *save* / *lend* you some money until the end of the month?

**4** I think I'll have to *lend* / *return* that shirt you gave me for my birthday. It's too small.

**5** I feel guilty if I *borrow* / *owe* someone money. I always pay them back right away.

**6** If you're not sure about a *seller* / *charity* you find online, don't buy their product.

**7** I'm sorry, but that color is out of *sale* / *stock* at the moment.

**8** Buying a house is probably the most expensive *purchase* / *buy* you'll ever make.

# LISTENING

**11** Listen to the short conversations and choose the correct pictures. 🎧 **71**

**1 a**

**c**

**b**

**2 a**

**c**

**b**

**3 a**

**c**

**b**
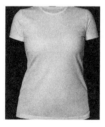

**12** Listen and choose the best description of the talk. 🎧 **72**

a the death of music CDs
b the rise of YouTube music stars
c the digital music revolution
d disappearing record companies

**13** Listen again and choose the correct options to complete the sentences. 🎧 **72**

**1** A *buck* is another way of saying _____.
   a a billion          c a device
   b a dollar

**2** A *cash cow* is _____.
   a something that earns you a lot of money
   b a very unusual, expensive animal
   c anything that costs an enormous amount of money

**3** *À la carte* allows you to _____.
   a create a menu       c pick and choose
   b buy the whole thing

**4** A word or phrase used by the speaker meaning *passed* is _____.
   a overtaken          c gone beyond
   b outdone

**5** *Heaven sent* is another way of saying _____.
   a an artist          c a fan
   b a gift

**6** A word used by the speaker meaning *memorable* is _____.
   a attractive         c catchy
   b likable

**14** Listen again and choose the correct answers to the questions. 🎧 **72**

**1** In what year did the iTunes store open?
   a 2003              c 2015
   b 2007

**2** What device brought about the digital revolution in music?
   a iTunes            c the iPod
   b the CD

**3** Who is Matt Kleinschmit?
   a a music analyst    c a music producer
   b a music artist

**4** Where does the phrase "à la carte" come from?
   a the music industry c many countries
   b France

**5** What is an example of "physical" music?
   a a download        c a CD
   b streaming

**6** When does the speaker expect CDs to completely disappear?
   a sometime very soon
   b not anytime soon
   c sometime in the near future

**7** What kind of place do you think Des Moines is?
   a a small, not very important city
   b a very important, powerful city
   c a big city with a lot of children

## GRAMMAR Passive voice

**15** Are the words in bold active (A) or passive (P)?

**1** Cheaper brands **can be found**, but they are not as good as the more expensive ones. _____

**2** I **bought** these shoes online, but I might return them. _____

**3** Customers **had** sometimes **been given** the wrong information. _____

**4** **Was** the loan ever **paid back**? _____

**5** Parents **donated** money to buy a new computer for the school. _____

**6** These products **are** often **manufactured** in India. _____

**7** I **didn't find** a new pair of headphones because they didn't have the ones I like. _____

**8** Shoppers **can pay** full price if they don't want to wait for the sale. _____

**16** Choose the correct verb forms to complete the sentences.

**1** The way we spend our money *has been changed / is change / was change* by online shopping.

**2** I *wasn't recommend / don't recommend / been recommended* the department store on Main Street.

**3** One dollar *is donated / is donate / donated* to charity every time the song *is play / been played / is played*.

**4** Was the money *spend / been spent / spent* on something useful?

**5** My sister *is sold / sells / been sell* CDs she no longer wants on eBay.

**6** The TV *was returned / returned / has been return* and the customer *was been given / has been given / gave* a full refund.

**17** Put the words in the correct order to make passive sentences and questions.

**1** can / on / Sometimes, / be / great deals / found / the internet / .

_____

**2** identified / Who / been / as / the previous owner / had / ?

_____

**3** new / Gift cards / to / usually given / are / customers / .

_____

**4** donated / What / has / to / the / been / auction / ?

_____

**5** are / suits / only sold / These / Los Angeles store / our / in / .

_____

**6** been / by 10% / have / prices / increased / Last year's / .

_____

**18** Complete the second sentence in the correct passive form so that it means the same as the first.

**1** We sold the extra tickets for a reduced price.
The extra tickets _____ for a reduced price.

**2** They can repair the broken guitar pretty easily.
The broken guitar _____ pretty easily.

**3** The heavy rain had damaged his leather jacket.
His leather jacket _____ by the heavy rain.

**4** We have already returned the extra stock to the supplier.
The extra stock _____ to the supplier.

**5** Most of the salespeople wear a uniform.
A uniform _____ by most of the salespeople.

**6** They have sent a refund to every unhappy customer.
A refund _____ to every unhappy customer.

**7** We can buy these goods more cheaply in other countries.
These goods _____ more cheaply in other countries.

**19** Complete the sentences with the correct passive form of the verb and tense in parentheses.

**1** Students ___*have been given*___ the choice of using print or online textbooks. (give, present perfect)

**2** If the goods _____, they can't be returned. (damage, simple present)

**3** The last pair _____ just before we arrived. (sell, past perfect)

**4** The smaller sizes _____ to the back of the store. (take, simple past)

**5** _____ all the orders _____ yet? (deliver, present perfect)

**6** A lot of sports equipment _____ in China. (manufacture, simple present)

**7** This pretty dress _____ from recycled materials. (make, present perfect)

**8** There was absolutely no waste because nothing _____. (throw away, past perfect)

# 7B The Shopping Experience

## READING

**1** Read the text and choose the correct answers to the questions.

**1** What do many of us pay attention to when we shop, even though we don't realize it?
 **a** things we don't want
 **b** smells, sounds, and colors
 **c** the shape of certain vegetables
 **d** foods that we don't recognize

**2** How do supermarkets get shoppers to spend more time in the store?
 **a** They try to distract shoppers.
 **b** They sell fruit and vegetables.
 **c** They pay attention to shoppers.
 **d** They have more than one door.

**3** How do supermarkets try to make the things they sell attractive to shoppers?
 **a** They only sell natural foods that are good for you.
 **b** They sell things that make you feel both energized and hungry.
 **c** They sell fruit and vegetables that were picked that morning.
 **d** They have carefully organized areas, like the fruit and vegetable department.

**4** Why do stores often play music?
 **a** People who listen to music don't shop rationally.
 **b** People spend more time shopping in stores that play music.
 **c** Listening to music makes people buy things they don't want.
 **d** People who enjoy music usually spend more.

**5** Why do supermarkets place more expensive products at eye level?
 **a** Researchers have found that products placed at eye level sell faster.
 **b** There isn't enough room on end-caps for expensive products.
 **c** Products placed at eye level are easier to see and reach.
 **d** They don't want people to feel tired when they shop.

**2** Read the statements. Are the sentences true (T), false (F), or is the information not given (NG)?

**1** Supermarkets and other stores know how to manipulate your shopping experience. _____
**2** Supermarkets would like you to spend as little time as possible in the store. _____
**3** Some supermarkets only sell organic, naturally grown produce. _____
**4** Special lights are used to make supermarket fruit and vegetables look attractive. _____

**5** After about 40 minutes of shopping, people begin to buy things they hadn't planned to buy. _____
**6** "End-caps" are used to display products that the store doesn't want to sell. _____

**3** Choose the correct words to complete the sentences.

**1** Whether we know it or not, most of us do pay attention to how things are _____ in a supermarket.
 **a** wanted          **c** bought
 **b** arranged        **d** stored

**2** Supermarkets want shoppers to _____ as much time as possible in the store.
 **a** pay            **c** spend
 **b** shop           **d** browse

**3** Supermarkets make sure that they arrange fruit and vegetables very _____.
 **a** emotionally     **c** carefully
 **b** quickly         **d** naturally

**4** Research has found that music encourages shoppers to spend more time _____ in stores.
 **a** singing         **c** listening
 **b** browsing        **d** talking

**5** Expensive brands are usually kept at eye level in supermarkets because they're more _____ seen and reached there.
 **a** normally        **c** completely
 **b** rationally      **d** easily

## VOCABULARY BUILDING  Adverbs

**4** Complete each sentence with an adverb formed from the adjective in parentheses.

**1** They serve delicious fish dishes that are always _____ cooked. (perfect)
**2** Sorry, but the coffee machine is _____ out of service. (temporary)
**3** I try not to eat too much chocolate, but I _____ give myself a treat. (occasional)
**4** Slow down a little—you're driving too _____! (fast)
**5** This excellent restaurant is famous for its _____ prepared food. (careful)
**6** Why don't you ever get your hair cut _____? (professional)
**7** Choose your words _____—you don't want to make her angry! (careful)
**8** I always sleep _____ after a long walk. (good)

# Tricks of the Trade: How Supermarkets Influence Shoppers

🎧 **73** Do you notice the music playing in the background when you're shopping in a supermarket? Do you care how the fruit and vegetables are arranged? Though we may not realize it, most of us do pay attention to things like colors, sounds, and even smells when we shop. Shopping for groceries in a supermarket is a good example of how stores manipulate* your shopping experience in order to persuade you to buy more or to buy something you didn't know you wanted.

Supermarkets want you to spend as much time as possible in the store. They know that the longer you stay, the more you'll see and want to buy, so while you're there, they try to distract* you to make you spend a little more money. How do they do it? For one thing, once you enter a supermarket, it's not always easy to get out again, and that's not accidental. Most supermarkets have only one entrance. To find the way out, you're forced to walk through most of the store, past tempting displays of products for sale.

Once you're in the door, the first thing you'll see in most supermarkets is the fruit and vegetable department, packed with smells, colors, and textures that make you feel both energized and hungry. This gives the supermarket a welcoming impression, a colorful place filled with natural foods that are fresh and good for you. The truth is that this department is the first of several carefully organized areas. Special lighting is used to make the fruit and vegetables on display appear bright and colorful. Even the mist that periodically sprays produce in some supermarkets is only there for effect. Though it makes fruit and vegetables look as if they were picked that morning, the spray serves no practical purpose and rather than keeping them fresh, actually causes them to rot more quickly than normal.

Music also helps to keep shoppers browsing. One study found that people spend up to 34% longer shopping in stores that play music. That's significant because research has also found that after about 40 minutes, people stop shopping rationally* and carefully, and instead shop emotionally, buying things they hadn't planned to buy.

Another trick involves the placement of goods for sale. In most supermarkets, the more expensive items are kept on shelves at eye level, where they're easily seen and reached. Bargain or cheaper brands are placed closer to the floor, so that you have to bend down to get them. The displays at the ends of aisles*, known as "end-caps," are also designed to catch your eye and convince you to buy the items placed there. Researchers have found that products placed on end-caps sell eight times faster than they would if put elsewhere in the store!

What can you do to avoid spending all afternoon buying things you didn't think you wanted? If you want to get your shopping done efficiently, make a list and stick to it! Don't go shopping when you're hungry or because you're bored. And keep your eyes and ears open. Don't let a store trick you into buying something you don't need!

**manipulate** *to control*
**distract** *to make someone stop giving their attention to something*

**rationally** *based on practical reasons and not emotions*
**aisle** *a long narrow space between the rows of shelves in a supermarket*

# 7C Services in My Town

## GRAMMAR *have / get something done*

**1** Listen and complete the sentences. 🎧 **74**

1 They _____ every spring.
2 We _____ to a different address.
3 I need to _____.
4 You should _____. It would look so much better.
5 Penny _____ while she's at work.
6 Max _____ before he bought the car.
7 If you need the recording next week, I'll _____ to you tomorrow.

**2** Complete the sentences using *have / get something done*.

1 I _____ every three weeks.
   (have / hair / cut)
2 The Luong family _____ every summer. (have / a family portrait / take)
3 My gym _____ last week.
   (get / a new sound system / install)
4 It was so nice—Kyung _____ for everyone at the meeting. (have / coffee and donuts / bring)
5 I _____ to see if I needed glasses, but they said they were fine. (have / my eyes / check)
6 He usually _____ before each concert. (have / the piano / tune)
7 We _____ after we'd finished studying. (have / pizza / deliver)
8 You should _____—it's really dirty! (get / your car / wash)

**3** Write who did the action in bold. Write *don't know* if it is not clear.

1 The classroom was very cold, so our teacher **turned** the temperature **up**. _____
2 Santosh got his phone **fixed**. _____
3 The music at the restaurant was too loud, so we got it **turned down**. _____
4 I have the newsletter **delivered** to my inbox every week. _____
5 The students **put** the books on the shelves. _____
6 Sima **drove** her aunt to the airport so that she didn't have to take the bus. _____

7 We had our bags **checked** as we entered the stadium. _____
8 The company has every phone **tested** before it leaves the factory. _____

**4** Are the words in bold correct or incorrect? Correct those that are incorrect.

1 We had breakfast **delivering** to our room while we were on vacation. _____
2 We **have our tickets checked** as we went into the concert. _____
3 Professor Sales **had** signs put up all over campus to advertise the lecture. _____
4 He has the weekly report **got copy** before he sends it to Josefina. _____
5 She had the invitations **be sent** a week before the party. _____
6 They **have flowers delivered** to their grandmother on her birthday. _____
7 The librarian had the books **put has got** back on the shelves. _____
8 Anisa **gets** her mail sent to her school. _____

**5** Look at Nadia's to-do list from yesterday. Write sentences with *have / get something done* to talk about what Nadia did and didn't get done.

get new passport photo [✔]
electrician here to fix lights – 3:00 [✔]
take phone to store to get fixed [✘]
Sandy here to clean windows – midday [✔]
haircut – 4:30 [✔]
dentist for teeth cleaning – 9:15 [✘]

1 *She got her passport photo taken.*
   (her passport photo)
2 _____
   (the lights)
3 _____
   (her phone)
4 _____
   (the windows)
5 _____
   (her hair)
6 _____
   (her teeth)

**6** Complete the second sentence with *have / get something done.*

**1** They asked the groundskeeper to check the soccer field to see if it was too wet.

They *had the soccer field checked* to see if it was too wet.

**2** The optician fixed his glasses after he broke them at the concert.

He _____ after he broke them at the concert.

**3** She asked the company to make a sign for her coffee shop.

She _____ for her coffee shop.

**4** He asked Carlos to forward his calls to his phone.

He _____ to his phone.

**5** She told the clerk to send the bill to her mother.

She _____ to her mother.

**6** We asked them to bring breakfast to our hotel room.

We _____ to our hotel room.

**7** I asked a plumber to repair the kitchen faucet.

I _____ by a plumber.

**7** Read and listen to the questions. Choose the correct answers. 🎧 75

**1** Where do you get your car fixed?
  **a** I get it fixed at Quick Auto Repair, on Main Street.
  **b** I had got it fixing at Quick Auto Repair, on Main Street.

**2** Do you have a new student ID yet?
  **a** Yes. I had taking a new picture already.
  **b** No. I haven't had a new picture taken yet.

**3** Is everything ready for the party?
  **a** Yes! I had the food delivered this morning and the house cleaned this afternoon.
  **b** Well, tomorrow I still need to had the food delivered and got the house cleaned.

**4** Do you think you need to get new glasses?
  **a** No. I got my eyes checked last month and the glasses I have are fine.
  **b** No. My optician got my eyes had checked and the glasses I have are fine.

**5** Did Dr. Jensen give you anything for your sore throat?
  **a** Yes. She got sent a prescription to the pharmacy.
  **b** Yes. She had a prescription sent to the pharmacy.

**6** Are you ready to eat dinner?
  **a** No. I was really hungry earlier, so I had some pizza delivered.
  **b** Yes. I'm really hungry, so let's got some pizza delivered.

**7** Is your computer still broken?
  **a** No. I'm having it fixed last week.
  **b** No. I had it fixed last week.

**PRONUNCIATION** Sentence stress

**8** Listen and underline the two or three words that are stressed in each sentence. Then practice saying the sentences. 🎧 76

**1** Have you ever had anything stolen?
**2** I've never had my room painted.
**3** Have you ever had your car fixed?
**4** Has she ever had her eyes tested?
**5** Have they ever had their groceries delivered?
**6** We've never had the television repaired.

# 7D  Grow Your Own Clothes

## TEDTALKS

## AUTHENTIC LISTENING SKILLS

**1** Read the excerpts from Parts 2 and 3 of the TED Talk. Choose the sentences that you think follow. Then listen and check your answers. 🎧 **77**

**1** At this point, it's really heavy.
  **a** So we start by brewing the tea.
  **b** And then we're ready to add the living organism.
  **c** It's over 90 percent water.

**2** What I can't yet do is make it water-resistant.
  **a** Possibly a good performance piece, but definitely not ideal for everyday wear.
  **b** So, if I was to walk outside in the rain wearing this dress today, I would immediately start to absorb huge amounts of water.
  **c** After about three days, the bubbles will appear on the surface of the liquid.

**3** And in fact, we could make it from a waste stream.
  **a** So, we only grow what we need.
  **b** So, for example, a waste sugar stream from a food processing plant.
  **c** And as it evaporates, it will knit itself together, forming seams.

**4** What I'm not suggesting is that microbial cellulose is going to be a replacement for cotton, leather, or other textile materials.
  **a** But I do think it could be quite a smart and sustainable addition to our increasingly precious natural resources.
  **b** So they're spinning these tiny nano-fibers of pure cellulose.
  **c** And they're sticking together, forming layers, and giving us a sheet on the surface.

**5** Ultimately, maybe it won't even be fashion where we see these microbes have their impact.
  **a** The dress would get really heavy and eventually the seams would probably fall apart.
  **b** What I'm looking for is a way to give the material the qualities that I need.
  **c** We could, for example, imagine growing a lamp, a chair, a car, or maybe even a house.

## WATCH ▶

**2** Watch Parts 1 and 2 of the TED Talk. Put the sentences in the correct order.

  **a** Brew 30 liters of tea and add two kilos of sugar. _____
  **b** Cool tea to below 30 degrees C (86 degrees F) and add the living organism and acetic acid. _____
  **c** Cut out shapes and sew, or use the material to form a 3-D shape. _____

  **d** Maintain an optimum temperature for the growth. _____
  **e** Pour tea into a growth bath. _____
  **f** To harvest, take out of the bath, wash it, spread it out, and let it evaporate. _____
  **g** When bubbles appear on the surface of the liquid, fermentation has begun. _____
  **h** Within two to three weeks, a one-inch sheet has formed. _____

**3** Watch Part 3 of the TED Talk. Choose the correct words or phrases to complete the sentences.

**1** Suzanne Lee is excited by how *efficient / economical / fast* microbe use is in textile production.
**2** Lee thinks fabric could be *spread out / poured / made* from the sugar that is thrown away at food factories.
**3** When Lee says that microbial cellulose can biodegrade naturally with vegetable peelings, she means *it's good for the environment / it's easy to clean / it can be made from vegetables*.
**4** Lee feels that microbial cellulose should *replace / not replace / be an addition to* other materials.
**5** When she says, "maybe it won't even be fashion where we see these microbes have their impact," she means *they may never be used / they might be used in another area / they may never become popular in fashion*.

## VOCABULARY IN CONTEXT

**4** Choose the correct words to complete the sentences.

**1** _____ the cake mixture out in the pan so it bakes evenly.
  **a** Pour  **b** Spread  **c** Extend
**2** In the bathroom, there were ants and other _____ crawling all over the floor.
  **a** birds  **b** leaves  **c** bugs
**3** In many parts of the world, clean water is a _____ resource.
  **a** precious  **b** beautiful  **c** wasteful
**4** The box is _____, so you can see everything inside it.
  **a** liquid  **b** transparent  **c** 3-D
**5** I'm not surprised you feel cold, you're practically _____! Put some more clothes on!
  **a** stupid  **b** naked  **c** wet
**6** _____ the liquid into the bowl and mix it with the other ingredients.
  **a** Pour  **b** Catch  **c** Fall
**7** I was very impressed by the speed and _____ of the process.
  **a** waste  **b** concept  **c** efficiency

# 7E Buying and Selling

## SPEAKING

**1** Complete the conversation with these phrases. Then listen and check your answers. 🎧 **78**

It's OK, I'm just browsing.
I need a size large.
Where are the changing rooms?
I'm looking for something classier.
Is it the right size?
It looks really good on you.
We only have red ones
I'll take it.
do you have these in a larger size?

**Salesperson** Hi. Can I help you with anything?

**Customer (1)** _____

**S** No problem. Let me know if you need anything.

**C** Thanks. Actually, I wonder, **(2)** _____

**S** The linen skirts? We might. I'll check. What size are you looking for?

**C (3)** _____

**S** OK. We also have these linen pants in a large.

**C** Yes, they're nice, but **(4)** _____

**S** OK. I'll be right back.

. . .

**S (5)** _____ in large. I've brought one and the blue in a medium—in case you want to try it.

**C** Thanks. **(6)** _____

**S** Over there on the right.

. . .

**C** Excuse me. Could I ask what you think?

**S** Of course.

**C (7)** _____

**S** Oh, yes! **(8)** _____

**C** Great. **(9)** _____

**2** When speaking English fast, some sounds in consonant clusters disappear or change. Look at the underlined consonant clusters and say the phrases quickly. Decide which consonant sound disappears/changes in fast speech. Listen again and check your answers. 🎧 **78**

**1** ju_st br_owsing… It's OK, I'm ju_st br_owsing.
**2** chang_ing r_ooms… where are the chang_ing r_ooms?
**3** righ_t s_ize… Is it the righ_t s_ize?
**4** loo_ks r_eally… It loo_ks r_eally good on you.

**3** Match the sentences (1–7) with the responses (a–g).

**1** Are you looking for anything in particular? _____
**2** We've got some great new t-shirts in stock. _____
**3** I need a size medium. _____
**4** Do you have these in a different color? _____
**5** Is it the right size? _____
**6** Where are the changing rooms? _____
**7** It looks really good on you. _____

**a** Great—I'll take it.
**b** Over there, next to the cash register.
**c** No, I'm just browsing.
**d** It's a little tight around the shoulders.
**e** I'm not sure we have any in stock, but they're coming in on the next delivery.
**f** Thanks, but I want something a little nicer.
**g** No, we only have the green ones.

**4** Practice conversations for the two situations below. Make notes on your ideas on a separate sheet of paper. Then listen to the sample conversations and compare your ideas. 🎧 **79**

Clothing store:

You want to buy some jeans. First the salesperson suggests a standard design, but you want something more fashionable. You're size 30 long. They have all colors in 30 regular but only black in 30 long. You ask to try both on. The black ones fit and you decide to buy them.

Phone store:

You want to get a new phone—something reliable with a large memory. First, the salesperson suggests an iPhone, but you want something at a lower price. She offers you a much cheaper, silver phone with 128GB—you like the design but want more storage. The store only has a black or white phone with more storage, and you ask to see the black one. You decide to buy this phone.

**5** Some people think it is better to go into stores to buy clothes. Others think it is better to buy clothes online. Which do you think is better? Explain why.

Make some notes on your ideas for this on a separate sheet of paper. Then listen to the sample answer and compare your ideas. 🎧 **80**

# WRITING  An announcement

**6** Choose four things you should <u>not</u> do when writing an announcement to sell an item online.

1 Use a clear heading with the name of the item. _____
2 Include fun facts even if they aren't relevant. _____
3 Post a photo of the item. _____
4 Provide the price and types of payment accepted. _____
5 Use rhetorical questions. _____
6 Write long, very detailed sentences. _____
7 Supply a description of the item, including age and condition. _____
8 Say what you dislike about the item. _____
9 Mention who the item would be suitable for. _____
10 Talk about the seller's background and hobbies. _____
11 Provide details about shipping. _____

**7** Read and choose the best sentences or phrases for a "for sale" announcement.

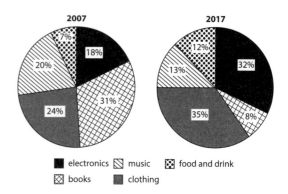

1 **a** <u>Telescope: Celestron Astromaster 76EQ!</u>
  **b** An old telescope with a very nice tripod.

2 **a** Do you want to own my telescope, which I've had for a year?
  **b** Want a cool telescope for an excellent price? Keep reading!

3 **a** Not bad condition. Probably suitable for someone who would not use it very often.
  **b** Good condition. Suitable for someone developing a new interest in astronomy.

4 **a** Not accepting any offers under $50.
  **b** Costs $100 new. Make me an offer.

5 **a** Once paid, I will ship the item as soon as I can.
  **b** Shipping within two days of receipt of payment.

**8** Look at the sentences in Activity 7 again. Then match the problems with the correct headings.

1 Not clear and sounds lazy. Buyers need to know when they will receive the item. _____
2 Not relevant or exact enough to attract a buyer's interest. _____
3 Too general; isn't clear about how much to pay. _____
4 Too boring, and doesn't really make anyone interested in finding out more. _____
5 Too negative. Doesn't provide a good reason to buy. _____

**a** condition / suitability
**b** heading
**c** opening question
**d** shipping
**e** price

**9** Complete the "for sale" announcement with these words or phrases.

| | | |
|---|---|---|
| bargain price | Brand new | Cash payment |
| Central Monterrey | for general travel | Lots of smaller |
| Price | quality | selling because |
| students | Suitable for | |

### Black backpack

(1) _____ : $35

Payment: Cash only

Seller: (2) _____

Need a comfortable backpack (3) _____? There is plenty of space in the main section.

(4) _____ pockets for convenience.

(5) _____ hiking, walking, or camping weekends. Ideal for (6) _____!

(7) _____ with the tags still on. Material is excellent (8) _____.

Only (9) _____ I received a similar backpack for my birthday.

These backpacks cost $50 in stores. I'm asking the (10) _____ of $35 for a quick sale. No shipping, sorry. (11) _____ and local pickup of item in Monterrey only.

**10** The pie charts show how online shopping trends among 20- to 30-year-olds changed over a period of ten years in one region of the UK.

Summarize the information by reporting the main features and make comparisons where relevant. Write at least 150 words.

**2007**
7% / 18% / 20% / 24% / 31%

**2017**
12% / 32% / 13% / 35% / 8%

■ electronics  ▨ music  ▩ food and drink
▨ books  ▆ clothing

# Review

**1** Read the definitions and complete the words. The first letter is given for you.

**1** a business or organization   c _ _ _ _ _ _ _

**2** something that costs much less than usual
b _ _ _ _ _ _

**3** to give money or goods to charity  d _ _ _ _ _

**4** a symbol or design on something   l _ _ _

**5** to give money to someone for a period of time
l _ _ _

**6** to look around a store without buying
b _ _ _ _ _

**7** to take money from someone for a period of time
b _ _ _ _ _

**2** Complete the second sentence so that it means the same as the first. Use no more than three words.

**1** I haven't owed money for a long time.
It's a long time since I've been in _____.

**2** I think you should donate more to charity.
If I were you, _____ more to charity.

**3** I prefer shopping around to buying everything at one place.
I'd rather _____ than buy everything at one place.

**4** If you don't send it back, you won't get a refund.
You won't _____ unless you send it back.

**5** If you don't like it, why don't you return it?
If you don't like it, why don't you _____ back?

**6** I asked my parents if I could borrow some money.
I asked my parents for a _____.

**3** What is the tense of these passive sentences? Choose the correct option.

**1** The cost of the repair is estimated at $500.
*simple present / present perfect / past perfect*

**2** All the carpets have been replaced.
*present perfect / past perfect / simple present*

**3** Are those phones manufactured in Mexico?
*simple past / simple present / past perfect*

**4** Many new products were photographed for the 2018 catalog. *simple present / simple past / past perfect*

**5** The price had been reduced because it was an old model.
*present perfect / simple past / past perfect*

**6** Has the concert been advertised on TV?
*simple present / present perfect / past perfect*

**7** A new range of products is introduced every season.
*present perfect / present continuous / simple present*

**8** The cost of tablet computers had been expected to decrease.
*simple past / present perfect / past perfect*

**4** Complete the sentences to change the active sentences to passive and the passive sentences to active. Leave out the agent in the passive sentences.

**1** People often buy books and electronic items online.
Books and electronic items _____.

**2** The price has been reduced by the salesperson because of the damage.
The _____ because of the damage.

**3** They had paid the loan back by the end of the year.
The _____ by the end of the year.

**4** The logo was removed from her coats by the designer.
_____ from her coats.

**5** The payment was sent to the credit card company by my bank.
My _____ to the credit card company.

**5** Choose the correct options to complete the sentences.

**1** Pedro was picked up _____ a taxi to go to the airport.
**a** from　　**b** for　　**c** by　　**d** with

**2** We had the presentation _____ with our school's logo.
**a** designed　　　**c** make
**b** was designed　　**d** designed by

**3** The door _____ by my friend Katya.
**a** has opened　　**c** has got opened
**b** was opened　　**d** was opening

**4** They like to _____ the carpets cleaned every few years.
**a** have get　**b** had　**c** got　**d** get

**5** The tickets were _____ up a couple of days ago.
**a** picked　**b** got　**c** pick　**d** picking

**6** Put the words in the correct order to make sentences with *have / get something done*.

**1** computers / our / new / teacher / installed / got / .
_____

**2** made / have / I / a / every / birthday / cake / year / for / my / father's / .
_____

**3** Thursdays / grass / they / get / the / cut / on / .
_____

**4** taken / we / that / years / photo / five / ago / had / .
_____

**5** before / Chao / his / college / repaired / laptop / got / went / to / he / .
_____

**6** the school / having / website / made / is / new / a / .
_____

# 8 Effective Communication

## 8A Getting Your Message Out

### VOCABULARY Effective communication

**1 Review** Match the two parts of the sentences.

1 I can't leave my office _____
2 I'll probably be driving then, _____
3 She sent me a message _____
4 My dad can't text, _____
5 You need to speak louder _____
6 If you need to talk to me, _____

a so send me a text and I'll read it later.
b because I'm expecting an important call.
c because I can't understand you.
d so he calls me instead.
e call my cellphone.
f to say that she wasn't coming tonight.

**2 Review** Put the words in the correct order to make sentences and questions.

1 understand / I / saying / what / are / you / don't / .
   _____
2 me / text / if / send / you / need / a / me / .
   _____
3 well / you / English / communicate / how / can / in / ?
   _____
4 teacher / the / spoke / I / to / the / test / about / .
   _____
5 listening / me / to / anyone / is / ?
   _____
6 I / your / view / of / point / understand / .
   _____
7 got / I / important / an / message / boss / my / from / .
   _____

**3 Review** Read the sentences. Is each underlined word a noun (N) or a verb (V)?

1 He told me to give him a <u>call</u> this weekend. _____
2 Send me a <u>text</u> when you get to the restaurant. _____
3 Did she <u>email</u> them with the directions yet? _____
4 We called Lena but there was no <u>answer</u>. _____
5 Don't ever <u>text</u> me when you're driving. _____
6 She checks her <u>email</u> every evening. _____

7 The phone's ringing—could someone <u>answer</u> it? _____
8 Please <u>call</u> me when you get there. _____

**4** Complete the expressions about communication.

1 pay a __ __ __ __ __ __ __ __
2 g __ __ my m __ __ __ __ __ __ out
3 get d __ __ __ __ __ __ __ __ d
4 interpersonal s __ __ __ __ __
5 post on s __ __ __ __ __ m __ __ __ __
6 r __ __ __ __ __ to texts
7 s __ __ __ __ photos
8 make c __ __ __ __ __ __ __ __ s

**5** Choose the correct words to complete the sentences.

1 When I study in my room, I *get / make* distracted far too easily.
2 My sister always takes forever to *post / respond* to texts.
3 It's important to *get / pay* attention in class.
4 We won't be able to *send / share* texts while we're traveling.
5 You can *share / respond* photos on the new website.
6 Using social media is a great way to *make / share* connections with new people.

**6** Choose the word or phrase that does <u>not</u> collocate with the verbs.

1 pay        *attention / a fine / a text*
2 get        *connection / distracted / into an argument*
3 make       *connections / friends / messages*
4 respond    *to a text / to a friend / to a phone*
5 share      *photos / chat / computers*
6 post       *on a forum / on social media / on an email*

**7** Choose the correct options.

1 usually informal, between friends: *a conversation / a debate*
2 angry, emotional: *a debate / an argument*
3 serious, giving ideas: *a discussion / a chat*
4 informal, short, friendly: *an argument / a chat*
5 between teams, to give a point of view: *a debate / a discussion*

**8** Put the words in the correct order to make sentences.

**1** get / message / I / to / need / out / my / .

_____

**2** skills / teacher / Jack's / interpersonal / terrible / has / .

_____

**3** old / she / trying / is / with / connect / friends / to / .

_____

**4** careful / social / post / media / what / you / be / on / .

_____

**5** distracted / by / your / don't / get / friends / .

_____

**6** he / photos / his / website / on / share / likes / to / .

_____

**7** attention / when / pay / someone / talking / is / .

_____

**9** **Extension** Complete the sentences with the correct forms of these verbs.

| argue | call | chat | debate | discuss | question |
|-------|------|------|--------|---------|----------|

**1** The teams were _____ whether animals should be used for scientific purposes.

**2** My manager and I need to _____ my new work schedule.

**3** Don't _____ with me—you know that you're wrong!

**4** I'm just _____ whether this is something we really need.

**5** Why don't you _____ me after work and we can talk?

**6** We were _____ before the lesson started, but then the teacher asked us to be quiet.

**10** **Extension** Choose the correct words to complete the sentences.

**1** Have you heard the latest *chat* / *gossip* about Jan? She's moving to Spain.

**2** You can all have some—there's no need to *quarrel* / *discuss* about it.

**3** The whole group was in *argument* / *agreement* about what they should do.

**4** If he forgets to pay, they usually send him a *reminder* / *call*.

**5** Plans for the new building have attracted a lot of *argument* / *criticism*.

**6** He gave a wonderful *lecture* / *speech* at Min and Kai's wedding.

## LISTENING

**11** Listen and choose the correct answers to the questions.
🎧 **81**

**1** Why is the man apologizing?
**a** He doesn't want to be around Tom.
**b** He can't accept the woman's invitation.
**c** He has something else he has to do.
**d** He wasn't invited to the party.

**2** Why does the man not want to be around Tom?
**a** Tom was invited first.
**b** He thinks Tom is selfish.
**c** The woman likes Tom.
**d** He can't stand Tom.

**3** What do the man and woman agree on?
**a** Tom can't stand the woman.
**b** Tom is selfish.
**c** Tom is not very polite.
**d** Tom always changes his mind.

**4** Why does the man want to talk to the woman?
**a** He feels really terrible.
**b** He's been thinking.
**c** He wants her to be honest.
**d** He and Tom have talked.

**5** What does the man not want?
**a** to let Tom win
**b** to be around Tom
**c** to avoid Tom
**d** to be polite to Tom

**6** What does the woman tell the man he must do?
**a** avoid Tom
**b** come to the party
**c** be himself
**d** ask Tom not to come

**12** Listen and choose the best summary.  🎧 82

**a** Tim Baird is afraid new technology is destroying the traditional culture.
**b** Tim Baird sees both positives and negatives in new technology.
**c** Tim Baird generally thinks technology makes the Maasai people's lives better.
**d** Tim Baird worries that the Maasai culture could disappear.

**13** Listen again. Are the statements true (T) or false (F)?  🎧 82

**1** The Maasai people depend on their cows. _____
**2** The Maasai are taking technology tests. _____
**3** Tim Baird is an anthropology professor. _____
**4** The availability of new information is changing Maasai life. _____
**5** Maasai business was traditionally done in person. _____
**6** Taking photographs is allowed in Maasai culture. _____
**7** Baird used to believe that technology was interfering with Maasai culture. _____
**8** The Maasai are worried that technology is changing their culture. _____

## GRAMMAR  Reported speech (1)

**14** Are these sentences direct (D) or reported (R) speech?

**1** "Some animals use special chemicals to communicate." _____
**2** Our teacher asked, "Do pets react when they hear the word *treat*?" _____
**3** She told us that some animals used special chemicals to communicate. _____
**4** Juan said that his dog scratches the door when he wants to go outside. _____
**5** "Do pets react when they hear the word *treat*?" _____
**6** He said, "My dog scratches the door when he wants to go outside." _____
**7** She asked if pets reacted when they heard the word *treat*. _____

**15** Choose the sentence that means the same as the first.

**1** Jose Luis: "Do you like to text your friends?"
  **a** He asked if we liked to text our friends.
  **b** He asked that we liked to text our friends.
**2** Mina: "I spend a lot of time texting my friends."
  **a** She said that she spent a lot of time texting my friends.
  **b** She said that she spent a lot of time texting her friends.
**3** Mustapha: "I text really fast. I use a lot of abbreviations."
  **a** He commented that he had texted really fast and that he had used a lot of abbreviations.
  **b** He commented that he texted really fast and that he used a lot of abbreviations.
**4** Natalia: "Texting is the best way to communicate with my friends."
  **a** She said that texting was the best way to communicate with her friends.
  **b** She said that texting will be the best way to communicate with your friends.
**5** Javier: "I even taught my grandmother how to text!"
  **a** He admitted that he had even taught his grandmother how to text.
  **b** He admitted that he was even teaching his grandmother how to text.
**6** Sue: "I text my best friend if I'm having trouble with my homework."
  **a** She explained that her best friend texts her if she is having trouble with her homework.
  **b** She explained that she texted her best friend if she was having trouble with her homework.

**16** Choose the correct options to complete the sentences.

**1** Hara: "What time did my boss tell me that I have to be at work?"

Hara asked what time her boss *tells* / *did tell* / *told* her that she *had* / *have* / *has had* to be at work.

**2** Ellie: "We have to make sure the store is ready for the morning before going home."

Ellie said that they *have had* / *had* / *are having* to make sure the store *was* / *has been* / *had been* ready for the morning before going home.

**3** Jin: "My sister cooks dinner during the week and I cook it on weekends."

Jin told me that his sister *has cooked* / *is cooking* / *cooked* dinner during the week and he *is cooking* / *cooked* / *has cooked* it on weekends.

**4** Carla: "I'm learning how to use the cash register tomorrow."

Carla explained that she *was learning* / *learn* / *has been learning* how to use the cash register the next day.

**5** Oliver: "We got a new puppy named Prince!"

Oliver posted on social media that they *get* / *are getting* / *had got* a new puppy named Prince.

**6** Fatima: "Saturday is always busier than Sunday."

Fatima commented that Saturday *is being* / *was* / *has been* always busier than Sunday.

**17** Put the words in the correct order to complete the sentences in reported speech.

**1** she / that / complained / had / she

_____

too much responsibility in her job.

**2** replied / had / working / enjoyed / he / he / that

_____

at his father's company.

**3** suggested / that / she / she / show / could

_____

the manager one of the reports.

**4** wasn't / he / admitted / he / that

_____

really comfortable using a computer.

**5** worked / claimed / she / had / she / that

_____

at the store for two years.

**6** to / he / find / needed / replied / he / that

_____

someone who could work on Saturdays.

**18** Complete each sentence with the correct form of the verb in parentheses.

**1** "Are we going to study in the library after school?"

She asked if we _____ (study) in the library after school.

**2** "Who knows the best way to study for the science test?"

He asked who _____ (know) the best way to study for the science test.

**3** "Where is Gena today? I haven't seen her."

She asked where Gena _____ (be) and said that she _____ (not see) her.

**4** "Can you help me with an essay question?"

She asked if I _____ (can help) her with an essay question.

**5** "Did anyone write down the page number?"

She asked whether anyone _____ (write) down the page number.

**6** "Why do you always wait until the last minute?"

She asked him why he always _____ (wait) until the last minute.

**7** "Juan has already passed his driving test."

He said that Juan _____ (already pass) his driving test.

**8** "When will we know our grades on the test?"

He asked when we _____ (know) our grades on the test.

# 8B Communication

## READING

**1** Read the statements. Are the sentences true (T), false (F), or is the information not given (NG)?

1 It's possible that plants of the same type recognize one another as members of a related group. _____

2 Plants may use chemical signatures to send messages through their leaves. _____

3 Sea-rocket is a plant you can eat and it tastes like fresh seafood. _____

4 Some plants seem to know that certain neighbors can help prevent the growth of competing weeds. _____

5 A plant called "thale cress" produces a poisonous oil when it feels that an insect is eating its leaves. _____

6 Scientists have discovered that plants all speak the same language. _____

**2** Read the text and match the paragraphs (1–5) with the main ideas (a–g). You may use a number more than once.

a how plants defend themselves _____
b how plants "hear" their relatives and friends _____
c unanswered questions about plant communication _____
d plants don't communicate like us _____
e how plants use chemical signatures to communicate _____
f the "hidden but complicated" social life of plants _____
g plants know when they're being eaten _____

**3** Read the text again and match the statements (1–5) with the place or person (a–e).

1 Plants can recognize when a good neighbor is growing next to them. _____

2 Chili seedlings sprout more quickly when grown next to good neighbors. _____

3 Closely-related plants work together to succeed in their environment. _____

4 Plants such as cress are able to defend themselves from plant-eating insects. _____

5 Plants have a hidden but complicated social life. _____

a Susan Dudley
b McMaster University
c University of Missouri
d Monica Gagliano
e University of Western Australia

## VOCABULARY BUILDING  Negative prefixes

**4** Complete the sentences with these negative prefixes and the adjectives in parentheses. You may use some of the prefixes more than once.

| im- | in- | ir- | un- |
|-----|-----|-----|-----|

1 Though it may seem _____, researchers now agree that plants are able to communicate. (believable)

2 Obviously, plants are _____ to send texts or make phone calls. (able)

3 Whether or not plants can "talk" may be _____ to some people, but to many scientists, it's a fascinating topic. (relevant)

4 Without sophisticated technology, it would be _____ to record the sounds a caterpillar makes. (possible)

5 The idea that plants can talk does seem like an _____ concept. (usual)

6 Imagine having an _____ conversation with a plant! (formal)

# Do Plants Talk?

1  🎧 **83** Is a flower a member of a "family"? Does a plant recognize other plants like it, as part of a group? Research has recently shown that both possibilities may be true. Like animals and people, it seems that plants are able to recognize friends and relatives in order to work together. Obviously, plants can't send texts, make phone calls, or post photos on social media, so how do they communicate?

2  Some researchers believe that plants may connect with one another by sending messages through their roots, using chemical "signatures" specific to each plant's family in order to identify themselves. One study found that plants from the same species of sea-rocket, a coastal wildflower, grow aggressively alongside unrelated neighbors, but are less competitive when they share space with their siblings*. Researchers at McMaster University, Ontario, suggest that this may be an example of kin* selection, a behavior in which closely-related individuals work together to succeed in their environment. As Dr. Susan Dudley of the university says, "Plants have this kind of hidden but complicated social life."

3  In addition to chemical signals, it's possible that plants "hear" one another and use what they hear to recognize their relatives and good neighbors. A study conducted by the University of Western Australia has shown that the seedlings* of chili plants sprouted* more quickly when grown next to basil seedlings. The chili seedlings seem to know that these neighbors help prevent the growth of competing weeds and damage by insects. "We have shown that plants can recognize when a good neighbor is growing next to them," says Monica Gagliano, an evolutionary ecologist at the university.

4  Plants have even demonstrated that they know when they're being eaten! Not surprisingly, they don't seem to like it, and, luckily for them, they're not unable to defend themselves! Researchers at the University of Missouri made recordings of the vibrations* a caterpillar makes as it eats the leaves of a plant called thale cress. Their experiment showed that the cress produced extra mustard oil, a substance that's mildly poisonous and disliked by caterpillars, when it heard or felt vibrations similar to those made by a munching* caterpillar. Other plants, by sending chemical distress* signals while under attack from insects, are able to attract predators* that attack those same insects.

5  Scientists accept that research into plant communication is in its early days. There are still many unanswered questions. Do plants intentionally communicate with one another? If they do, do they all speak one language or are there as many languages as there are types of plants? And can we, as humans, really understand what plants are saying?

**siblings** *brothers and sisters*
**kin** *family and relatives*
**seedlings** *very young plants*
**sprout** *to begin to grow*

**vibration** *a very small, fast shaking movement*
**munch** *to eat in a noisy way*
**distress** *unhappiness or pain*
**predator** *an animal that kills and eats other animals*

# 8C He Said, She Said

## GRAMMAR Reported speech (2)

**1** Listen and complete the sentences. 🎧 84

1 He _____ the play.
2 Dottie _____ enough to eat.
3 Diego _____ my suggestion.
4 We _____ at Lee's place.
5 I _____ about our ten o'clock meeting.
6 He _____ outside to see the beautiful sunset.

**2** Choose the sentence that means the same as the first.

1 She said she needed a rest before we went to the concert.
   a "I have rested before we go to the concert."
   b "I need a rest before we go to the concert."

2 I offered to sing at the concert that day.
   a "I'm available to sing at the concert today."
   b "I'll sing at the concert the next day."

3 I told him he could stay up late to see the fireworks the next day.
   a "You would stay up late to see the fireworks the previous day."
   b "You can stay up late to see the fireworks tomorrow."

4 He said he wanted to stay up for another half an hour.
   a "I've been wanting to stay up for half an hour before."
   b "I want to stay up for another half an hour."

5 He claimed he hadn't seen the car on the corner.
   a "I didn't see the car on the corner."
   b "I won't see the car on the corner."

6 She said she'd finished the essay.
   a "I would finish the essay."
   b "I've finished the essay."

7 He asked if he could get a pet rabbit.
   a "Can I get a pet rabbit?"
   b "Will I get a pet rabbit?"

8 He explained that Camilla would be flying in from Bogotá the next day.
   a "Yesterday, Camilla flew in from Bogotá."
   b "Camilla will be flying in from Bogotá tomorrow."

**3** Complete the chart with these words. You may use some of them more than once. Then complete the example sentences using reported speech.

| can/can't | past continuous | past perfect |
|---|---|---|
| present perfect | simple present | would/wouldn't |

| direct speech | example | reported speech | example |
|---|---|---|---|
| _____ _____ | "I speak French." | simple past | She said that _____. |
| present continuous | "I am speaking French." | _____ _____ | She said that she was speaking French. |
| simple past | "I spoke French." | _____ | She said that _____. |
| _____ _____ | "I have spoken French." | past perfect | She said that _____. |
| will/won't | "I'll speak French." | _____ | She said that _____. |
| _____ _____ | "I can't speak French." | could/ couldn't | She said that _____. |

**4** Complete the chart with these words.

| our | that | that day | then |
|---|---|---|---|
| there | they | tomorrow | yesterday |

| direct speech | reported speech |
|---|---|
| (1) _____ | the next day |
| now | (4) _____ |
| we | (5) _____ |
| (2) _____ book | their book |
| today | (6) _____ |
| this book | (7) _____ book |
| here | (8) _____ |
| (3) _____ | the day before |

**5** Find and correct the mistakes in the words in bold. One sentence is correct.

1 She asked if I got to **meet the president?**
2 I saw Chau a couple of days ago—she complained that her car had broken down **yesterday**.
3 As we were finishing the meeting, I **added that I thought** we needed to do more research.
4 My little brother **admitted to he lost** his pet lizard.
5 **Asked Brigit** if I could turn off the TV.
6 He **said Sara** he'd like to play tennis with them.

**6** Choose the correct options to complete the sentences.

**1** Elia: "Should I type the note or write it out?"
Elia asked if *I / she* should type the note or write it out.

**2** My sister: "We should move to a bigger apartment."
Me: "A bigger apartment might be too expensive."
My sister suggested *moving / to move* to a bigger apartment. I *replied that / replied to* a bigger apartment might be too expensive.

**3** Oleg: "Sure, I can help you make dinner."
Oleg *agreed to help / would agree to help* us make dinner.

**4** Me: "I could go shopping with you tomorrow, Mom."
I offered to go shopping with my mom *tomorrow / the next day*.

**5** Cara: "Why don't you join us at the movies?"
She invited *me to join / to join* them at the movies.

**6** My dad: "I'll pay you back next week."
He *promised / promised to* pay me back the following week.

**7** Moira: "When I was in high school, I played lacrosse."
Moira said *to she play / that she'd played* lacrosse in high school.

**8** My sister: "Amal still hasn't replied to my email!"
She complained that Amal still *wasn't replying / hadn't replied* to her email.

**7** Complete the sentences in reported speech using the verbs in parentheses.

**1** My sister: "I'm going to jump over that chair."
My sister _____ over the chair. (say)

**2** Me to my brother: "Have you fed the dog yet?"
I _____ (ask)

**3** My aunt: "Isla, did you go to the movies on Friday?"
My aunt _____ on Friday. (ask)

**4** Mr. Vasquez: "I'll text Jen to ask her if she left her bag in class."
Mr. Vasquez _____ her bag in class. (promise)

**5** My uncle to me: "I have tickets to the game on Saturday, so I can't go to the play with you."
My uncle _____
_____. (explain)

**6** Me to my brother: "Do you have any homework to do this afternoon?"
I _____ that afternoon. (ask)

**7** Me to my sister: "I'll take you to the mall after your band rehearsal."
I _____ band rehearsal. (offer)

**8** My friends to me: "Do you want to go sailing at the lake on Saturday?"
My friends _____ at the lake the next Saturday. (invite)

## PRONUNCIATION  Contrastive stress

Remember that the same sentence can have different meanings depending on which words are stressed.

**8** Listen to the sentences. Underline the words that the speaker stresses. Then practice saying the sentences and think about the differences in meaning. 🔔 **85**

**1** Paul argued that we all connect on social media before we meet in person.

**2** Paul argued that we all connect on social media before we meet in person.

**3** Paul argued that we all connect on social media before we meet in person.

**4** Can you believe Sarah shared those photos of me on her blog?

**5** Can you believe Sarah shared those photos of me on her blog?

**6** Can you believe Sarah shared those photos of me on her blog?

**9** Listen again and choose the option that is most likely to follow each sentence. 🔔 **85**

**1** Paul argued that we all connect on social media before we meet in person.
 **a** Not just some of us.
 **b** He didn't want to wait until after.
 **c** It wasn't Susan who recommended it.

**2** Paul argued that we all connect on social media before we meet in person.
 **a** Not just some of us.
 **b** That way we could come together as a group.
 **c** It wasn't Susan who recommended it.

**3** Paul argued that we all connect on social media before we meet in person.
 **a** He didn't want to wait until after.
 **b** Not just some of us.
 **c** That way we could come together as a group.

**4** Can you believe Sarah shared those photos of me on her blog?
 **a** And I'm one of her best friends!
 **b** She, of all people, should know better!
 **c** They were so embarrassing!

**5** Can you believe Sarah shared those photos of me on her blog?
 **a** She, of all people, should know better!
 **b** And I'm one of her best friends!
 **c** That's the worst possible place!

**6** Can you believe Sarah shared those photos of me on her blog?
 **a** They were so embarrassing!
 **b** That's the worst possible place!
 **c** And I'm one of her best friends!

# 8D 10 Ways to Have a Better Conversation

## TEDTALKS

## AUTHENTIC LISTENING SKILLS

**1** Listen to the TED Talk excerpts. Choose the correct words or phrases to complete the sentences. Listen again and check your answers. 🎧 86

**1** Don't multitask. And I don't mean just set down your cellphone or your tablet or your car keys or _____ your hand.
   **a** whatever is in    **b** what's in    **c** what else is in

**2** Start your _____ with *who, what, when, where, why,* or *how.*
   **a** concerns    **b** questions    **c** requests

**3** If I ask you, "Were you terrified?" you're going to respond to the most powerful word in that sentence, which is "terrified," and _____ "Yes, I was" or "No, I wasn't."
   **a** it always is    **b** the answer is    **c** the word is

**4** And we stop listening. _____ and ideas are going to come to you.
   **a** Stories    **b** Stores    **c** Reports

**5** I cannot tell you how many really important people have said that listening is perhaps the most, the number one most important skill that you _____ develop.
   **a** should    **b** can    **c** could

**6** I don't have to hear anything I'm not interested in. I'm the _____.
   **a** sense of adventure    **c** communication
   **b** center of attention

**7** People would come over to talk to my grandparents, and after they would leave, my mother would _____, and she'd say, "Do you know who that was?"
   **a** care for us    **c** come over to us
   **b** come home with us

## WATCH ▶

**2** Watch Part 1 of the TED Talk. Choose the correct option to complete each sentence.

**1** Celeste Headlee's TED Talk is about how to have good *speeches / interviews / conversations.*

**2** Every conversation has the potential to become *a disagreement / important / an important event.*

**3** Many young people today are able to share ideas *in groups, but not individually / online, but not face-to-face / face-to-face, but not online.*

**4** Celeste Headlee works as *a professional interviewer / a secondary school teacher / a communications expert.*

**5** Celeste Headless *agrees with / disagrees with / doesn't know* the advice the audience may have heard before about how to listen.

**6** She is going to teach the audience *how to show that you're listening / the skills she uses in her profession as an interviewer / how not to be bored when having a conversation.*

**3** Watch Parts 2 and 3 of the TED Talk. Match the rules (1–6) with the explanations (a–f).

**1** Don't multitask. _____
**2** Don't pontificate. _____
**3** Use open-ended questions. _____
**4** Go with the flow. _____
**5** Try not to repeat yourself. _____
**6** Stay out of the weeds. _____

**a** Don't expect people not to have an opinion about what you're saying.
**b** Don't worry about giving all the details. Nobody cares.
**c** Encourage the person you're talking to to think about their answer.
**d** Give the person you're speaking to your full attention.
**e** Learn to listen and forget about what you want to say.
**f** Stop making the same point again and again.

## VOCABULARY IN CONTEXT

**4** Choose the correct word or phrase to complete each sentence.

**1** My father _____ my love of music. He just wants me to take over the family business.
   **a** avoids    **c** came up with
   **b** doesn't care about

**2** He got the job _____ his connections with the right people.
   **a** in conflict with    **c** due to
   **b** surrounded by

**3** It's best to _____ getting into an argument.
   **a** avoid    **b** count on    **c** try to

**4** Some people think it's polite to _____ and smile; it shows that you're listening.
   **a** whisper    **b** nod    **c** text

**5** Do you _____ ? If so, then let's hear it.
   **a** have a care    **c** show your view
   **b** have a point to make

**6** It's not easy to _____ as an actor. You have to be really good or have the right connections.
   **a** make a living    **c** make a comment
   **b** make a point

# 8E I Hear What You're Saying

## SPEAKING

**1** Choose the correct options to complete the conversation. Then listen and check your answers. 🎧 **87**

**A** Excuse me. Err, I wonder, can you help me?

**B** Yes?

**A** Well, I just went outside to answer a phone call and when I came back, my laptop was missing. Could anyone have moved it?

**B** Ah, well, I don't think so, but I'll check with the other staff.

**A** Thanks.

**C** Hi, Tom! Working hard? Oh, what's wrong?

**A** My laptop's missing.

**C** Oh, I **(1)** *see / hear*.

**B** Excuse me. I'm **(2)** *scared / afraid* that no one's seen your laptop.

**A** Then where is it?

**B** I'm sorry to **(3)** *say / tell* it looks like someone's taken it.

**A** What? My work!

**C** Oh, Tom. **(4)** *There's / That's* awful!

**A** Haven't you got CCTV or something?

**B** Err… **(5)** *Occasionally / Unfortunately*, our system is being upgraded and the cameras aren't recording.

**A** So you can't check?

**C** That is **(6)** *frustrating / complaining*. A security system that doesn't work.

**B** I **(7)** *hear / listen* what you're saying, but we do say that the library can't be responsible for personal items.

**A** But it's got all my work on it!

**B** Well, I'm sorry to **(8)** *say / hear* that. Do you have a backup?

**A** Well, I did, it's **(9)** *almost / just* that the wifi isn't working and I've been here all day.

**C** That's **(10)** *such / what* a shame.

**B** Yes, you see, the **(11)** *something / thing* is, the whole computer system's being updated, including the network.

**C** I understand, **(12)** *and / but* that's not the point. I do think you should take some responsibility for this.

**B** OK, let's call the police and see what they advise.

**2** Listen again and decide where the intonation goes up and down when showing sympathy. Practice using sympathetic intonation. 🎧 **87**

**1** I'm sorry to hear that.
**2** That is frustrating.
**3** That's such a shame.
**4** That's awful!
**5** I see.
**6** I hear what you're saying, but…
**7** I understand, but…
**8** You see, the thing is…
**9** It's just that…
**10** Unfortunately,…
**11** I'm afraid that…
**12** I'm sorry to say…

**3** Read and complete the conversation with your own answers to show sympathy. Then listen to the sample answer and compare your ideas. 🎧 **88**

**Eva** I've had a very bad week. I had an accident on my bike on Monday.

**You (1)** _____. What happened? Were you hurt?

**Eva** I'm OK, but unfortunately I hit a car.

**You (2)** _____! So what about your bike—and the car?

**Eva** Well, my front wheel was broken, but the worst thing was the car. I damaged the door and scratched the paint.

**You (3)** _____.

**Eva** The driver told me he was glad I wasn't injured, but that I would have to pay to repair the damage. So I have to work extra hours during the holidays to pay my parents back.

**You (4)** _____—so you won't have much free time, then?

**Eva** No, and that's not the only thing. I'm afraid I'm not going to finish my history homework on time.

**You** What? No! **(5)** _____. How come?

**Eva** I didn't start it early enough. I've been working hard on it this week, but last night I was so tired that I just fell asleep at my desk and woke up in the morning.

**You (6)** _____. Maybe you should ask for more time?

**4** Read the scenarios and think about the conversations in these situations. How would you show understanding or disagree politely with the other person? Make notes on your ideas. Then listen to the sample conversations and compare your ideas. 🎧 **89**

**a** You are a salesperson. A customer comes into the store wanting to return some headphones that don't work, but he doesn't have the receipt. The shop doesn't give refunds without a receipt.

**b** You're in a café and the service is very slow. You have been waiting for half an hour and the waiter brings you the wrong order. This isn't the first time you've had slow service here.

**c** Your friend calls to say that she is flying home, but the airline has canceled her flight and she can't leave until tomorrow. You're both involved in a group presentation for your course the next morning. Your friend says that the group will have to do it without her.

# WRITING  A complaint email

**5** Read the sentences. Are the words and phrases in bold expressing contrast (C), result (R), or addition (A)?

1 The fabric was cheap and, **in addition**, the sleeve was torn. _____

2 The laptop was faulty and, **therefore**, I lost a lot of important work. _____

3 The waitress was inefficient and, **furthermore**, she was pretty rude. _____

4 The item was delivered on time, **however**, it was damaged when it arrived. _____

5 No one has replied to me, **even though** I've emailed three times! _____

6 The taxi arrived far too late and, **because of this**, I missed my flight. _____

7 **In spite of** explaining the problem twice, I was asked to explain it again. _____

8 You sent it in the wrong color and, **moreover**, it was the wrong size. _____

**6** Label the parts of the complaint email.

| | |
|---|---|
| background to the problem | details of the problem |
| formal ending | formal greeting |
| how she feels | items attached |
| reason for writing | request for a reply |
| what she wants them to do | |

FROM: LiNa.Sung@messages.com

TO: CARE@funfones.com

SUBJECT: Complaint – account number 778429

(1) _____ To Whom It May Concern:

(2) _____ I am writing to complain about some ongoing customer service issues that I have had with your company.

(3) _____ Over three weeks ago, I was invited to upgrade my phone. I was assured there would be no charge for the phone and that my contract would continue for two years at the same rate of monthly payments. I was also told that the phone would be delivered to my home the following day.

(4) _____ First of all, the phone was not delivered on time. I was given a new date three times and the phone arrived more than two weeks later. Furthermore, when my bank statement arrived, I discovered I had been charged the full cost of the phone in spite of being promised I would have nothing to pay. Your customer service agents now tell me that a refund cannot be processed.

(5) _____ It has been an extremely frustrating situation that still has not been resolved. I have been a loyal customer for four years, but my confidence in your company has now declined.

(6) _____ I would like you to immediately send a full refund, in addition to an apology, or cancel my contract.

(7) _____ I am attaching copies of my bank statement, as well as a list showing details of every call I've had with customer service about this matter.

(8) _____ I look forward to hearing from you very soon.

(9) _____ Sincerely,
Li Na Sung

**7** Read the passage and then listen to the lecture. Summarize the points made in the lecture, being sure to explain how they oppose specific points made in the reading passage.  🎧 90

Unless you are someone who actually enjoys arguing, you may find it difficult to make a complaint calmly and clearly. Unlike their friends in the United States, making complaints causes many people in Britain to feel anxious. In fact, a common stereotype of British people is being so polite that they will accept great inconvenience rather than complain. Why is this?

First of all, fear. Many are afraid to speak out and risk being challenged. When service is poor, for example, it often seems easier to say nothing. The British, in particular—world famous for their extreme politeness— are also afraid to appear difficult; they don't want to cause trouble, and actually prefer to apologize than to complain.

A second theory is negative expectations—the belief that the situation won't be handled properly, or at all. What is the point of complaining if nothing is going to be done? Furthermore, people may perceive negativity in complainers. We don't want to be labeled in a negative way, so we choose not to complain at all.

Finally, according to experts, it is not that people don't want to complain, but rather, that they don't know how to complain effectively. It has been suggested that we might be happier and healthier if we could learn techniques that helped us to present our complaints more confidently. We can learn how to deliver a firm and clear message while still remaining polite. Studies show that unspoken frustrations can build up and cause a different range of problems such as anger and stress, which then put significant strain on our well-being. So, let's start complaining!

# Review

**1** Match the two parts of the sentences.

1 Having poor interpersonal skills _____
2 You can use social media _____
3 You should never send or respond _____
4 I'll miss you when you move, _____
5 Online forums are not _____
6 We need to get the message out _____

**a** to connect with new people at your university.
**b** a good place to get medical advice.
**c** about climate change.
**d** can be bad for your career.
**e** but we can have long phone conversations.
**f** to texts when you are driving.

**2** Read the text below and choose the correct options.

Next year, I'm starting college and I'm worried about losing touch with my old friends. We're going to try to stay connected **(1)** _____ each other by using social **(2)** _____. I'll **(3)** _____ photos of my new friends and my life at college, and I'll **(4)** _____ updates about what I'm doing and learning every week. Of course, I'll also make sure that I **(5)** _____ to texts when I'm not too busy. I guess it will be important not to get **(6)** _____ by my social life and forget to go to class! I'm sure though, that my old friends and I will still have great **(7)** _____ and a lot of fun when we see each other during breaks.

1 **a** with    **b** for    **c** by    **d** from
2 **a** texts    **b** media    **c** connections    **d** forums
3 **a** share    **b** send    **c** get    **d** talk
4 **a** take    **b** make    **c** download    **d** post
5 **a** respond    **b** post    **c** get    **d** make
6 **a** texted    **b** connected    **c** distracted    **d** shared
7 **a** debates    **b** conversations    **c** forums    **d** texts

**3** Read the sentences and write what each person said.

1 Jake and Maria admitted that they didn't understand what the teacher wanted them to do.
   *"We don't understand what the teacher wants us to do."*

2 He told me that the project was taking longer than he had expected.
   _____

3 The teacher reminded the students that they needed to finish their projects by Thursday.
   _____

4 He commented that no one had followed the directions.
   _____

5 She explained that the test would be worth 30% of their final grades.
   _____

6 Monica added that they always enjoyed English class.
   _____

7 Jens said that he could lend me a dictionary.
   _____

**4** Complete the reported speech with the correct form of the verbs in parentheses.

1 Ana: "I always pay attention when people talk to me."
   She claimed that she always _____ (pay) attention when people _____ (talk) to her.

2 Jakub: "You interrupt people too much."
   He said that I _____ (interrupt) people too much.

3 Haruto: "If I forget the English word for something, I can check the dictionary on my phone."
   He reminded us that if he _____ (forget) the English word for something, he _____ (can check) the dictionary on his phone.

4 Sophia: "I haven't spoken English in England, but I've visited the US."
   She told them that she _____ (not speak) English in England, but she _____ (visit) the US.

5 Hasan: "It's hard to understand people who speak quietly."
   He explained that it _____ (be) hard to understand people who _____ (speak) quietly.

**5** Complete the sentences with these words and phrases.

| admitted | could | he'd do | invited |
| that | the next day | there | told |
| was making | | | |

1 He _____ ice hockey was more challenging than he thought it would be.
2 Nadir _____ the boys for a meal before the play.
3 He said he _____ lasagna and that they _____ have it for lunch.
4 Anya _____ me she cried when she watched him on TV.
5 Joan agreed to go to town with me _____.
6 Ramon said _____ his homework later.
7 She said that they had lived _____ many years ago, in _____ small house near the church.

## **9A** Entertain me!

### VOCABULARY Creative arts

**1 Review** Match the examples with the nouns.

| | | | |
|---|---|---|---|
| **1** | The Prado, The Louvre, MoMA | **a** | art |
| **2** | painting, drawing | **b** | color |
| **3** | classical, hip hop, pop | **c** | instrument |
| **4** | bright, dark | **d** | music |
| **5** | guitar, piano, violin | **e** | photograph |
| **6** | digital, old | **f** | museum |

**2 Review** Choose the correct options to complete the sentences.

**1** Their first attempt to climb the mountain ended in _____.
   **a** failure   **b** failed   **c** fail   **d** successful

**2** I'm so disappointed—my application to theater school has been _____.
   **a** failed   **b** rejected   **c** accept   **d** failure

**3** It was one of the most _____ exhibitions that the museum had ever organized.
   **a** perfection   **b** successful   **c** accepting   **d** failed

**4** The painting was beautiful, even with the small _____ in the corner.
   **a** perfection   **b** imperfection   **c** failure   **d** fail

**5** Some of the most famous artists were _____ during their lifetimes.
   **a** success   **b** failure   **c** failed   **d** unsuccessful

**6** Those shoes look great with your dress—they're the _____ color.
   **a** perfect   **b** imperfect   **c** perfection   **d** rejection

**7** Some people say that art is _____ if it doesn't make people think.
   **a** failure   **c** successful
   **b** perfection   **d** unsuccessful

**3** Complete the chart with these words.

| | | | |
|---|---|---|---|
| audience | gallery | listeners | stadium |
| studio | theater | viewers | visitors |

| People | Venues |
|---|---|
| | |

**4** Match the sentences with the correct types of art or entertainment.

**1** It was a spectacular show—the singers and dancers were amazing!   **a** a play

**2** It was made of stone, but it looked like a real person.   **b** a portrait

**3** The queen looks very young in this picture, but also confident and serious.   **c** a sculpture

**4** The paintings showed how art changed in Spain from the 1920s to the 1960s.   **d** a mural

**5** This incredible painting covers the whole wall of the building.   **e** an exhibition

**6** I loved the show—the acting was wonderful and I cried at the end.   **f** a musical

**5** Choose the correct options to complete the text.

Last Friday evening, the band Pop Shop did a small
**(1)** _____ at a new music
**(2)** _____ in town. The band's
**(3)** _____ was exciting and full of
energy, and the small **(4)** _____ of about
50 people seemed to love it. My only complaint was that
it was difficult to hear the **(5)** _____ of
some of the songs because the crowd was so loud! But in
any case, it was a great night of **(6)** _____
entertainment.

**1 a** production   **b** concert   **c** musical
**2 a** program   **b** venue   **c** production
**3 a** musical   **b** entertainment   **c** performance
**4 a** concert   **b** listeners   **c** audience
**5 a** lyrics   **b** audience   **c** performance
**6 a** exhibition   **b** live   **c** theater

**6** Choose the correct options to complete the sentences.

**1** The most successful songs always have a catchy *tune* / *lyrics*.

**2** Over 10,000 fans packed into the *exhibition* / *stadium* to watch the concert.

**3** The lead singer sang the first *verse* / *lyrics* and then the others joined in.

**4** This early morning radio show has over 2 million *listeners* / *viewers*.

**5** The president is going to make a live *entertainment* / *broadcast* to the country tonight.

**6** I never liked that series because the *characters* / *audience* seemed really unrealistic.

**7** What's your favorite *broadcast* / *form of entertainment*— music, TV, or theater?

**7** Complete the words in the sentences. The first letter is given for you.

**1** A new g _ _ _ _ _ _ was opened in the city to display the paintings.

**2** The final p _ _ _ _ _ _ _ _ _ _ _ on Broadway was over twenty years ago.

**3** She asked the children to do a d _ _ _ _ _ _ of themselves with a pencil and paper.

**4** I think p _ _ _ _ are often too serious, so I prefer musicals.

**5** My brother's going to paint a p _ _ _ _ _ _ _ _ of my mother for her birthday.

**6** The artist has been working on a large m _ _ _ _ covering the east side of the building.

**7** I love the band's music, but their l _ _ _ _ _ don't make any sense!

**8** **Extension** Complete the chart with these adjectives.

| appealing | awful | boring | creative | imaginative |
|-----------|-------|--------|----------|-------------|
| inspirational | moving | slow | tedious | |

| Positive | Negative |
|----------|----------|
|          |          |

**9** **Extension** Read the text and choose the correct options to complete the sentences.

**1** The Whitney Museum of American Art in New York opened its new building in 2015. This modern, _____ space was designed by the Italian architect Renzo Piano.
   **a** contemporary
   **b** boring
   **c** lifelike
   **d** moving

**2** The museum now has large galleries that are full of light to display the _____.
   **a** designs
   **b** work of art
   **c** works of art
   **d** masterpiece

**3** The galleries are large and bright, making them more _____ to young people.
   **a** controversial
   **b** emotional
   **c** moving
   **d** appealing

**4** Many artists say they find the new museum _____ and enjoy visiting it when they need new ideas.
   **a** emotional
   **b** inspirational
   **c** award-winning
   **d** lifelike

**5** Visitors also have a chance to be _____ when they are at the museum. There are many large outdoor spaces where people can paint, draw, or write.
   **a** creative
   **b** appealing
   **c** boring
   **d** inspirational

**6** The new museum building is so beautifully designed that many people say it is a _____.
   **a** works of art
   **b** design
   **c** fine arts museum
   **d** masterpiece

**10** **Extension** Complete the sentences with these adjectives. There are two adjectives you don't need.

| abstract | award-winning | controversial | emotional |
|----------|---------------|---------------|-----------|
| imaginative | lifelike | modern | moving |

**1** The sculpture is incredibly _____—it looks exactly like him.

**2** The painting doesn't show objects as they really appear; it's a piece of _____ art.

**3** It's a _____ art museum displaying the work of contemporary artists.

**4** The artist has made very _____ use of recycled objects.

**5** The museum has an _____ design which has inspired many other buildings.

**6** These portraits of politicians in comical situations have proved _____.

# LISTENING

**11** Listen to a tour guide in Paris, France, and match the statements with the photos (a, b, or c). 🎧 **91**

1 It's from about the 2nd century. _____
2 The portrait is a masterpiece. _____
3 It's one of the finest examples of French Gothic architecture. _____
4 It was painted between 1503 and 1506. _____
5 It's made of marble. _____
6 It's made of limestone. _____
7 It's on permanent display at the Louvre. _____
8 The sculptor is unknown. _____

a

Mona Lisa

b

Winged Victory

c

Notre-Dame

**12** Listen to the talk. What is the speaker's purpose? 🎧 **92**

a to persuade the listener
b to argue against something
c to give a detailed description
d to compare and contrast

**13** Listen again. Match the adjectives with the nouns. 🎧 **92**

| | | | |
|---|---|---|---|
| 1 | chilly | a | door |
| 2 | ghoulish-looking | b | patterns |
| 3 | creepy | c | welcome |
| 4 | infamous | d | tunnels |
| 5 | famous | e | buildings |
| 6 | artistic | f | gallery |
| 7 | threatening | g | air |
| 8 | spiral | h | staircase |
| 9 | frightening | i | skull |
| 10 | spooky | j | guillotine |

**14** Listen again and choose the correct answers to the questions. 🎧 **92**

1 What place is being described?
   a the subway      c the catacombs
   b an art museum

2 How does it feel down there?
   a cool      c hot
   b warm

3 Where did all the bones come from?
   a the tunnels      c the churches
   b the cemeteries

4 In what year were the bones moved to the tunnels?
   a 1786      c 1876
   b 1678

5 Who ordered the bones to be arranged into artistic patterns?
   a Napoleon I      c Napoleon III
   b Napoleon II

6 What language is the sign in?
   a French and English      c French
   b English

7 What kinds of bones are described as smiling?
   a arms      c faces
   b skulls

8 What do people sometimes try to steal?
   a bags      c bones
   b signs

# GRAMMAR Defining relative clauses

**15** Choose the correct relative pronouns to complete the sentences. Choose (-) where a relative pronoun is not needed.

1 They've just played that song *who / that* you like!
2 It's a special keyboard *that / -* is designed to be more comfortable.
3 When we go to Lima, we're going to visit the gallery *- / who* John told us about.
4 Is that the woman *- / who* discovered those valuable paintings?
5 It was a surprise to see a museum *which / -* featured digital images.
6 The paintings *that / whom* the museum owns are not for sale.
7 My favorite poster is of a painting *who / that* I saw at the Metropolitan Museum in New York.
8 She's the artist *which / who* is going to teach a class here next month.

**16** Read the sentences. Are the relative pronouns necessary (N) or unnecessary (U)?

1 The musicians **that** opened the concert have been playing together for five years. _____
2 The drummer uses a kit **which** her father bought her for her sixteenth birthday. _____
3 The singer **who** writes songs for the band is also a poet. _____
4 Together, they make music **that** speaks to young people around the world. _____
5 The song **that** we just heard is one of their most popular ones. _____
6 When they first started, they played in a small club **which** their friend owned. _____
7 The keyboard player also designs the t-shirts **that** are for sale at each show. _____
8 Anyone **who** didn't get a ticket will have to listen on the radio. _____

**17** Put the words in the correct order to complete the sentences with relative clauses.

1 It's a famous Argentinian art museum   famous / many / paintings / by / Latin American artists / has / which

_____.

2 The Museum of Modern Art in Warsaw is a museum modern artists / on / which / Polish / focuses

_____.

3 The São Paulo Museum of Art has a collection which / European and South American / painters / many different / includes / from / countries

_____.

4 Os Gêmeos are Brazilian street artists   over / murals / who / all / the world / paint / colorful

_____.

5 John Singleton Copley was an artist   paintings / of / known / who / for / was / famous and important people / his

_____.

6 The Whitney Museum of American Art is a place   of / sometimes / exhibitions / artists / hosts / that / up-and-coming

_____.

**18** Read the sentences. Are the relative pronouns the subject (S) or object (O) of the clauses?

1 The bus which stops on the corner goes directly to the art gallery. _____
2 Kids often spend a lot of time watching videos which they find online. _____
3 A guy who I know from school is working at the ticket office. _____
4 I bought a second-hand book that has excellent examples of Impressionist art. _____
5 Some films have characters who you can really relate to. _____
6 She's excited to see a play which is based on one of her favorite books. _____
7 The movie theater which is near my house has luxury seats with tables. _____
8 She saw the documentary that she'd read about online. _____

**19** Combine the two sentences into one with a relative clause.

1 The artist creates masterpieces. The masterpieces are made of different colored lights.
   *The artist creates masterpieces that are made of different colored lights.*
2 The painter bought new paintbrushes. The paintbrushes were made in Italy.

_____

3 The ancient Romans decorated their homes with paintings. The paintings were later discovered by archaeologists.

_____

4 M. C. Escher was a famous graphic artist. He was from the Netherlands.

_____

5 The tango is a well-known dance. The dance is from Argentina and Uruguay.

_____

6 Graphic novels are a new kind of literature. Graphic novels are enjoyed by kids around the world.

_____

# 9B Fast Art, Big Art

## VOCABULARY BUILDING Expressions with *make*

**①** Complete the sentences with these phrases. There are two phrases you don't need.

| | | |
|---|---|---|
| make a decision | make a difference | make a living |
| make a splash | make friends | make sense |
| make the most | make time | make way |

1 Unless you're very famous, it's not very easy to _____ as an actor.

2 Because he's so pleasant and generous, Dev has never found it difficult to _____.

3 The weather was gorgeous, so we decided to _____ of it and have a picnic.

4 I know it's tricky when there are so many choices, but very soon you'll have to _____.

5 Did my explanation of the homework _____ to you?

6 I'm not available today, but I'd be happy to _____ to see you tomorrow.

7 Spending even a little time with an older person can really _____ in their life.

## READING

**②** Choose the best headings for the paragraphs (1–6) in the text.

1 **a** The Importance of the Arts
  **b** Rapid Changes in Cuba Today
2 **a** The Changing Face of Cuban Music
  **b** The Music of Geovani del Pino
3 **a** The Importance of Live Percussion
  **b** Manana, a Place Where Musicians Meet
4 **a** A Mixture of Rhythms
  **b** A Family of Cuban Performers
5 **a** Fashion in Popular Magazines
  **b** The Growth of Fashion in Cuba
6 **a** Young Designers in Cuba
  **b** What's next for Cuba?

**③** Choose the correct options to complete the sentences.

1 Geovani del Pino is a Cuban musician who's always preferred to *experiment / play* traditional music.

2 At Manana, Mililian Galis took part in a *performance / gallery* of Cuban, American, and Iranian music.

3 A typical *concert / venue* at Manana might include musicians playing a mix of rumba, electronic music, and hip hop.

4 Now that travelers from all over the world are able to visit, Cuban artists are starting to reach wider *broadcasts / audiences* than ever before.

5 Young fashion designers in Cuba dream of taking part in *studios / exhibitions* with designers from all over the world.

**④** Read the text and choose the correct answers to the questions.

1 Why is Cuba today visited by travelers from all over the world?
  **a** Cubans are embracing visitors and the ideas they bring.
  **b** Cuba is no longer cut off from the rest of the world.
  **c** Cuba attracts a lot of artists.
  **d** New styles are emerging in the arts in Cuba.

2 According to paragraph 2, why is music an important art form for Cuba?
  **a** Many Cuban musicians prefer to play traditional music.
  **b** Young Cuban musicians are mixing modern and traditional music.
  **c** Music is an expression of Cuban style.
  **d** Rumba is famous all over the world.

3 According to paragraph 3, what is one result of Cuba being more open to the world?
  **a** Young Cuban musicians are performing with musicians from around the world.
  **b** Mixing rumba and electronic music produces interesting results.
  **c** DJs are no longer playing European or American music.
  **d** Traditional artists such as Mililian Galis are able to perform at music festivals.

4 What does Yissy Garcia mean when she says, "All the rhythms that we make aren't pure"?
  **a** Yissy thinks Cuban music is undeveloped.
  **b** Yissy and her band use a lot of percussion instruments in their music.
  **c** Yissy and her band mix Cuban music with other types of music.
  **d** Yissy & Bandacha play mostly funk and jazz.

5 According to Miguel Leyva, how are young Cuban designers breaking the stereotype of Cuban fashion?
  **a** More young Cuban designers are now paying attention to popular magazines.
  **b** Young Cubans who work at government jobs now buy more fashionable clothes.
  **c** More young Cubans would like to be able to buy the things they see in magazines.
  **d** Young Cuban designers are being influenced by new ideas and creating their own fashion.

# The Changing State of the Arts in Cuba

1 🎧 93 Cuba is a country that's experiencing rapid and significant changes. Not surprisingly, the arts are playing an important role in moving those changes forward. Cut off from daily contact with much of the world for many years, Cuba is today flooded with travelers. Cubans are embracing these visitors and the ideas they bring. As a result, new styles are emerging in almost every aspect of the arts.

2 Music is one art form that's always been enormously important in Cuba. "It's an expression of Cuban style," says Geovani del Pino, the director of a fifteen-piece band known internationally for playing traditional Cuban rumba*. While musicians like Geovani prefer to stick to historic and traditional styles, many young Cuban artists are today feeling free to experiment with the rhythms they learned as children. These young musicians are taking traditional Cuban musical styles and mixing them with funk*, electronic music, and reggaeton*, with interesting results.

3 "Cuba is changing now. It is opening to the world," says Alain Garcia Artola, a member of a rap group and an organizer of Manana, a music festival that aims to combine traditional Cuban sounds with international electronic music. At Manana, a respected traditional artist such as Mililian Galis, known as one of the greatest Afro-Cuban drummers, performs new music with American and Iranian musicians, mixing Iranian tunes with elements of rumba and electronic music. Another artist, DJ Jigüe, combines hip hop, classic Caribbean music, and electronica, accompanied by live percussion*. "We're trying to find new sounds based on what belongs to us," Jigüe explains. "Doing the same music as a European DJ or an American DJ wouldn't sound like us and would be a failure."

4 Yissy Garcia agrees. Yissy is a young drummer who was brought up in a family of musicians. She recently released her first album which mixes jazz, funk, electronica, and Afro-Cuban rhythms. Yissy says, "All the rhythms that we make aren't pure. They're more like developed rhythms, more fusion*. For example, we love to use a street conga* and mix it with a little drum and bass, funk; mix it up with the rumba." Yissy and her band are called Yissy

& Bandacha, and they describe their music as "high-speed Cuban jazz."

5 Fashion is another area that's developing in Cuba. Not long ago, the only option for most young people was working in a government job and making very little money—usually less than $100 a month. But that's changing, too. Miguel Leyva is a fashion blogger in Havana. He sees new opportunities in fashion as an example of how things in Cuba are developing. He writes about young people who are making a difference, adapting to new influences and using them to create their own fashion. He looks forward to a day when Cubans will be able to look at popular magazines without feeling that they'll never have the things in them. "This generation is doing something new," Leyva said. "They're breaking the stereotype* of Cuban fashion. It's an important first step."

6 What comes next for Cuba? If the youth of Cuba has anything to say about it, the future will be full of exciting performances, eye-catching exhibitions, and satisfied audiences. Fans will be able to attend concerts in which they'll hear traditional artists and new musicians working side by side, taking steps towards a more open, inclusive* future.

**rumba** *a type of dance and music originally from Cuba*
**funk** *a type of popular music with a strong beat*
**reggaeton** *a type of Latin American music influenced by hip hop and Caribbean music*
**percussion** *musical instruments that you play by hitting or shaking*

**fusion** *a combination of things*
**conga** *a tall drum shaped like a barrel*
**stereotype** *a fixed and often unfair idea about a group of people*
**inclusive** *includes everyone*

# 9C  A Bit of Culture

## GRAMMAR  Defining and non-defining relative clauses

**1** Read the sentences and complete the chart.

1  I got my driver's license two years ago and it expires when I'm 21.
2  Our teacher usually wears a red tie and is always laughing.
3  Our teacher, who usually wears a red tie, is always laughing.
4  The driver's license that I got two years ago expires when I'm 21.
5  The teacher that usually wears a red tie is always laughing.
6  Two years ago, I got my driver's license, which expires when I'm 21.

| defining relative clause | non-defining relative clause | no relative clause |
|---|---|---|
|  |  |  |

**2** Choose what the words in bold refer to in the sentences.

1  The storm **that** knocked down several trees in our garden last year also caused a lot of damage in our town.
   a  several trees
   b  the storm
   c  our town
2  My friends thought the cake, **which** I made last night, was delicious.
   a  last night
   b  my friends
   c  the cake
3  The guide, **who** had already been to the White Mountains, was talking to the boys about their next trip.
   a  the guide
   b  the White Mountains
   c  the boys
4  My friend **who** studied anthropology got a job in Belize.
   a  my friend
   b  Belize
   c  anthropology
5  You should talk to your teacher, **who** can always give you ideas to help you study better.
   a  you
   b  ideas
   c  your teacher
6  There's always a lot of traffic on the Severn Bridge, **which** connects England and Wales.
   a  traffic
   b  the Severn Bridge
   c  England and Wales

7  The hotel **that** we stayed at on our trip to Sedona was on a golf course.
   a  the trip
   b  the golf course
   c  the hotel
8  My sister Amal, **who** has just sent me an email, has gone to Spain with her friends.
   a  an email
   b  my sister Amal
   c  my sister's friends

**3** Complete the second sentence so that it means the same as the first. Use one word only.

1  We watch that show every week. I love it!
   I love that show, _____ we watch every week.
2  Whitby is a seaside town in England. It is on the northeast coast.
   Whitby is a seaside town in England _____ is on the northeast coast.
3  A detective solved the crime. She asked me questions.
   The detective _____ solved the crime asked me questions.
4  Death Valley, a park in California and Nevada, is the hottest and driest national park in the US.
   Death Valley, _____ is a park in California and Nevada, is the hottest and driest national park in the US.
5  Varanasi is a beautiful city in India. It is on the Ganges River.
   A beautiful Indian city is Varanasi, _____ is on the Ganges River.
6  The mayor of our town used to be a baseball player. He's very popular.
   The mayor of our town, _____ used to be a baseball player, is very popular.

**4** Underline the relative pronouns that can be replaced by *that*.

1  My friend who lives in Oregon invited us to go walking along the Pacific Trail.
2  Yesterday's concert, which was the last one this year, had the biggest audience ever.
3  The man who was sitting across from me was very quiet.
4  The seafood which we had at that restaurant near the beach was delicious.
5  My mom, who has always been interested in art, went to Florence, Italy last month.
6  Our friends who moved to Singapore email us every week.
7  He gave all the money to Angela, who decided to spend it on a car.

**5** Choose the correct options to complete the sentences.

**1** The car *that / who* I want costs $40,000.

**2** The *article, which / article which* I read in my English class, was about early Chinese history.

**3** Our teacher said there will be a quiz on the *article, that / article that* we read in our English class today.

**4** The man, *who / which* was reading a book while he waited, looked just like my brother.

**5** The photo *who's / that's* on my bedroom wall was taken by my grandma.

**6** I bought the *dictionary, that / dictionary that* we need online.

**7** Jamal, *who / which* is one of my best friends from college, is starting a teaching job.

**8** My red and gold shirt is the one *who / that* I wore to my audition.

**6** Choose the option which is closest in meaning to the first sentence.

**1** My brother who plays the clarinet had a concert last night.
 **a** I have more than one brother. One of them plays the clarinet and he had a concert last night.
 **b** I have one brother. He plays the clarinet and he had a concert last night.

**2** My roommate who has a history degree helped me study for my African history exam.
 **a** Several of my roommates have history degrees. One of them helped me study for my African history exam.
 **b** I have more than one roommate. The one who has a history degree helped me study for my African history exam.

**3** Some of the first superheroes that Stan Lee wrote about were the Fantastic Four.
 **a** Stan Lee was the first person to write about superheroes, the Fantastic Four.
 **b** When Stan Lee began writing about superheroes, the Fantastic Four were some of the first he wrote about.

**4** The man that was wearing the green tie asked me where the elevator was.
 **a** There were several men wearing green ties. One of them asked about the elevator.
 **b** There were several men around. The one with the green tie asked about the elevator.

**5** The letter, which I received on Thursday, said I had won the scholarship.
 **a** On Thursday, I received a letter saying I had won the scholarship.
 **b** I received a scholarship on Thursday. I also received a letter.

**6** My dog that always barks at the mail carrier is very loud.
 **a** I have one dog. It's very loud when it barks at the mail carrier.
 **b** I have more than one dog. One of them barks at the mail carrier and is very loud.

**7** Put the words in the correct order to make sentences.

**1** won / she's / the / who / the / big award / teacher / .
_____

**2** which / is / her / , / , / hair / short / is / dark brown / very / .
_____

**3** moved / my friend / who / to / texts / every now and then / me / La Paz / .
_____

**4** which / wrote / people / loved / his / many / third / album, / he / in  2015 / .
_____

**5** Toshi is / play / my friend / who / in / school / starred / the / .
_____

**6** the song / that / was / the album / not / she / good enough / to / wrote / put / on / .
_____

**7** a story / told / about / her time / us / which / wasn't / true / Padma / in Helsinki / .
_____

**8** Are the words in bold correct or incorrect? Correct those that are incorrect.

**1** The piano is the **instrument who** he plays in the band.

**2** The **postcard who** she sent from Sicily, shows a beautiful picture of the Mediterranean Sea.

**3** I hung the **diploma I** received at graduation on my bedroom wall.

**4** The **menu who** the waiter gave me was sticky and dirty.

**5** The **photographer took** pictures at our graduation will post the photos online.

**6** Karen's **neighbor, loves** to bake, often gives us homemade cakes.

**7** The **man which** Joy talked to yesterday said he was a professional soccer player.

**8** The **ruler who** I use in math class has both centimeters and inches.

## PRONUNCIATION  Relative clauses

Remember that defining relative clauses give information which is necessary for understanding exactly who or what is being talked about. Non-defining relative clauses give extra information about someone or something.

**9** Listen to the sentences. Do you hear a defining relative clause (D) or a non-defining relative clause (N)? Choose the correct options. 🎧 **94**

**1** *D / N*      **4** *D / N*
**2** *D / N*      **5** *D / N*
**3** *D / N*      **6** *D / N*

# 9D  The World's Most Boring Television… and Why It's Hilariously Addictive

## TEDTALKS

## AUTHENTIC LISTENING SKILLS

**1** Listen to the TED Talk excerpts. Complete the summary with sentences a–d.  🎧 **95**

**(1)** _____ 1.2 million Norwegians watched the program and Slow TV became a big success. One week later, the producers began planning their next show.

**(2)** _____ They broadcast the journey live in June 2011.

**(3)** _____ After that, Slow TV became a buzzword and they started to look for other ideas, such as birdwatching or knitting. The producers now think that Slow TV is a nice way to tell a story.

**(4)** _____

**a** It became the longest documentary ever made.

**b** Slow TV first began in November 2009 with the broadcast of a seven-hour train journey across Norway.

**c** They decided to film a five-and-a-half-day voyage by ship around the coast of Norway.

**d** They like to organize a Slow TV event once or twice a year.

## WATCH ▶

**2** Watch Part 1 of the TED Talk. Then read the quotes and choose the best explanations of what they mean.

**1** "Even the elections this past week passed without much drama. And that's the Norwegian media in a nutshell: not much drama."
*Norway's media was exciting during the elections. / is never very exciting.*

**2** "A few years back, Norway's public TV channel NRK decided to broadcast live coverage of a seven-hour train ride—seven hours of simple footage, a train rolling down the tracks. Norwegians, more than a million of them according to the ratings, loved it. A new kind of reality TV show was born, and it goes against all the rules of TV engagement."
*NRK came up with a new kind of TV program that, surprisingly, people liked. / NRK broadcast a seven-hour train ride that a few Norwegians liked.*

**3** "For the past two months, Norwegians have been watching a cruise ship's journey up the coast and there's a lot of fog on that coast."
*Norwegians are watching the cruise ship journey on TV even though the fog means it's hard to see the coastline. / no longer watching the cruise ship journey on TV due to the fog.*

**4** "Executives at Norway's National Broadcasting Service are now considering broadcasting a night of knitting nationwide. On the surface, it sounds boring, because it is, but something about this TV experiment has gripped Norwegians."
*Even though knitting is boring, Norwegians find this form of TV fascinating. / Knitting is boring to watch on TV, even for Norwegians.*

**3** Watch Parts 2 and 3 of the TED Talk. Match the descriptions with these numbers.

| 1.2 million | 100 years | 14 hours |
|---|---|---|
| 148 | 23 | 3,000 |
| 7 hours and 4 minutes | 8,040 | 87 days |

**1** kilometers of the Norwegian coastline journey

**2** the anniversary of the Bergen Railway in 2009

**3** the length of the birdwatching project called "Peep Show" on the web

**4** the length of the birdwatching project called "Peep Show" on TV

**5** the length of the train journey across Norway from east to west

**6** the number of minutes of the Norwegian coastline journey show

**7** the number of nations able to view the video of the Norwegian coastline journey

**8** the number of Norwegians who watched the Bergen Railway show on TV

**9** the number of people who went on the coastal ship to film the show

## VOCABULARY IN CONTEXT

**4** Choose the correct words or phrases to complete the sentences.

**1** It's hard to believe that a TV show where nothing really happens has _____ an entire nation.
**a** pulled    **b** gripped    **c** pushed

**2** A lot of people _____ for the free concert.
**a** got up    **b** warmed up    **c** showed up

**3** The government has been criticized for the way it _____ the problem.
**a** handled    **b** gripped    **c** argued

**4** He's been voted best actor for four years _____.
**a** in a line    **b** in a row    **c** in a series

**5** The TV producer _____ a great idea by creating "slow TV." It's fascinating to watch!
**a** teamed up with    **b** came up with    **c** put up with

# 9E Well Worth Seeing

## SPEAKING

**1** Look at the words in bold in the sentences and correct the mistakes. Listen and check your answers. 🎧 **96**

**1** The museum is a **could-see**. _____
**2** It was alright, I **propose**. _____
**3** The new Bond movie is **worth well seeing**.

_____
**4** What **have** you think about it? _____
**5** I highly **recognize** it. _____
**6** You might like it if you don't have **nothing** else to do.

_____
**7** Is it worth **to visiting**? _____
**8** I didn't **consider** it was great. _____
**9** I don't **practically** like musicals, but this one has a good story. _____
**10** You won't want to **lose** this. _____
**11** Is **thing** any good? _____
**12** You must **to go**! _____
**13** It'll **like** to anyone who enjoys thrillers.

_____
**14** It's worth **watch**. _____

**2** Listen again. Are the sentences asking for a recommendation (A), giving a recommendation (G), or showing reservation (S)? 🎧 **96**

| | | |
|---|---|---|
| **1** _____ | **6** _____ | **11** _____ |
| **2** _____ | **7** _____ | **12** _____ |
| **3** _____ | **8** _____ | **13** _____ |
| **4** _____ | **9** _____ | **14** _____ |
| **5** _____ | **10** _____ | |

**3** Complete the conversation with the missing words or phrases. Then listen and check your answers. 🎧 **97**

**A** What are we going to do this weekend?
**B** Well, **(1)** _____ doing something outdoors? My cousin sometimes goes camping in the forest north of here. He says it's a **(2)** _____. There are small lakes and waterfalls, and places to fish.
**C** **(3)** _____ like camping, but that sounds alright. [checking phone] But oh, the weather forecast is for rain.
**A** Really? Is **(4)** _____ going? I don't want to camp in that.
**B** No, well, maybe another time. He **(5)** _____, though. If you like the idea, I'll **(6)** _____ the link.
**A** Great! Thanks! But what about this weekend, then? A movie?

**C** Well, there's that new comedy they've been talking about.
**B** I saw it, actually. I would **(7)** _____ to people who enjoy that kind of thing, but it's not for everyone.
**C** [checking phone] Oh, hang on, you won't **(8)** _____.
**A** What?
**C** The new Bond movie comes out this weekend. We could go and see that.
**A** Is **(9)** _____? I saw the last one and I didn't **(10)** _____.
**B** Well, it was **(11)** _____.
**C** Well, this review says "It's **(12)** _____ watching." Five stars.
**A** I don't know.
**C** Come on! You **(13)** _____ if you don't have anything else to do.
**B** And then we can go to that new Brazilian restaurant on Queens Street. I went last week and it's so good. **(14)** _____!
**A** Well, OK. That's Saturday figured out. What about the rest of the weekend?
**B** Why don't we play that new video game? I've played it and it's awesome.
**A** Well, I **(15)** _____ video games, but if you say it's that good, I'll try it.

**4** Make notes for short conversations with friends recommending different things to do. Then listen to some sample answers and compare your ideas. 🎧 **98**

**a** movies to watch
**b** music for a party
**c** things to do on the weekend

**5** Read the speaking test task below and make notes about how you would speak alone about the topic. Then listen to the sample answer and compare your ideas. 🎧 **99**

Describe a place that you like to go to relax.
You should:
say what it is
say why you like going there
say what you do there
and explain who else would enjoy this place.

# WRITING An email describing a place and its culture

**6** Choose the correct options to complete the sentences.

1 It's an area of Colombia *where / that* has rainforests and a very wet climate.
2 I live in a town *which / who* has a lot of ancient history.
3 There's a sense of culture *what / that* you feel as soon as you arrive at the airport.
4 Florence is well known as the city *where / who* Michelangelo is buried.
5 Ha-yun is the friend *who / which* I told you about—he can show you around when you arrive.
6 In San Francisco, there's an area called Chinatown *that / where* you can eat delicious noodles.

**7** Put the paragraphs in the correct order (1–6) to complete the email.

FROM: Hiroto_K@sendmail.net.jp

TO: jorge.91@telcoms.com.mx

SUBJECT: Japan to Mexico!

Hi Jorge,

**a** Finally, I know you love art, so you'll have to come and see the Yonago Museum of Art. Some of the paintings are amazing, but it also has an incredible collection of photographs, which I think you'll enjoy. _____

**b** First of all, Yonago is a city on the west coast of Japan. It's not a very big city—about 150,000 people live here—although my cousin, who lives in the countryside, thinks it's huge! The first thing you have to do when you come here is relax on the beach. There are some gorgeous beaches and the best thing is that we have natural hot springs. Very good for your health! _____

**c** How are things? Thanks so much for your last email. I really enjoyed reading all about your life in Mexico City. It sounds so exciting! _____

**d** Next, Yonago has a pretty famous castle. It's almost 600 years old. It's on a mountain over the river and it looks pretty cool. It's not in good condition any more, but you can still walk around it and imagine what life was like there. _____

**e** So, you asked me to tell you about Yonago, where I've lived all my life. I'm afraid it might sound boring compared to Mexico City, where there's so much to do. Luckily, I like living here, though. _____

**f** Well, I have to go now, Jorge, it's almost midnight. I'll probably dream about Mexico City! Hey, maybe you could come to Japan during the holidays next year? Let's make a plan! _____

All the best,

Hiroto

**8** Read Hiroto's email again and match the two parts of the sentences. Two sentence endings are not needed.

1 We can assume that Hiroto _____
2 The first thing Hiroto recommends in Yonago _____
3 The second thing he recommends _____
4 The last thing he recommends to Jorge _____
5 Hiroto is writing his email _____
6 We can infer that Jorge _____
a is the museum.
b is the countryside.
c is the beach.
d is sleeping.
e has never been to Mexico City.
f is the castle.
g has never been to Yonago.
h late at night.

**9** Read the passage and then listen to the lecture. Summarize the points made in the lecture, making sure to explain how they oppose specific points made in the reading passage. 🎧 **100**

The radio, once an important invention which, at one time, had a central place in most homes, is almost forgotten today.

First of all, times have changed. In the past, when everybody listened to the radio, many presenters and disc jockeys (DJs) became household names. Some DJs had an extremely important influence on the popularity of new bands. That doesn't happen so much today because the radio is an old-fashioned form of broadcasting whose significance is disappearing.

Everything began to change in the 1990s, largely due to developments in technology. New portable devices reduced the popularity of the radio and the DJ was no longer king. People had "personal stereos," which they could take anywhere. They could choose to play the albums they liked best, first on cassette, and later on CD. Then, of course, we had the rise of the internet. With the ability to stream and download music, the radio is not as relevant anymore.

Finally, if we look beyond music to the other reasons for listening to traditional radio, we can see that they have all been replaced by more modern options. For example, people today do not need the radio in order to listen to the news or to sports coverage, like football games. They can get all of this information online.

So, the radio is a pleasant reminder of a different time in our history, but it no longer has a real place in our lives.

# Review

**1** Complete the sentences with the correct pairs of words.

| | |
|---|---|
| concert + lyrics | gallery + drawings |
| listeners + show | live + form |
| musical + theater | play + characters |

**1** The _____ was performed at an old _____ in the city center.

**2** I wanted to like the _____, but the _____ weren't remotely interesting.

**3** This _____ only sells _____ by local artists.

**4** Broadcast data shows that most _____ turned the _____ off halfway through.

**5** _____ music is the most exciting _____ of entertainment, in my opinion.

**6** The _____ was great, but I couldn't hear the _____ very well.

**2** Correct the mistakes in the sentences with relative clauses. Each sentence contains one mistake.

**1** She's taking an art class which it meets on Saturdays at the college.
_____

**2** The gallery who is owned by my artist friend is open on the weekend.
_____

**3** Our teacher showed us photos of objects which she had seen them in the museum.
_____

**4** Performance art is not something who I usually understand.
_____

**5** The paintings are most valuable are in the gallery downstairs.
_____

**6** Not all the countries that competes in the Eurovision Song Contest are European.
_____

**7** Jazz is a kind of music which not everyone can appreciate that.
_____

**3** Make sentences using defining relative clauses.

**1** The novelist / she wrote the award-winning book / she often writes about her childhood.
*The novelist who wrote the award-winning book*
*often writes about her childhood.*

**2** I met a director / she has won many awards for her documentaries about nature.

**3** The actors / they were chosen for the movie / they are traveling to the set by helicopter.
_____

**4** The artist's inspiration for the drawing was a windmill / he had seen the windmill in the Netherlands.
_____

**5** The poet writes about subjects / the subjects come from his personal life.
_____

**6** The painter started with a red square / the red square represented loneliness for her.
_____

**4** Underline the relative pronouns that can be omitted.

**1** This is the picture that my cousin Lydia painted.

**2** Every few hours he checks Facebook, which he thinks is a great way to keep up with friends.

**3** The presenters of the show, who are usually pretty funny, were very serious this evening.

**4** Charles is the friend who I was telling you about.

**5** The artist that gave a lecture at our school was very inspiring.

**6** The birthday card that I sent my brother was hilarious.

**7** *Star Wars* was the movie that made him very famous.

**8** The flight that I took to Kuala Lumpur was late.

**5** Choose the correct words or phrases to complete the sentences.

**1** A hurricane, _____ a type of storm called a tropical cyclone, forms over tropical or subtropical waters.
**a** whom      **c** which is
**b** who is      **d** what's

**2** A hurricane is a storm _____ winds of over 70 miles per hour.
**a** that has      **c** who's
**b** who has      **d** has

**3** Each hurricane's name, _____ chosen from an alphabetical list of names, is unique.
**a** who's      **c** that had
**b** who is      **d** which is

**4** The National Ocean Service in the United States says every year there's a "Hurricane Season" _____ starts on June 1st and ends on November 30th.
**a** who      **c** which is
**b** that      **d** whom

**5** The National Oceanic and Atmospheric Administration (NOAA), _____ part of the US government, "strives to understand the mechanics of these complex storms."
**a** whom      **c** who is
**b** who have      **d** which is

**6** The NOAA is an organization _____ helps towns examine and talk about environmental issues.
**a** who      **c** which is
**b** which      **d** that,

# 10 Time

## 10A  Spend Your Time Wisely

### VOCABULARY  Phrasal verbs about time

**1** **Review**  Choose the correct option to complete the sentences.

1  I told the children to be quiet *during* / *after* the performance.
2  Make sure you put on sunscreen *during* / *before* you go outside.
3  It's important to stretch *before* / *until* you do any sport.
4  You will feel much better *after* / *during* a good night's sleep.
5  We didn't want to *be late* / *wait* long for a table, so we found a restaurant that was less busy.
6  It's always better to be *before* / *early* for an interview rather than late.
7  I saw a celebrity *once* / *during* when I was in New York.

**2** **Review**  Put the words in the correct order to make sentences.

1  late / be / don't / football / game / for / the / .
_____
2  people / during / movie / the / kept / talking / the / .
_____
3  don't / until / your / says / doctor / exercise / OK / it's / .
_____
4  arrive / try / to / early / theater / at / the / .
_____
5  before / their arguments / both teams / should / research / a debate / .
_____
6  I / can't / until / lend / you / money / any / more / next / month / .
_____
7  vegetarian / before / liked / steak / she / became / a / she / .
_____

**3** Match these words to make phrasal verbs about time.

| | | | |
|---|---|---|---|
| 1 | fall | **a** | off |
| 2 | hang | **b** | up |
| 3 | put | **c** | behind |
| 4 | catch | **d** | to |
| 5 | look forward | **e** | for |
| 6 | wait around | **f** | out |

**4** Complete the sentences with the correct forms of the phrasal verbs in Activity 3.

1  Hurry! We need to _____ with the rest of the tour group.
2  We don't have time to _____ you to browse every book in the store.
3  I am really _____ your wedding in Thailand next March.
4  If you miss too many classes, you will _____ at school.
5  I'm _____ with my friends after school this Friday.
6  If you _____ your work all weekend, you'll just have more to do on Sunday night.

**5** Read the statements. Are the sentences true (T) or false (F)? Correct the false sentences.

1  If you never get around to exercising, you exercise a lot. _____
2  Someone who holds on to a job stays at that job for a while. _____
3  Looking forward to something means being excited about something happening in the future. _____
4  If you run out of time, you have a large amount of time left. _____
5  When you move something up, you make it happen earlier. _____
6  If you try to fit something in, you try to find extra time to do it. _____
7  When you hang out, you are usually busy. _____

**6** Listen and complete the phrases.  🎧 101

1  _____ _____
_____ planning
2  _____ _____
_____ patients
3  _____ _____
_____ from my job
4  _____ _____ with my work
5  _____ appointments _____
6  _____ _____ until

**7** Read and complete the text with phrasal verbs about time.

Studies show that students who miss lessons regularly **(1)** _____ _____ with their school work. When this happens, it can be very difficult to **(2)** _____ _____ with the rest of the class. Studies also show that students who are behind are more likely to **(3)** _____ _____ homework and other tasks because they feel they will never have enough time to do it all. If you are behind at school, it's important to make a plan to help you **(4)** _____ everything _____ . Your teacher can help with this. If you work hard, you might even be able to **(5)** _____ some tasks on your plan _____ . Don't be afraid to ask for help from teachers, family, and friends.

**8** **Extension** Unscramble the letters to make phrases about time.

| | |
|---|---|
| **1** in the ___ ___ ___ ___ | s t a p |
| **2** in the ___ ___ ___ ___ ___ ___ | f t e r u u |
| **3** in the first ___ ___ ___ ___ ___ | a p l c e |
| **4** as ___ ___ ___ ___ as | o n o s |
| **5** at ___ ___ ___ ___ | s t l a |
| **6** run ___ ___ ___ ___ | a t l e |
| **7** on ___ ___ ___ ___ | t m e i |

**9** **Extension** Complete the sentences with the phrases in Activity 8.

**1** I'm sorry you don't like this restaurant, but I didn't want to come here _____!

**2** Call me _____ your plane lands in Rio de Janeiro.

**3** We've been waiting forever for my grandparents' flight to arrive, but they're here _____!

**4** People _____ used much less technology than we do today.

**5** I like the trains in Japan because they seem to run _____ most days.

**6** _____, I'd like to focus on my painting.

**7** I don't like it when friends _____ and don't call to let me know.

**10** **Extension** Complete the sentences with *meanwhile, finally,* or *currently*.

**1** I want to travel to Mexico, but I'm _____ in Canada visiting family.

**2** The manager _____ called to offer me the job after three weeks of waiting.

**3** She's _____ performing in a musical on Broadway, but it finishes next month.

**4** My parents boarded the flight to Madrid. _____ I was shopping in the airport!

**5** You can play basketball when your arm is better, but _____, you need to rest.

**6** Have you _____ decided to sell your house? It's been years since you first talked about it.

## LISTENING

**11** Listen to two people talking. What is the main topic of their conversation? 🎧 **102**

**a** how bad the woman is feeling because of jet lag

**b** the effect of time zones on travel

**c** traveling to Shanghai in China

**d** time travel and its effect on aging

**12** Listen to the conversation again and choose the correct options. 🎧 **102**

**1** How is the woman feeling?
  **a** unwell      **c** disoriented
  **b** pretty good      **d** very tired

**2** Where did the woman's flight depart from?
  **a** Singapore      **c** Shanghai
  **b** Los Angeles      **d** Beijing

**3** What time did the flight depart?
  **a** 4 am      **c** 9 am
  **b** 1 pm      **d** 11 pm

**4** What time did the flight arrive?
  **a** 4 am      **c** 9 am
  **b** 1 pm      **d** 11 pm

**5** What did her flight pass through many of?
  **a** time zones          **c** date lines
  **b** oceans              **d** weekdays

**6** In what direction was the woman traveling?
  **a** north               **c** east
  **b** south               **d** west

**⑬** Listen to the talk. What do you think the speaker might be promoting or advertising? 🎧 **103**

  **a** Sven Hagemeir        **c** Honolulu, Hawaii
  **b** *Guinness World Records*  **d** birthdays

**⑭** Listen again and choose the correct options to complete the sentences. 🎧 **103**

  **1** *Guinness World Records* is published
  _____.
    **a** weekly              **c** annually
    **b** every six months

  **2** Sven Hagemeir kept his birthday going for
  _____.
    **a** 46 hours    **b** 24 hours    **c** 35 hours

  **3** Hagemeir's journey began in _____.
    **a** New Zealand   **b** Hawaii    **c** Australia

  **4** The International _____ Line is an imaginary line in the middle of the Pacific Ocean.
    **a** Time        **b** Date        **c** Hour

  **5** Nargis Bhimji of Karachi _____ the record before Hagemeir.
    **a** knew        **b** gave        **c** held

  **6** The time in Brisbane, Australia, is 20 hours _____ Honolulu, Hawaii.
    **a** behind      **b** ahead of    **c** before

  **7** Time _____ differences allow people to celebrate holidays more than once.
    **a** zone        **b** line        **c** date

## GRAMMAR Third conditional

**⑮** Complete the chart with these conditional sentences.

  **1** Carlo would have read more if he hadn't had to work so many hours.
  **2** I read books if I have free time.
  **3** I would go to the movie night if I was invited.
  **4** If he has enough time, he will join a yoga class.
  **5** If she knew how long it was going to take to fix her bike, she would be able to plan her weekend.
  **6** If we don't have any homework on Friday, no one takes their books home for the weekend.
  **7** If we had been there on time, we would have seen the surprised look on his face.
  **8** If we had studied more, the test would have been easier.

**9** She would have invited more people to the party if she had known everyone's email addresses.
**10** The time would pass more quickly if you tried to enjoy the trip.
**11** You'll never get better if you don't practice.

| Zero / first conditional | Second conditional | Third conditional |
|---|---|---|
|  |  |  |

**⑯** Choose the sentence that means the same as the first.

  **1** The football game started early. I was not on time.
    **a** If the football game had started early, I would have been on time.
    **b** If the football game hadn't started early, I would have been on time.
    **c** If the football game hadn't started early, I wouldn't be on time.

  **2** The concert was sold out. We didn't try to get tickets.
    **a** If the concert hadn't been sold out, we would have tried to get tickets.
    **b** If the concert had been sold out, we would have tried to get tickets.
    **c** If the concert hadn't been sold out, we would try to get tickets.

  **3** The amusement park was closed. They didn't ride the rollercoaster.
    **a** If the amusement park will be closed, they would ride the rollercoaster.
    **b** If the amusement park hadn't been closed, they will ride the rollercoaster.
    **c** If the amusement park hadn't been closed, they would have ridden the rollercoaster.

  **4** The hockey equipment was stolen. We didn't play in the finals.
    **a** If the hockey equipment hadn't been stolen, we would have played in the finals.
    **b** If the hockey equipment was stolen, we wouldn't have played in the finals.
    **c** If the hockey equipment hadn't been stolen, we will play in the finals.

  **5** Her car broke down. She didn't give us a ride to the beach.
    **a** If her car wasn't broken down, she will give us a ride to the beach.
    **b** If her car hadn't broken down, she would give us a ride to the beach.
    **c** If her car hadn't broken down, she would have given us a ride to the beach.

**17** Choose the correct options to complete the sentences.

**1** We wouldn't have spent so long looking for the hotel if he *brought / had brought / would bring* a map like I suggested.

**2** If they had looked up how to cook lobster, they *wouldn't have ruined / didn't ruin / ruined* their meal.

**3** I *will be / would have been / was* happy with a lower score if I hadn't had unrealistic expectations.

**4** If she *hadn't been / wasn't / isn't* so busy, she would have realized how tired she actually was.

**5** We would have gone to the museum if it *rained / would rain / had rained*.

**6** If the flight hadn't been canceled, we *will arrive / would have arrived / would arrive* on Tuesday.

**7** We would have played video games all weekend if our game console *isn't broken / will be broken / hadn't been broken*.

**8** If I *hadn't forgotten / forgot / wouldn't forget* my sneakers, we would have gone running before breakfast.

**18** Choose the correct options to complete the sentences.

**1** If they _____ the tent at home, no one _____ in the car.
   **a** hadn't left; will have to sleep
   **b** had had left; would have had to sleep
   **c** hadn't left; would have had to sleep

**2** If Tran _____ to bring food, they _____ anything to eat.
   **a** had forgotten; wouldn't have had
   **b** would forget; wouldn't have
   **c** would forget; wouldn't have had

**3** Akito wished he _____ his camera, so they _____ photos of their camping trip.
   **a** brought; would have had
   **b** had brought; have had
   **c** had brought; would have had

**4** If Mei _____ the campsite, they _____ someone for help.
   **a** hadn't found; had to ask
   **b** haven't found; would have had to ask
   **c** hadn't found; would have had to ask

**5** If Jörg _____ the beehive alone, no one _____ by the bees.
   **a** would leave; had been stung
   **b** had left; would have been stung
   **c** had left; was stung

**6** If Anika _____ the matches, they _____ to make a fire.
   **a** hadn't forgotten; would have been able
   **b** hasn't forgotten; be able
   **c** hasn't forgotten; would be able

**7** If only Jan _____ on the rock.
   **a** hasn't tripped   **b** would trip   **c** hadn't tripped

**19** Complete the sentences with the correct form of the verbs in parentheses.

**1** The police don't know what happened. They can't arrest anyone.
   If the police _____ (know) what happened, they _____ (arrest) someone.

**2** He caused the accident. He wasn't paying attention to the road.
   He _____ (not cause) the accident if he _____ (pay) attention to the road.

**3** He was singing along to the radio. He didn't pay close attention.
   If he _____ (not sing) along to the radio, he _____ (pay) closer attention.

**4** It had rained. The street was wet.
   If it _____ (not rain), the street _____ (not be) wet.

**5** He skidded into the car in front of him. The street was wet.
   He _____ (not skid) into the car in front of him if the street _____ (not be) wet.

**6** The car in front of him didn't use its turn signal. He didn't know that the driver wanted to turn.
   If the car in front of him _____ (use) its turn signal, he _____ (know) that the driver wanted to turn.

**7** The car hit the pedestrian. The pedestrian stepped onto the crosswalk.
   The car _____ (not hit) the pedestrian if she _____ (not step) onto the crosswalk.

**20** Correct the mistake in each sentence.

**1** If you would study harder, you would have received better grades.

**2** If he would have took better notes, he could have studied more easily.

**3** They would have gotten better grades if they would have remembered to hand in their homework.

**4** If we wouldn't skip our classes, the test would have been much easier.

**5** We would have created a study group if we would know each other's phone numbers.

**6** If she would done the assignments on time, she wouldn't have fallen behind.

**7** If only we would have taken better notes when we read the articles.

**8** I wish that we would do some practice tests to help us study. We would have gotten better scores.

# 10B Mastering Time

## VOCABULARY BUILDING Expressions with *time*

**①** Choose the correct options to complete the sentences.

1 _____, I enjoy going downtown to watch a movie with my friends.
   a On time
   b Ahead of time
   c From time to time
   d Early

2 Rafik's three young cousins all wanted to play his guitar _____.
   a pass the time
   b in the past
   c at the same time
   d keep the time

3 Do you _____ right now to help me with something?
   a waste time
   b spend some time
   c find the time
   d have some time

4 I think it was _____ it took us to find this place.
   a find the time
   b worth the time
   c waste some time
   d pass some time

5 It usually _____ and effort to do things correctly.
   a lost time
   b takes time
   c on time
   d it's time

## READING

**②** Read the text and match the paragraphs (1–5) with the main ideas (a–f). You may use a number more than once.

a how biological clocks help our bodies work _____

b a definition of "circadian rhythm" _____

c our "inner alarm clock" _____

d plants and the sun _____

e how internal clocks affect our health _____

f plants and their biological clocks _____

**③** Read the statements. Are the sentences true (T), false (F), or is the information not given (NG)?

1 Our bodies are always exactly sure of the hour of the day. _____

2 Scientists have known for years that plants follow daily routines. _____

3 Most plants flower during the day, but some flower at night. _____

4 The word "circadian" comes from Latin roots. _____

5 The body's "master clock," which sends signals throughout the day, is located in the brain. _____

6 Scientists now know how to control the body's internal clock. _____

**④** Match the two parts of the sentences.

1 We all have _____
2 Researchers have recently discovered _____
3 A circadian period _____
4 Your "master clock" _____
5 Cycles of sleep and wakefulness _____

a that plant cells contain biological clocks.
b a type of "inner alarm clock."
c works with your body's circadian rhythms.
d affect our health and productivity.
e is approximately 24 hours long.

# Biological Clocks

1 🎧 104 Do you need an alarm clock to wake you up in the morning? Have you ever thought, "Oh, if I'd woken up on time, I wouldn't have missed that bus"? Or do you wake up at just about the same time every morning, with or without a clock?

You may not know it, but we all carry an inner "alarm clock" with us. Our bodies know more or less what time it is, even when we're not exactly sure of the hour of day. And it isn't only people who carry an internal* clock. Animals and plants know what time it is, too.

2 For years, scientists have known that plants, like humans and animals, have daily routines that include "going to sleep" and "waking up" on a regular basis. Recently, researchers have discovered that the cells within plants also contain their own biological clocks. They've learned that these clocks allow each cell, and the whole plant in turn, to make tiny adjustments as daylight changes throughout the day and even to adjust to changing seasons. "Having a biological clock is particularly important for plants to prepare for daylight and at night-time to store energy for growth," says Professor Andrew Millar, of the University of Edinburgh in Scotland.

3 Our internal clocks, like those of plants and animals, follow a pattern or rhythm called a "circadian rhythm." The word "circadian" comes from the Latin for "circa," meaning "about," and "dies," meaning "day." Each rotation* of the Earth, which takes about a 24-hour day to complete, represents a circadian period in the life of an organism. Plants, because they depend on the sun and its light for food, need to know on a daily basis how long or short the day will be, when and where the sun will rise and set, and how much daylight they'll receive. To ensure their long-term* survival, plants must also keep track of when the sun will be hot, strong, and high overhead, and when it will be low on the horizon, and therefore weak, distant, and cold. They can't afford to wait around to see how each day will turn out to be.

4 Similarly, our own biological clocks help manage the complex work our bodies do every day. Our organs, for example, need to know when to get to work and when to take time off. At around noon, your stomach may tell you it's time to eat. About 30 minutes after you've eaten, your liver knows that it's time to start doing its job. Your kidneys, glands*, and even fat cells also get to work, creating and storing energy, and processing what you've eaten. The human body's "master clock," a type of control center located in the brain, coordinates all of this activity and sends signals throughout the day that tell your body what to do. In the morning, for example, it raises your body temperature to make you feel alert and then at night drops it down again when it's time to sleep. This master clock works with your body's circadian rhythms, and, like the biological clocks found in plants, takes its cues from the sun.

5 Researchers look forward to unlocking the mysteries of circadian rhythms, from discovering how to control our internal clocks to knowing exactly where in the brain the clocks are located. Health and productivity* are both linked to cycles of sleep and wakefulness*, and to our internal clocks. "We have found over 35 medical conditions that are affected by the body's internal clock," says Michael Smolensky, professor of environmental physiology at the University of Texas-Houston School of Public Health. "That concept is revolutionary and there's more coming."

**internal** *located on the inside of something*
**rotation** *the process of moving or turning around a central point*
**long-term** *involving a long period of time*
**glands** *organs in the body that makes a substance used by the body*

**productivity** *the rate at which goods are produced or work is completed*
**wakefulness** *the state of not sleeping or not being able to sleep*

# 10C Plenty of Time!

## GRAMMAR Modals: past speculation, deduction, and regret

**1** Underline the modals that express past speculation, deduction, or regret.

In 1526, explorer Hernán Cortés recorded tales of fabulously rich towns hidden in the Honduran interior.

He must have heard similar stories from a variety of people. If early explorers hadn't heard stories of a ruined city rising above the jungle, archaeologist Chris Fisher might not have flown to the mountains of La Mosquitia in early 2015 to look for the ruins of a lost city. Fisher did not believe in the legends of "Ciudad Blanca"—a mythical city built of white stone. He thought it couldn't have existed.

Though the Mosquitia are among the most mysterious of ancient cultures in the Americas, Fisher *did* believe the mountains of La Mosquitia must contain the ruins of a real lost city, which had been abandoned for at least 500 years.

When archaeologists first began to explore Mosquitia in the 1930s, they uncovered some settlements. They thought the area may once have been occupied by a widespread, sophisticated culture. Some archaeologists have proposed that a group of Maya warriors may have taken control of Mosquitia. Others think that the local culture could have simply embraced the characteristics of the Maya.

There is no evidence yet that the Mosquitia built with stone. When their buildings were decorated and painted, they may have been as remarkable as some of the great temples of the Maya. But once abandoned, they dissolved in the rain and rotted away. If the Mosquitia had built their buildings of stone, we might know more about them.

**2** Choose the sentence that means the same as the first.

**1** I didn't hear my alarm and missed my bus.
   **a** If I had heard my alarm, I wouldn't have missed my bus.
   **b** If I had missed my bus, I might have heard my alarm.

**2** I can't make it to practice because I have to stay after school for a meeting.
   **a** I couldn't make it to practice so maybe I have to stay after school.
   **b** If I didn't have a meeting, I could come to practice.

**3** I ate so much at lunch that I don't have room for dessert.
   **a** I might have had room for dessert if I had eaten so much at lunch.
   **b** If I hadn't eaten so much at lunch, I might have had room for dessert.

**4** I was late to school because I had a doctor's appointment this morning.
   **a** Because I had a doctor's appointment this morning, I could have been late for school.
   **b** If I hadn't gone to see the doctor, I wouldn't have been late for school.

**5** You didn't tell me about the concert, so I didn't go with you.
   **a** If you had told me about the concert, I would have gone with you.
   **b** I may have told you about the concert so you could go with me.

**6** I didn't have time to write my paper about the Mosquitia last night.
   **a** I would have written my paper about the Mosquitia if I had had more time last night.
   **b** I could have had more time last night to write my paper about the Mosquitia.

**7** My favorite jeans were on sale. I only bought one pair.
   **a** I should have bought more than one pair of my favorite jeans when they were on sale.
   **b** When my favorite jeans were on sale, I wouldn't have bought one pair.

**8** I rode my bike to school in the rain. Now I'm all wet.
   **a** I shouldn't have ridden my bike in the rain because now I'm all wet.
   **b** If I'm riding my bike to school in the rain, I might be all wet.

**3** Read the statements and choose the correct answers to the questions.

**1** If Alexander Graham Bell hadn't been a curious child, he might not have developed the telephone.
   Was Bell a curious child? *yes / no*

**2** Amelia Earhart wouldn't have been the first female pilot to fly alone across the Atlantic Ocean if she hadn't been adventurous.
   Was Earhart the first female pilot to fly alone across the Atlantic Ocean? *yes / no*

**3** Usain Bolt may not have won so many Olympic medals if he had taken a lot of time off from training.
   Did Bolt take a lot of time off from training? *yes / no*

**4** If Jonas Salk hadn't discovered one of the first polio vaccines, many more people would be affected by the disease today.
   Did Salk discover one of the first polio vaccines? *yes / no*

**5** If Florence Nightingale had been born in the 1400s, she probably wouldn't have started a nursing school.
   Was Nightingale born in the 1400s? *yes / no*

**6** Georgia O'Keeffe may have painted scenes of the Gobi Desert if she had lived in China.
   Did O'Keeffe live in China? *yes / no*

**4** Are the words in bold correct or incorrect? Correct those that are incorrect.

**1** If he **hadn't moving** to California, we might still be best friends.
**2** I **would has gone** backpacking with you if my parents had let me.
**3** He knew all of the answers in class—he **must have read** ahead in his math book.
**4** If Kyle had been at the game, we **might have winned**.
**5** Why didn't you take your phone with you? Rick **could have called** while you were out.
**6** I **would have went** to the party if he had invited me.
**7** That building **must have been built** in the 1700s—it looks really old.

**5** Read the sentences and questions. Choose the sentences that you think follow them.

**1** Have you heard about the annual camel beauty pageant in Abu Dhabi?
  **a** Yes, if I hadn't read about it, I wouldn't have believed the pageant was real.
  **b** Yes, if I had read about it, I can't have believed the pageant was real.
**2** A winning camel should have a big head.
  **a** I know. That camel over there shouldn't have won because it has such a small head.
  **b** Sure. That camel over there should have won because its head is so small.
**3** I can't believe my camel didn't win!
  **a** If your camel's hump were bigger, you shouldn't have won.
  **b** Your camel might have won if its hump were bigger.
**4** We can look at history to understand the importance of camels.
  **a** If Bedouin life hadn't centered on movement, they might not have come to depend on camels.
  **b** If Bedouin life hadn't depended on camels, their history would have centered on movement.
**5** Sorry I'm late!
  **a** You should have arrived earlier to get a good seat. Now you might not have a good view.
  **b** You shouldn't have arrived earlier to get a good seat. Now you would not have a good view.

**6** Choose the correct options to complete the sentences.

**1** I *shouldn't* / *should* have spoken to my friend during the exam.
**2** Bill Gates *might not* / *can't* have started Microsoft if he and Paul Allen hadn't been friends.
**3** He *couldn't* / *may* have studied in Berlin. He doesn't speak any German.
**4** I *must* / *should* have let my tea cool more before I drank it—it was so hot!
**5** I *might not* / *should* have lost my book if I had kept it in my bag.

**7** Listen and choose the correct answers. 🎧 **105**

**1** Was Nero ruling Rome in the year 83?
  **a** Nero may have ruled Rome in the year 83 because he died in 68.
  **b** Nero couldn't have ruled Rome in the year 83 because he died in 68.
**2** I was so worried—where were you?
  **a** Sorry! I should have called to let you know I'd be late.
  **b** My apologies. If I had been late I couldn't have called you.
**3** Did you know Kate Middleton and Prince William went to college together?
  **a** No, Kate shouldn't have met William at St Andrew's if she had studied there.
  **b** Yes! If Kate hadn't studied at St Andrew's, she might not have met William.
**4** Why does he have his glasses with him at dinner?
  **a** If he had his glasses, he may be able to read the menu.
  **b** He wouldn't be able to read the menu if he had forgotten his glasses.
**5** Was she close to winning the election?
  **a** Yes, if she had received just 2,500 more votes, she would have won.
  **b** Yes, she received fewer votes and shouldn't have won.
**6** What do you know about Caroline Herschel?
  **a** She was born in 1750 and made discoveries about space. If she had lived in the 20th century, she might have taught astronomy at a university.
  **b** She was born in 1750 and should have made discoveries about space. If she was living in the twentieth century, she can't have taught astronomy at a university.

## PRONUNCIATION Weak forms: *have*

Remember that sometimes sounds in a word are not pronounced to make the word easier to say.

**8** Listen to the sentences with *have*. Underline *have* in the sentences where the whole word is pronounced. Then practice saying the sentences. 🎧 **106**

**1** He could have done better if he had studied.
**2** Have you had any luck finding a job?
**3** They can't come because they have to study tonight.
**4** I should have started earlier. Now it's too late.
**5** We might have missed the plane if we hadn't taken a taxi.
**6** Would you really have helped me if I'd asked you?
**7** The test must have been very difficult.
**8** Have the exam results been posted yet?

# 10D Inside the Mind of a Master Procrastinator

## TEDTALKS

## AUTHENTIC LISTENING SKILLS

**1** Listen to the TED Talk excerpts. Choose the correct options to replace the words or phrases in bold. 🎧 **107**

**1** And one day I woke up with three days until the **deadline**, still not having written a word, and so I did the only thing I could: I wrote 90 pages over 72 hours, pulling not one but two **all-nighters**…
   **a** end date, all-night study sessions
   **b** race, days of work
   **c** test, evenings

**2** So the Rational Decision-Maker will make the rational decision to do something **productive**, but the Monkey doesn't like that plan, so he actually **takes the wheel**…
   **a** smart, steals        **c** interesting, gives up
   **b** useful, takes control

**3** Now, the Panic Monster is **dormant** most of the time, but he suddenly wakes up any time a deadline gets too close or there's danger of public embarrassment, a career disaster, or some other scary **consequence**.
   **a** home, idea        **c** afraid, series
   **b** asleep, outcome

**4** So, if you wanted to have a career where you're a **self-starter**— something in the arts, something entrepreneurial— there's no deadlines on those things at first, because nothing's happening at first, not until you've gone out and done the hard work to get some **momentum**, to get things going.
   **a** beginner, time        **c** motivated person,
   **b** busy person, ahead        energy

## WATCH ▶

**2** Watch Parts 1 and 2 of the TED Talk. Put the sentences in the correct order.

   **a** He started writing his senior thesis three days before the deadline. _____
   **b** He wrote a blog post about procrastination. _____
   **c** He wrote all his papers the day before the deadlines. _____
   **d** Tim started blogging. _____
   **e** Tim Urban majored in government in college. _____
   **f** Tim was given a year to spend on his senior thesis. _____

**3** Watch Parts 2 and 3 of the TED Talk. Choose the correct options to complete the sentences.

**1** According to Tim Urban, one way the Panic Monster helps the procrastinator is by *saving him or her from a potentially bad outcome / defeating the rational decision maker / embarrassing the Gratification Monkey.*

**2** When Tim Urban was first asked to do the TED Talk, he *started planning it right away / procrastinated for the first five months before planning it / decided to wait two months before he planned it.*

**3** When he wrote about procrastination on his blog, *only a few people saw the article / mostly students emailed him / people from many different backgrounds emailed him.*

**4** Tim Urban decided after studying procrastination that there is *more than one kind / only one kind.*

**5** Tim Urban believes that procrastinators who don't have deadlines *may never achieve their goals / are the lucky ones / should find new jobs.*

## VOCABULARY IN CONTEXT

**4** Choose the correct words or phrases to complete the sentences.

**1** I have a lot _____ at the moment. I'm busy and I don't have time for my family.
   **a** in conflict with        **c** handled
   **b** on my mind

**2** The students were _____ at the clock. They were ready to go home.
   **a** lighting up        **c** staring
   **b** nodding

**3** At my new job, being late for work is not a _____. The boss doesn't mind as long as we work late.
   **a** damage        **c** big deal
   **b** piece of cake

**4** My _____ goal is to learn how to stop procrastinating. I hope to stop doing it by next year.
   **a** tremendous        **c** transparent
   **b** long-term

**5** I use social media so I can stay _____ what's happening in the world.
   **a** damage        **c** spread
   **b** aware of

**6** She was so upset about her missing children she thought she would _____.
   **a** lose her mind        **c** light up
   **b** make a living

# 10E Studying

## SPEAKING

**1** Put the words in the correct order to make sentences. Then listen and check your answers. 🎧 **108**

**1** studying / the / develop / purpose / abilities / of / to / your / is / .

_____

**2** at school / is / studying / that / interest / boredom / caused / things / don't / by / you / .

_____

**3** I / why / that's / practical / learning / subjects / like / .

_____

**4** point / to / the / learning / enjoy / more / is / your / of / something / life / .

_____

**5** like / practical / cooking / I / because / nature / its / of / very / .

_____

**6** to / order / we / eat / to / have / in / live / .

_____

**7** cooking / skill / consequently, / practical / is / most / the / .

_____

**8** and / should / eating / be / therefore, / cooking / enjoyable / .

_____

**9** that / learned / cook / more / food / could / I / so / to / I / enjoy / .

_____

**10** of / I / the / creativity / cooking / reasons / the / like / is / main / one / that / of / .

_____

**11** the / chef / that's / I / to be / want / reason / a / .

_____

**2** Match the facts with the explanations or consequences.

**1** I have a very logical brain. _____
**2** I want to help people. _____
**3** I love having debates in class. _____
**4** I don't get stressed by tests. _____
**5** I really love making music. _____
**6** I have to work a lot after school. _____
**7** I really enjoy being outside. _____
**8** I want to become a doctor. _____
**9** I'm the captain of the football team. _____
**10** I have a bad memory. _____
**11** Exams make me really stressed. _____

**a** **Consequently**, I'm often tired in class.
**b** I have to invent special rhymes **so that** I can remember all my notes.
**c** I need good grades **in order to** get into medical school.
**d** I think it**'s caused by** the fear of failure.
**e** It's a huge commitment **because of** training and planning.
**f** **One of the main reasons is that** it gives me a rush.
**g** **That's the reason** I'm planning to study nursing.
**h** **That's why** I'm good at math.
**i** **The point of** taking tests is to demonstrate your knowledge.
**j** **The purpose of** discussing topics is to develop your opinions.
**k** **Therefore**, I'd like to study environmental science.

**3** Complete the text with the phrases in bold in Activity 2.

**Why review?**

**(1)** _____ reviewing is to prepare yourself for a test. **(2)** _____ we can't remember most things on our first encounter—we need to go back to them. **(3)** _____ some classes spend a lot of time on review sessions after each topic is studied. You have to plan ahead **(4)** _____ review effectively.
**(5)** _____ a lot of people do poorly on tests, **(6)** _____ not planning review time carefully. Often, getting behind with your review **(7)** _____ tiredness and lack of focus.
**(8)** _____, a good study plan is important when you plan your review. It's important that you know where you are in your review, **(9)** _____ you have time for breaks to refresh yourself and don't fall behind. **(10)** _____, reviewing should be a fun and rewarding part of studying. After all, **(11)** _____ learning something is to use it in real life, which means you have to remember it first!

**4** Read the text and answer the question. Make notes on your ideas on a separate sheet of paper. Then listen to the sample conversation and compare your ideas. 🎧 **109**

There are big changes to the exam system this year and the school has reorganized its test schedule as a result. All exams are going to be in the final two years, so students can relax in their first two years, but that means we are going to have much more to do during junior and senior year. This may have an impact on participation in school clubs and sports. Classwork is also being reduced as part of the assessment in all subjects. Classwork will be worth a maximum of 50 percent of final grades, which means we all have more exams to take.

**Question:** What is the writer's opinion? Explain the reasons he gives for having that opinion.

# WRITING A pro and con essay

**5** Read and choose the correct discourse markers to complete the sentences.

1 Texting while driving is dangerous and irresponsible. _____, it is illegal.
   **a** Even so   **b** Furthermore   **c** On the other hand

2 I don't agree that public transportation should be free. _____, I do agree that it should be significantly cheaper.
   **a** However   **b** What's more   **c** Not only that but

3 There are many problems with this approach. _____, it would cost too much. Secondly, it would take too long.
   **a** Thirdly   **b** First of all   **c** In conclusion

4 To conclude, I feel that violent video games should be banned. _____, I believe these games increase aggression and bullying, and I do not accept that they are harmless.
   **a** Even so   **b** However   **c** Overall

**6** Complete the text with these words.

| discourse marker | First of all | in favor of |
|---|---|---|
| linking words | own opinion | reasons |
| relevant | structure | the topic |
| third paragraph | | |

When writing a pro and con essay, there is a
**(1)** _____ to follow.
The first paragraph introduces **(2)** _____.
For example, you can: describe the current situation; say
why it's **(3)** _____ or important now;
explain that it's something people disagree on; compare the past and present situations.
The second paragraph presents arguments
**(4)** _____ the topic. Include two or three
**(5)** _____ to support your arguments.
Use **(6)** _____ , also called discourse markers, to make your essay clearer for the reader. These include expressions such as **(7)** _____ ,
*What's more…* , *Not only that, but…*, etc.
The **(8)** _____ presents arguments against the topic. Again, include two or three reasons or examples. Make sure you start this paragraph with a
**(9)** _____ that introduces arguments against the statement.
Finally, conclude with your **(10)** _____
about the statement. Make sure you clearly state what you believe.

**7** Complete the pro and con essay with the correct sentences (a–f).

"University education has become so expensive that many can no longer afford it. Fees should be completely abolished." Discuss.

**(1)** _____ They spend years working very hard just for the chance to go to college and get a degree in the subject of their choice. But is it fair that, for many, increasingly high fees are now making this dream impossible?

It is clear that expensive fees are a serious problem for several reasons. **(2)** _____ This means that they have to apply for student loans to pay for their tuition and books, and it can take many years to repay these loans. Secondly, most have to leave home and move to the city, or even another country, where their university is.

**(3)** _____ Furthermore, while at college, many need to find part-time jobs to support themselves financially, which takes valuable time away from their studies.

**(4)** _____ Firstly, it costs money to retain excellent academics and other members of staff. Personally, I believe the quality of teaching would suffer if fees were abolished. **(5)** _____ Many young people are supported by their parents or other family members. Lastly, college students have a lot of free time every year, which makes it easier to balance their studies with part-time work.

**(6)** _____ While I accept that fees are too high and should be reduced, I do not believe that they should be completely abolished.

**a** On the other hand, fees are necessary in order to run universities.
**b** This comes with significant additional expense.
**c** Secondly, loans are not the only means of paying for college.
**d** First of all, young people typically do not have much money of their own.
**e** In conclusion, I do not fully agree with the statement.
**f** The ultimate goal for most high school students is to go to college.

**8** Write at least 250 words about why you agree or disagree with this opinion.

> Tests are unfair because they put students under too much pressure to perform well on a single day. All tests should be abolished in favor of continuous assessment.

# Review

**1** Put the words in the correct order to make sentences.

**1** I / wait / for / you / won't / around / longer / much / .

_____

**2** so / busy / I'm / falling / at / work / that / I'm / behind / .

_____

**3** took / so / catch / long / to / up / it / .

_____

**4** can / take / off / this / year / time / you / ?

_____

**5** to / calling / around / get / never / I / her / .

_____

**6** put / studying / failed / and / my / I / test / off / .

_____

**2** Choose the correct options to complete the sentences.

**1** Can you move the appointment with the doctor

_____?

**a** up                          **c** behind
**b** around                      **d** on

**2** We are looking _____ to seeing you all again at the wedding.

**a** around                      **c** on
**b** up                          **d** forward

**3** I tried to read the book before today's class, but I ran

_____ time.

**a** into                        **c** up with
**b** out of                      **d** behind

**4** When do you think you'll get _____ to finishing the painting?

**a** up                          **c** forward
**b** around                      **d** on

**5** I'm afraid I fell _____ and I didn't finish the report you asked for.

**a** out                         **c** behind
**b** off                         **d** around

**6** Could you fit _____ a meeting with the chief executive tomorrow?

**a** in                          **c** up
**b** on                          **d** out

**7** I can't wait for the weekend, when I can hang

_____ with my friends and relax.

**a** in                          **c** up
**b** on                          **d** out

**3** Choose the correct options to complete the sentences.

**1** Emma Thompson _____ have been making movies in 1955 because she wasn't born until 1959.

**a** could                       **c** should
**b** couldn't                    **d** may

**2** I _____ have ordered a steak if the restaurant hadn't just sold the last one.

**a** might                       **c** can't
**b** should                      **d** shouldn't

**3** He _____ have broken his arm if he'd fallen from that tree.

**a** couldn't                    **c** maybe
**b** can't                       **d** could

**4** The trip by sea from New York to Tokyo _____ take a lot longer if the Panama Canal hadn't been built.

**a** would                       **c** may
**b** can                         **d** should

**5** There _____ be less pollution if more people rode their bikes to school and work.

**a** maybe                       **c** would
**b** may be                      **d** can't

**6** If we had checked the weather before we left, we _____ not have become stuck in this blizzard.

**a** should                      **c** can't
**b** may                         **d** could

**7** If workers along the Yangtze River hadn't found a buried wooden timber 36 feet long in 1962, historians _____ not now believe that fifteenth-century Chinese explorer Zheng He had ships many times larger than those of Christopher Columbus.

**a** maybe                       **c** can
**b** should                      **d** might

**8** I _____ not speak Hindi so well if I hadn't studied in India.

**a** maybe                       **c** can
**b** should                      **d** might

**4** Put the words in the correct order to make sentences.

**1** I / not / if / have / met / had / my best friend / we / might / gone / to different schools / .

_____

**2** wouldn't / I / hadn't / been / found / last week / my passport / , / I / have / if / able / to / fly home / .

_____

**3** eaten / must / all the candy / have / Shana / .

_____

**4** you / have / all that music / streamed / shouldn't / .

_____

**5** he / done / have / well / on his test / must / .

_____

**6** have / cut / shouldn't / I / my hair / .

_____

**7** the river / if / it / hadn't / be lower / rained so much / would / last week / .

_____

# UNIT 1

## Review

| | |
|---|---|
| afraid (adj) | /əˈfreɪd/ |
| angry (adj) | /ˈæŋgri/ |
| bored (adj) | /bɔrd/ |
| excited (adj) | /ɪkˈsaɪtɪd/ |
| pleased (adj) | /plizd/ |
| unhappy (adj) | /ʌnˈhæpi/ |
| upset (adj) | /ʌpˈsɛt/ |
| worried (adj) | /ˈwɜrid/ |

## Unit Vocabulary

| | |
|---|---|
| annoyed (adj) | /əˈnɔɪd/ |
| anxious (adj) | /ˈæŋkʃəs/ |
| ashamed (adj) | /əˈʃeɪmd/ |
| confused (adj) | /kənˈfjuzd/ |
| delighted (adj) | /dɪˈlaɪtɪd/ |
| embarrassed (adj) | /ɪmˈbærəst/ |
| lonely (adj) | /ˈloʊnli/ |
| nervous (adj) | /ˈnɜrvəs/ |
| relaxed (adj) | /rɪˈlækst/ |
| scared (adj) | /skeərd/ |
| stressed (adj) | /strɛst/ |

## Extension

| | |
|---|---|
| cheerful (adj) | /ˈtʃɪərfəl/ |
| disappointed (adj) | /ˌdɪsəˈpɔɪntɪd/ |
| grateful (adj) | /ˈgreɪtfəl/ |
| impatient (adj) | /ɪmˈpeɪʃənt/ |
| jealous (adj) | /ˈdʒɛləs/ |
| proud (adj) | /praʊd/ |
| selfish (adj) | /ˈsɛlfɪʃ/ |

## Vocabulary Building

| | |
|---|---|
| confused (adj) | /kənˈfjuzd/ |
| confusion (n) | /kənˈfjuʒən/ |
| depressed (adj) | /dɪˈprɛst/ |
| depression (n) | /dɪˈprɛʃən/ |
| disappointed (adj) | /ˌdɪsəˈpɔɪntɪd/ |
| disappointment (n) | /ˌdɪsəˈpɔɪntmənt/ |
| embarrassed (adj) | /ɪmˈbɛrəst/ |
| embarrassment (n) | /ɪmˈbærəsmənt/ |
| excited (adj) | /ɪkˈsaɪtɪd/ |
| excitement (n) | /ɪkˈsaɪtmənt/ |
| exhausted (adj) | /ɪgˈzɔstɪd/ |
| exhaustion (n) | /ɪgˈzɔstʃən/ |
| friendliness (n) | /ˈfrɛndlinɪs/ |
| friendly (adj) | /ˈfrɛndli/ |
| happiness (n) | /ˈhæpinɪs/ |
| happy (adj) | /ˈhæpi/ |
| loneliness (n) | /ˈloʊnlinɪs/ |
| lonely (adj) | /ˈloʊnli/ |
| nervous (adj) | /ˈnɜrvəs/ |
| nervousness (n) | /ˈnɜrvəsnɪs/ |
| sad (adj) | /sæd/ |
| sadness (n) | /ˈsædnɪs/ |
| selfish (adj) | /ˈsɛlfɪʃ/ |
| selfishness (n) | /ˈsɛlfɪʃnɪs/ |

## Vocabulary in Context

| | |
|---|---|
| characteristic (n) | /ˌkærɪktəˈrɪstɪk/ |
| curiosity (n) | /ˌkjʊəriˈɒsɪti/ |
| gender (n) | /ˈdʒɛndər/ |
| homesick (adj) | /ˈhoʊmˌsɪk/ |
| joy (n) | /dʒɔɪ/ |
| wrinkle (n) | /ˈrɪŋkəl/ |

# UNIT 2

## Review

| | |
|---|---|
| airport (n) | /ˈɛərˌpɔrt/ |
| bus (n) | /bʌs/ |
| drive (v) | /draɪv/ |
| fly (v) | /flaɪ/ |
| holiday (n) | /ˈhɒlɪˌdeɪ/ |
| hotel (n) | /hoʊˈtɛl/ |
| plane (n) | /pleɪn/ |
| station (n) | /ˈsteɪʃən/ |
| tourist (n) | /ˈtʊərɪst/ |
| train (n) | /treɪn/ |
| travel (v) | /ˈtrævəl/ |
| traveler (n) | /ˈtrævələr/ |
| visit (v) | /ˈvɪzɪt/ |
| visitor (n) | /ˈvɪzɪtər/ |

## Unit Vocabulary

| | |
|---|---|
| car (n) | /kɑr/ |
| catch (v) | /kætʃ/ |
| commute (v) | /kəˈmjut/ |
| cruise (n) | /kruz/ |
| destination (n) | /ˌdɛstɪˈneɪʃən/ |
| excursion (n) | /ɪkˈskɜrʒən/ |
| expedition (n) | /ˌɛkspəˈdɪʃən/ |
| flight (n) | /flaɪt/ |
| get (v) | /gɛt/ |
| get off (phr v) | /ˌgɛt ˈɔf/ |
| get on (phr v) | /ˌgɛt ˈɒn/ |
| get to (phr v) | /ˈgɛt ˌtu/ |
| get to know (phr) | /ˈgɛt tə ˈnoʊ/ |
| go for (a bike ride) (phr) | /ˈgoʊ fər (ə ˈbaɪk ˌraɪd)/ |
| go on (a flight) (phr) | /ˈgoʊ ɒn (ə ˈflaɪt)/ |
| lift (n) | /lɪft/ |
| ride (n) | /raɪd/ |
| route (n) | /rut/ |
| ship (n) | /ʃɪp/ |
| take (v) | /teɪk/ |
| voyage (n) | /ˈvɔɪɪdʒ/ |

## Extension

| | |
|---|---|
| board (v) | /bɔrd/ |
| depart (v) | /dɪˈpɑrt/ |
| journey (n) | /ˈdʒɜrni/ |
| know (v) | /noʊ/ |
| land (v) | /lænd/ |
| leave (v) | /liv/ |

| | |
|---|---|
| outing (n) | /ˈaʊtɪŋ/ |
| sight (n) | /saɪt/ |
| sightseeing (n) | /ˈsaɪtˌsiɪŋ/ |
| stay (v) | /steɪ/ |
| way (n) | /weɪ/ |

## Vocabulary Building

| | |
|---|---|
| backpacking (n) | /ˈbækˌpækɪŋ/ |
| horseback riding (n) | /ˈhɔrsˌbæk ˈraɪdɪŋ/ |
| public transportation (n) | /ˈpʌblɪk ˌtrænspɔrˈteɪʃən/ |
| sightseeing (n) | /ˈsaɪtˌsiɪŋ/ |
| skyscraper (n) | /ˈskaɪˌskreɪpər/ |
| viewpoint (n) | /ˈvjuˌpɔɪnt/ |
| walking tour (n) | /ˈwɔkɪŋ ˌtʊər/ |
| zip-line (n) | /ˈzɪp ˌlaɪn/ |

## Vocabulary in Context

| | |
|---|---|
| a handful of (phr) | /ə ˈhændfʊl əv/ |
| don't get me wrong (phr) | /ˈdoʊnt ˌgɛt mi ˈrɒŋ/ |
| shame (n) | /ʃeɪm/ |
| shy (adj) | /ʃaɪ/ |
| surrounded by (trees) (phr) | /səˈraʊndɪd baɪ (ˈtriz)/ |
| team up with (phr v) | /ˈtim ˈʌp ˌwɪθ/ |

# UNIT 3

## Review

| | |
|---|---|
| baseball (n) | /ˈbeɪsˌbɔl/ |
| basketball (n) | /ˈbæskɪtˌbɔl/ |
| boxing (n) | /ˈbɒksɪŋ/ |
| football (n) | /ˈfʊtˌbɔl/ |
| ice hockey (n) | /ˈaɪs ˌhɒki/ |
| ice skating (n) | /ˈaɪs ˌskeɪtɪŋ/ |
| rugby (n) | /ˈrʌgbi/ |
| running (n) | /ˈrʌnɪŋ/ |
| skiing (n) | /ˈskiɪŋ/ |
| surfing (n) | /ˈsɜrfɪŋ/ |
| swimming (n) | /ˈswɪmɪŋ/ |
| tennis (n) | /ˈtɛnɪs/ |
| volleyball (n) | /ˈvɒliˌbɔl/ |
| yoga (n) | /ˈjoʊgə/ |

## Unit Vocabulary

| | |
|---|---|
| achieve (v) | /əˈtʃiv/ |
| beat (v) | /bit/ |
| board (n) | /bɔrd/ |
| boat (n) | /boʊt/ |
| climbing (n) | /ˈklaɪmɪŋ/ |
| club (n) | /klʌb/ |
| coach (n) | /koʊtʃ/ |
| court (n) | /kɔrt/ |
| diving (n) | /ˈdaɪvɪŋ/ |
| encourage (v) | /ɛnˈkɜrɪdʒ/ |
| equipment (n) | /ɪˈkwɪpmənt/ |

| field (n) | /fild/ |
|---|---|
| gymnastics (n) | /dʒɪmˈnæstɪks/ |
| helmet (n) | /ˈhɛlmɪt/ |
| karate (n) | /kəˈrɑti/ |
| mountain (n) | /ˈmaʊntən/ |
| net (n) | /nɛt/ |
| opponent (n) | /əˈpoʊnənt/ |
| player (n) | /ˈpleɪər/ |
| pool (n) | /pul/ |
| racket (n) | /ˈrækɪt/ |
| referee (n) | /ˌrɛfəˈri/ |
| represent (v) | /ˌrɛprɪˈzɛnt/ |
| rink (n) | /rɪŋk/ |
| score (n) | /skɔr/ |
| spectator (n) | /ˈspɛkteɪtər/ |
| surfing (n) | /ˈsɜrfɪŋ/ |
| track (n) | /træk/ |
| train (v) | /treɪn/ |
| win (v) | /wɪn/ |

## Extension

| do (v) | /du/ |
|---|---|
| go (v) | /goʊ/ |
| go ice skating (phr) | /ˌgoʊ ˈaɪs ˌskeɪtɪŋ/ |
| go horseback riding (phr) | /ˌgoʊ ˈhɔrs ˌbæk ˈraɪdɪŋ/ |
| play (v) | /pleɪ/ |
| play polo (phr) | /ˈpleɪ ˈpoʊloʊ/ |
| snowboarding (n) | /ˈsnoʊˌbɔrdɪŋ/ |
| table-tennis (n) | /ˈteɪbəl ˌtɛnɪs/ |
| windsurfing (n) | /ˈwɪndˌsɜrfɪŋ/ |

## Vocabulary Building

| give up (phr v) | /ˈgɪv ˈʌp/ |
|---|---|
| join in (phr v) | /ˈdʒɔɪn ˈɪn/ |
| keep up (phr v) | /ˈkip ˈʌp/ |
| knock out (phr v) | /ˈnɒk ˈaʊt/ |
| take on (phr v) | /ˈteɪk ˈɒn/ |
| take up (phr v) | /ˈteɪk ˈʌp/ |
| warm up (phr v) | /ˈwɔrm ˈʌp/ |
| work out (phr v) | /ˈwɜrk ˈaʊt/ |

## Vocabulary in Context

| barely (adv) | /ˈbɛərli/ |
|---|---|
| costume (n) | /ˈkɒstum/ |
| ensure (v) | /ɛnˈʃʊər/ |
| fresh water (n) | /ˈfrɛʃ ˈwɔtər/ |
| I believe in you (phr) | /ˈaɪ bɪˈliv ɪn ˈju/ |
| swollen (adj) | /ˈswoʊlən/ |

# UNIT 4

## Review

| apple (n) | /ˈæpəl/ |
|---|---|
| cake (n) | /keɪk/ |
| chicken (n) | /ˈtʃɪkɪn/ |
| chili powder (n) | /ˈtʃɪli ˌpaʊdər/ |
| chocolate (n) | /ˈtʃɔkəlɪt/ |
| coffee (n) | /ˈkɔfi/ |
| curry (n) | /ˈkɜri/ |
| French fries (n) | /ˈfrɛntʃ ˈfraɪz/ |
| ice cream (n) | /ˈaɪs ˌkrim/ |

| lemon (n) | /ˈlɛmən/ |
|---|---|
| pasta (n) | /ˈpɑstə/ |
| potato chips (n) | /pəˈteɪtoʊ ˌtʃɪps/ |
| prawn (n) | /prɒn/ |
| strawberry (n) | /ˈstrɔˌbɛri/ |
| tomato (n) | /təˈmeɪtoʊ/ |

## Unit Vocabulary

| boiled (adj) | /bɔɪld/ |
|---|---|
| cooked (adj) | /kʊkt/ |
| delicious (adj) | /dɪˈlɪʃəs/ |
| disgusting (adj) | /dɪsˈgʌstɪŋ/ |
| fresh (adj) | /frɛʃ/ |
| fried (adj) | /fraɪd/ |
| healthy (adj) | /ˈhɛlθi/ |
| junk food (n) | /ˈdʒʌŋk ˌfud/ |
| meat-eater (n) | /ˈmit ˌitər/ |
| mild (adj) | /maɪld/ |
| natural (adj) | /ˈnætʃərəl/ |
| processed food (n) | /ˈprɒsɛst ˈfud/ |
| raw (adj) | /rɔ/ |
| steamed (adj) | /stimd/ |
| strong (adj) | /strɒŋ/ |
| suitable for (phr) | /ˈsutəbəl fɔr/ |
| sweet (adj) | /swit/ |
| tasty (adj) | /ˈteɪsti/ |
| vegetarian (n) | /ˌvɛdʒəˈtɛəriən/ |
| well-balanced (adj) | /ˈwɛl ˈbælənst/ |

## Extension

| appetite (n) | /ˈæpəˌtaɪt/ |
|---|---|
| apple pie (n) | /ˈæpəl ˈpaɪ/ |
| bread and butter (n) | /ˈbrɛd ən ˈbʌtər/ |
| cake (n) | /keɪk/ |
| chocolate cake (n) | /ˈtʃɔkəlɪt ˈkeɪk/ |
| diet (n) | /ˈdaɪɪt/ |
| grill (n) | /grɪl/ |
| main course (n) | /ˈmeɪn ˈkɔrs/ |
| mashed potato (n) | /ˈmæʃt pəˈteɪtoʊ/ |
| roast chicken (n) | /ˈroʊst ˈtʃɪkən/ |
| salad (n) | /ˈsæləd/ |
| soup (n) | /sup/ |
| starter (n) | /ˈstɑrtər/ |
| steak (n) | /steɪk/ |
| stir-fry (n) | /ˈstɜr ˌfraɪ/ |
| tasteless (adj) | /ˈteɪstlɪs/ |

## Vocabulary Building

| deep-fried (adj) | /ˈdip ˈfraɪd/ |
|---|---|
| good-looking (adj) | /ˈgʊd ˈlʊkɪŋ/ |
| half-finished (adj) | /ˈhæf ˈfɪnɪʃt/ |
| home-made (adj) | /ˈhoʊm ˈmeɪd/ |
| old-fashioned (adj) | /ˈoʊld ˈfæʃənd/ |
| oven-baked (adj) | /ˈʌvən ˌbeɪkt/ |
| over-cooked (adj) | /ˈʌvən ˌkʊkt/ |
| sun-dried (adj) | /ˈsʌn ˌdraɪd/ |
| sweet-tasting (adj) | /ˈswit ˌteɪstɪŋ/ |
| well-known (adj) | /ˈwɛl ˈnoʊn/ |

## Vocabulary in Context

| combined (adj) | /kəmˈbaɪnd/ |
|---|---|
| come up with (phr v) | /ˈkʌm ˈʌp ˌwɪθ/ |
| damage (n) | /ˈdæmɪdʒ/ |

| in conflict with (phr) | /ˌɪn ˈkɒnflɪkt ˌwɪθ/ |
|---|---|
| raise (v) | /reɪz/ |
| risk (n) | /rɪsk/ |

# UNIT 5

## Review

| accountant (n) | /əˈkaʊntənt/ |
|---|---|
| architect (n) | /ˈɑrkɪˌtɛkt/ |
| chef (n) | /ʃɛf/ |
| chief executive (n) | /ˈtʃif ɪgˈzɛkjətɪv/ |
| doctor (n) | /ˈdɒktər/ |
| firefighter (n) | /ˈfaɪərˌfaɪtər/ |
| lawyer (n) | /ˈlɔjər/ |
| nurse (n) | /nɜrs/ |
| office worker (n) | /ˈɔfɪs ˌwɜrkər/ |
| paramedic (n) | /ˌpærəˈmɛdɪk/ |
| police officer (n) | /pəˈlis ˌɒfɪsər/ |
| salesperson (n) | /ˈseɪlzˌpɜrsən/ |
| store manager (n) | /stɔr ˌmænɪdʒər/ |
| teacher (n) | /ˈtitʃər/ |
| waiter (n) | /ˈweɪtər/ |
| waitress (n) | /ˈweɪtrɪs/ |

## Unit Vocabulary

| business (n) | /ˈbɪznɪs/ |
|---|---|
| career prospects (phr) | /kəˈrɪər ˌprɒspɛkts/ |
| competitive (adj) | /kəmˈpɛtɪtɪv/ |
| creative (adj) | /kriˈeɪtɪv/ |
| demanding (adj) | /dɪˈmændɪŋ/ |
| flexible (adj) | /ˈflɛksəbəl/ |
| in charge of (phr) | /ˌɪn ˈtʃɑrdʒ əv/ |
| industry (n) | /ˈɪndəstri/ |
| job (n) | /dʒɒb/ |
| out of work (phr) | /ˈaʊt əv ˈwɜrk/ |
| responsible for (phr) | /rɪˈspɒnsəbəl fɔr/ |
| stressful (adj) | /ˈstrɛsfəl/ |
| unemployed (adj) | /ˌʌnɪmˈplɔɪd/ |
| well-paid (adj) | /ˈwɛl ˈpeɪd/ |
| work (n) | /wɜrk/ |
| work for (phr v) | /ˈwɜrk ˌfɔr/ |
| work in (phr v) | /ˈwɜrk ˌɪn/ |
| work on (phr v) | /ˈwɜrk ˌɒn/ |

## Extension

| challenging (adj) | /ˈtʃælɪndʒɪŋ/ |
|---|---|
| find (v) | /faɪnd/ |
| need (v) | /nid/ |
| quit (v) | /kwɪt/ |
| resign (v) | /rɪˈzaɪn/ |
| retired (adj) | /rɪˈtaɪərd/ |
| rewarding (adj) | /rɪˈwɔrdɪŋ/ |
| supervisor (n) | /ˈsupərˌvaɪzər/ |
| trainee (n) | /ˌtreɪˈni/ |
| vacancy (n) | /ˈveɪkənsi/ |

## Vocabulary Building

| glance (v) | /glæns/ |
|---|---|
| identify (v) | /aɪˈdɛntəˌfaɪ/ |
| notice (v) | /ˈnoʊtɪs/ |
| observe (v) | /əbˈzɜrv/ |

recognize (v) /'rɛkəg,naɪz/
spot (v) /spɒt/

## Vocabulary in Context

a piece of cake (phr) /ə 'pis əv 'keɪk/
assignment (n) /ə'saɪnmənt/
count on (phr v) /'kaʊnt ,ɒn/
term (n) /tɜrm/
tough (adj) /tʌf/
turn out (phr v) /'tɜrn 'aʊt/

# UNIT 6

## Review

broken (adj) /'broʊkən/
chest (n) /tʃɛst/
elbow (n) /'ɛlboʊ/
finger (n) /'fɪŋgər/
hand (n) /hænd/
head (n) /hɛd/
knee (n) /ni/
neck (n) /nɛk/
nose (n) /noʊz/
pain (n) /peɪn/
patient (n) /'peɪʃənt/
seasick (adj) /'si,sɪk/
shoulder (n) /'ʃoʊldər/
stomach (n) /'stʌmək/
temperature (n) /'tɛmpərətʃər/
throat (n) /θroʊt/
virus (n) /'vaɪrəs/

## Unit Vocabulary

absorb (v) /əb'zɔrb/
bacteria (n) /bæk'tɪəriə/
blood cell (n) /'blʌd ,sɛl/
blood vessel (n) /'blʌd ,vɛsəl/
bone (n) /boʊn/
brain (n) /breɪn/
breathe (v) /brið/
digestion (n) /daɪ'dʒɛstʃən/
digestive system (n) /daɪ'dʒɛstɪv ,sɪstəm/
food (n) /fud/
heart (n) /hɑrt/
lung (n) /lʌŋ/
muscle (n) /'mʌsəl/
nutrient (n) /'nutriənt/
organ (n) /'ɔrgən/
oxygen (n) /'ɒksɪdʒən/
skeleton (n) /'skɛlɪtən/
skin (n) /skɪn/
tongue (n) /tʌŋ/

## Extension

eyebrow (n) /'aɪ,braʊ/
fingernail (n) /'fɪŋgər,neɪl/
hearing (n) /'hɪərɪŋ/
intestine (n) /ɪn'tɛstɪn/
liver (n) /'lɪvər/
rib (n) /rɪb/
sight (n) /saɪt/
skin (n) /skɪn/
smell (v) /smɛl/

spine (n) /spaɪn/
taste (v) /teɪst/
touch (v) /tʌtʃ/
vein (n) /veɪn/
wrist (n) /rɪst/

## Vocabulary Building

allow (v) /ə'laʊ/
enable (v) /ɛn'eɪbəl/
help (v) /hɛlp/
let (v) /lɛt/
prevent (v) /prɪ'vɛnt/
save (v) /seɪv/
stop (v) /stɒp/

## Vocabulary in Context

access (v) /'æksɛs/
concept (n) /'kɒnsɛpt/
extend (v) /ɪk'stɛnd/
light up (phr v) /'laɪt ʌp/
outcome (n) /'aʊt,kʌm/
tremendous (adj) /trə'mɛndəs/

# UNIT 7

## Review

advertise (v) /'ædvər,taɪz/
be in debt (phr) /'bi ɪn 'dɛt/
brand (n) /brænd/
create (v) /kri'eɪt/
design (n/v) /dɪ'zaɪn/
donate to charity (phr) /'doʊneɪt tə 'tʃærɪti/
get a refund (phr) /'gɛt ə 'rifʌnd/
give money away (phr) /'gɪv 'mʌni ə'weɪ/
grow (v) /groʊ/
manufacture (v) /,mænjə'fæktʃər/
material (n) /mə'tɪəriəl/
on sale (phr) /ɒn seɪl/
option (n) /'ɒpʃən/
pick (v) /pɪk/
produce (v) /prə'dus/
recycle (v) /ri'saɪkəl/
rough (adj) /rʌf/
sell (v) /sɛl/

## Unit Vocabulary

afford to (phr v) /ə'fɔrd tu/
bargain (n) /'bɑrgɪn/
browse (v) /braʊz/
earn (v) /ɜrn/
lend (v) /lɛnd/
logo (n) /'loʊgoʊ/
pay back (phr v) /'peɪ 'bæk/
pay for (phr) /'peɪ ,fɔr/
pay more (phr) /'peɪ 'mɔr/
pay off (phr v) /'peɪ 'ɔf/
shop around (phr v) /'ʃɒp ə'raʊnd/
spend money on (phr) /'spɛnd 'mʌni ,ɒn/
take something back (phr) /'teɪk 'sʌmθɪŋ 'bæk/
throw away (phr) /'θroʊ ə'weɪ/
waste money (phr) /'weɪst 'mʌni/

## Extension

buyer (n) /'baɪər/
consumer (n) /kən'sumər/
interest (n) /'ɪntrɪst/
loan (n) /loʊn/
out of stock (phr) /'aʊt əv 'stɒk/
owe (v) /oʊ/
purchase (n) /'pɜrtʃəs/
return (v) /rɪ'tɜrn/
save (v) /seɪv/
seller (n) /'sɛlər/
shop online (phr) /'ʃɒp ,ɒn'laɪn/

## Vocabulary Building

carefully (adv) /'kɛərfəli/
fast (adv) /fæst/
occasionally (adv) /ə'keɪʒənəli/
perfectly (adv) /'pɜrfɪktli/
professionally (adv) /prə'fɛʃənəli/
temporarily (adv) /,tɛmpə'rɛərəli/
well (adv) /wɛl/

## Vocabulary in Context

bug (n) /bʌg/
efficiency (n) /ɪ'fɪʃənsi/
naked (adj) /'neɪkɪd/
pour (v) /pɔr/
precious (adj) /'prɛʃəs/
spread (v) /sprɛd/
transparent (adj) /træns'pærənt/

# UNIT 8

## Review

answer (v) /'ænsər/
call (v) /kɔl/
check email (phr) /'tʃɛk 'i,meɪl/
communicate well (phr) /kə'mjunɪ,keɪt 'wɛl/
email (v) /'i,meɪl/
expect an important call (phr) /ɪk'spɛkt ən ɪm'pɔrtənt 'kɔl/
give someone a call (phr) /'gɪv 'sʌmwən ə 'kɔl/
listen (v) /'lɪsən/
ring (v) /rɪŋ/
send a message (phr) /'sɛnd ə 'mɛsɪdʒ/
send a text (phr) /'sɛnd ə 'tɛkst/
speak louder (phr) /'spik 'laʊdər/
text (v) /tɛkst/
understand (v) /,ʌndər'stænd/

## Unit Vocabulary

argument (n) /'ɑrgjəmənt/
chat (n) /tʃæt/
connect with (phr v) /kə'nɛkt ,wɪθ/
conversation (n) /,kɒnvər'seɪʃən/
debate (n) /dɪ'beɪt/
discussion (n) /dɪ'skʌʃən/
get distracted (phr) /'gɛt dɪ'stræktɪd/
get one's message out (phr) /'gɛt wʌnz 'mɛsɪdʒ 'aʊt/

| interpersonal skills (n) | /ˌɪntərˈpɜrsənəl ˈskɪlz/ |
|---|---|
| make connections (phr) | /ˈmeɪk kəˈnɛkʃənz/ |
| make friends (phr) | /ˈmeɪk ˈfrɛndz/ |
| online forum (n) | /ˈɒnˌlaɪn ˈfɔrəm/ |
| pay attention (phr) | /ˈpeɪ əˈtɛnʃən/ |
| post on social media (phr) | /ˈpoʊst ɒn ˈsoʊʃəl ˈmidiə/ |
| respond to texts (phr) | /rɪˈspɒnd tə ˈtɛksts/ |
| share photos (phr) | /ˈʃɛər ˈfoʊtoʊz/ |

## Extension

| agreement (n) | /əˈgrimənt/ |
|---|---|
| criticism (n) | /ˈkrɪtɪˌsɪzəm/ |
| gossip (n) | /ˈgɒsɪp/ |
| quarrel (v) | /ˈkwɒrəl/ |
| reminder (n) | /rɪˈmaɪndər/ |
| speech (n) | /spitʃ/ |

## Vocabulary Building

| impossible (adj) | /ɪmˈpɒsəbəl/ |
|---|---|
| informal (adj) | /ɪnˈfɔrməl/ |
| irrelevant (adj) | /ɪˈrɛləvənt/ |
| unable (adj) | /ʌnˈeɪbəl/ |
| unbelievable (adj) | /ˌʌnbɪˈlivəbəl/ |
| unusual (adj) | /ʌnˈjuʒʊəl/ |

## Vocabulary in Context

| avoid (v) | /əˈvɔɪd/ |
|---|---|
| care about (phr) | /ˈkɛər əˌbaʊt/ |
| due to (prep) | /ˈdu ˌtu/ |
| have a point to make (phr) | /ˈhæv ə ˈpɔɪnt tə ˌmeɪk/ |
| make a living (phr) | /ˈmeɪk ə ˈlɪvɪŋ/ |
| nod (v) | /nɒd/ |

# UNIT 9

## Review

| art (n) | /ɑrt/ |
|---|---|
| bright (adj) | /braɪt/ |
| classical (adj) | /ˈklæsɪkəl/ |
| color (n) | /ˈkʌlər/ |
| dark (adj) | /dɑrk/ |
| digital (adj) | /ˈdɪdʒɪtəl/ |
| drawing (n) | /ˈdrɔɪŋ/ |
| failure (n) | /ˈfeɪljər/ |
| guitar (n) | /gɪˈtɑr/ |
| hip hop (adj) | /ˈhɪp ˌhɒp/ |
| imperfection (n) | /ˌɪmpərˈfɛkʃən/ |
| instrument (n) | /ˈɪnstrəmənt/ |
| museum (n) | /mjuˈziəm/ |
| music (n) | /ˈmjuzɪk/ |
| painting (n) | /ˈpeɪntɪŋ/ |
| perfect (adj) | /ˈpɜrfɪkt/ |
| photograph (n) | /ˈfoʊtəˌgræf/ |
| piano (n) | /piˈænoʊ/ |
| pop (adj) | /pɒp/ |
| reject (v) | /rɪˈdʒɛkt/ |
| successful (adj) | /səkˈsɛsfəl/ |
| unsuccessful (adj) | /ˌʌnsəkˈsɛsfəl/ |
| violin (n) | /ˌvaɪəˈlɪn/ |

## Unit Vocabulary

| audience (n) | /ˈɔdiəns/ |
|---|---|
| broadcast (n/v) | /ˈbrɔdˌkæst/ |
| character (n) | /ˈkærɪktər/ |
| concert (n) | /ˈkɒnsərt/ |
| entertainment (n) | /ˌɛntərˈteɪnmənt/ |
| exhibition (n) | /ˌɛksɪˈbɪʃən/ |
| gallery (n) | /ˈgæləri/ |
| listener (n) | /ˈlɪsənər/ |
| live (adj) | /laɪv/ |
| lyrics (n) | /ˈlɪrɪks/ |
| mural (n) | /ˈmjʊərəl/ |
| musical (n) | /ˈmjuzɪkəl/ |
| performance (n) | /pərˈfɔrməns/ |
| play (n) | /pleɪ/ |
| portrait (n) | /ˈpɔrtrɪt/ |
| sculpture (n) | /ˈskʌlptʃər/ |
| stadium (n) | /ˈsteɪdiəm/ |
| studio (n) | /ˈstudiˌoʊ/ |
| theater (n) | /ˈθiətər/ |
| tune (n) | /tun/ |
| venue (n) | /ˈvɛnju/ |
| verse (n) | /vɜrs/ |
| viewer (n) | /ˈvjuər/ |
| visitor (n) | /ˈvɪzɪtər/ |

## Extension

| abstract (adj) | /ˈæbstrækt/ |
|---|---|
| appealing (adj) | /əˈpilɪŋ/ |
| award-winning (adj) | /əˈwɔrd ˌwɪnɪŋ/ |
| contemporary (adj) | /kənˈtɛmpəˌreri/ |
| controversial (adj) | /ˌkɒntrəˈvɜrʃəl/ |
| creative (adj) | /kriˈeɪtɪv/ |
| emotional (adj) | /ɪˈmoʊʃənəl/ |
| imaginative (adj) | /ɪˈmædʒɪnətɪv/ |
| inspirational (adj) | /ˌɪnspəˈreɪʃənəl/ |
| lifelike (adj) | /ˈlaɪfˌlaɪk/ |
| masterpiece (n) | /ˈmæstərˌpis/ |
| modern (adj) | /ˈmɒdərn/ |
| moving (adj) | /ˈmuvɪŋ/ |
| work of art (n) | /ˈwɜrk əv ˈɑrt/ |

## Vocabulary Building

| make a decision (phr) | /ˈmeɪk ə dɪˈsɪʒən/ |
|---|---|
| make a difference (phr) | /ˈmeɪk ə ˈdɪfrəns/ |
| make a living (phr) | /ˈmeɪk ə ˈlɪvɪŋ/ |
| make a splash (phr) | /ˈmeɪk ə ˈsplæʃ/ |
| make friends (phr) | /ˈmeɪk ˈfrɛndz/ |
| make sense (phr) | /ˈmeɪk ˈsɛns/ |
| make the most of (phr) | /ˈmeɪk ðə ˈmoʊst əv/ |
| make time (phr) | /ˈmeɪk ˈtaɪm/ |
| make way for (phr) | /ˈmeɪk ˈweɪ fɔr/ |

## Vocabulary in Context

| buzzword (n) | /ˈbʌzˌwɜrd/ |
|---|---|
| come up with (phr v) | /ˈkʌm ˈʌp wɪθ/ |
| gripped (adj) | /grɪpt/ |
| handle (v) | /ˈhændəl/ |
| in a row (phr) | /ˌɪn ə ˈroʊ/ |
| show up (phr v) | /ˈʃoʊ ˈʌp/ |

# UNIT 10

## Review

| after (prep) | /ˈæftər/ |
|---|---|
| be late (phr) | /ˌbi ˈleɪt/ |
| before (prep) | /bɪˈfɔr/ |
| during (prep) | /ˈdʊərɪŋ/ |
| early (adj) | /ˈɜrli/ |
| once (adv) | /wʌns/ |
| until (prep) | /ʌnˈtɪl/ |
| wait (v) | /weɪt/ |

## Unit Vocabulary

| catch up (phr v) | /ˈkætʃ ˈʌp/ |
|---|---|
| fall behind (phr v) | /ˈfɔl bɪˈhaɪnd/ |
| fit in (phr v) | /ˈfɪt ˈɪn/ |
| get around to (phr v) | /ˌgɛt əˈraʊnd tu/ |
| hang out (phr v) | /ˈhæŋ ˈaʊt/ |
| hold on (phr v) | /ˈhoʊld ˈɒn/ |
| hold on to (phr v) | /ˈhoʊld ˈɒn tu/ |
| look forward to (phr v) | /ˈlʊk ˈfɔrwərd tu/ |
| move up (phr v) | / muv ʌp / |
| put off (phr v) | /ˈpʊt ˈɔf/ |
| run out of (phr v) | /ˈrʌn ˈaʊt əv/ |
| take time off from (phr) | /ˈteɪk ˌtaɪm ˈɔf frʌm/ |
| wait around for (phr v) | /ˈweɪt əˈraʊnd fɔr/ |

## Extension

| as soon as (phr) | /ˌæz ˈsun æz/ |
|---|---|
| at last (phr) | /ˌæt ˈlæst/ |
| currently (adv) | /ˈkɜrəntli/ |
| finally (adv) | /ˈfaɪnəli/ |
| in the first place (phr) | /ˌɪn ðə ˈfɜrst ˌpleɪs/ |
| in the future (phr) | /ˌɪn ðə ˈfjutʃər/ |
| in the past (phr) | /ˌɪn ðə ˈpæst/ |
| meanwhile (adv) | /ˈminˌhwaɪl/ |
| on time (phr) | /ˈɒn ˈtaɪm/ |
| run late (phr) | /ˈrʌn ˈleɪt/ |

## Vocabulary Building

| ahead of time (phr) | /əˈhɛd əv ˌtaɪm/ |
|---|---|
| at the same time (phr) | /ˌæt ðə ˈseɪm ˈtaɪm/ |
| early (adj) | /ˈɜrli/ |
| find the time (phr) | /ˈfaɪnd ðə ˈtaɪm/ |
| from time to time (phr) | /frʌm ˈtaɪm tə ˈtaɪm/ |
| have some time (phr) | /ˈhæv sʌm ˈtaɪm/ |
| in the past (phr) | /ˈɪn ðə ˈpæst/ |
| it's time (phr) | /ˌɪts ˈtaɪm/ |
| keep the time (phr) | /ˈkip ðə ˈtaɪm/ |
| lost time (phr) | /ˈlɔst ˈtaɪm/ |
| on time (phr) | /ˈɒn ˈtaɪm/ |
| pass the time (phr) | /ˈpæs ðə ˈtaɪm/ |
| spend some time (phr) | /ˈspɛnd sʌm ˈtaɪm/ |
| take time (phr) | /ˈteɪk ˈtaɪm/ |
| waste time (phr) | /ˈweɪst ˈtaɪm/ |
| worth the time (phr) | /ˈwɜrθ ðə ˈtaɪm/ |

## Vocabulary in Context

| a big deal (phr) | /ə ˈbɪg ˈdil/ |
|---|---|
| aware of (phr) | /əˈwɛər əv/ |
| long-term (adj) | /ˈlɔŋ ˌtɜrm/ |
| lose one's mind (phr) | /ˈluz wʌnz ˈmaɪnd/ |
| on one's mind (phr) | /ˈɒn wʌnz ˈmaɪnd/ |
| stare (v) | /stɛər/ |

# CREDITS

**Photo Credits:**

**5** (cl) Berna Namoglu/Shutterstock.com, **7** (tl) Spotmatik Ltd/Shutterstock.com, **7** (tc) Monkey Business Images/Shutterstock.com, **7** (tc) wong yu liang/Shutterstock.com, **7** (tr) Ollyy/Shutterstock.com, **9** (t) Goran Bogicevic/Shutterstock.com, **15** (br) Chad McDermott/Shutterstock.com, **17** (cr) Krishna.Wu/Shutterstock.com, **19** (br) Ella Sarkisyan/Shutterstock.com, **20** (bl) Mihai Simonia/Shutterstock.com, **23** (bc) Emir Simsek/Shutterstock.com, **28** (tl) Blackregis/Shutterstock.com, **29** (br) KYTan/Shutterstock.com, **31** (t) Pavel Burchenko/Shutterstock.com, **27** (tr) Photodisc/Getty Images/Houghton Mifflin Harcourt, **39** (tr) Ruth Black/Shutterstock.com, **43** (t) Elena Schweitzer/Shutterstock.com, **44** (tl) racorn/Shutterstock.com, **47** (tl) Syda Productions/Shutterstock.com, **47** (cl) Elena Dijour/Shutterstock.com, **47** (bl) Syda Productions/Shutterstock.com, **42** (bl) © Valentyn Volkov/Shutterstock.com, **52** (tl) s_bukley/Shutterstock.com, **55** (br) Kadur, Sandesh Vishwanath/National Geographic Creative, **50** (bl) Golden Pixels LLC/Shutterstock.com, **67** (t) Pool/Getty Images, **71** (tl) Blend Images - KidStock/Getty Images, **71** (tr) ©Joey Schusler, **71** (cr) Bloomberg/Getty Images, **64** (tl) Impact Photography/Shutterstock.com, **74** (bl) leungchopan/Shutterstock.com, **76** (tl) v.schlichting/Shutterstock.com, **76** (tl) RTimages/Shutterstock.com, **76** (tr) Robynrg/Shutterstock.com, **76** (cl) sumire8/Shutterstock.com, **76** (cl) Sergiy Kuzmin/Shutterstock.com, **76** (cr) Mariyana M/Shutterstock.com, **76** (bl) nld/Shutterstock.com, **76** (bl) Early Spring/Shutterstock.com, **76** (br) elenovsky/Shutterstock.com, **79** (t) 06photo/Shutterstock.com, **84** (cl) razorbeam/Shutterstock.com, **84** (cr) Dja65/Shutterstock.com, **81** (tr) Minerva Studio/Shutterstock.com, **88** (tl) Virginia Polytechnic Institute and State University/National Geographic Creative, **91** (t) LookTarn.ss/Shutterstock.com, **98** (cr) Nejron Photo/Shutterstock.com, **100** (tl) muratart/Shutterstock.com, **100** (cl) muratart/Shutterstock.com, **100** (bl) PHOTOCREO Michal Bednarek/Shutterstock.com, **103** (tl) Roxana Gonzalez/Shutterstock.com, **111** (tl) Dragon Images/Shutterstock.com, **115** (tl) PhotoDisc/Getty Images,

**Text Credits:**

**39** "Chew on This," by Kay Boatner, National Geographic Kids, December 2013–January 2014, p. 6., **40** "The Joy of Food: Bringing Family and Friends Together," by Victoria Pope, National Geographic Magazine, December 2014, p. 37+., **52** "The Dog Whisperer," by Ruth A. Musgrave, National Geographic Kids, March 2012, p. 26+., **64** "No Arms, Amazing Feet," by James Dennehy, et al., National Geographic Kids, December 2011-January 2012, p. 28+., **88** "The Maasai: Changed, for Better or Worse, by Cell Phones," by Daniel Stone, National Geographic Magazine, March 2016, p. 24., **100** "City of Bones," by Bekah Wright, National Geographic Kids, October 2009, p. 24+. **103** "Cuba's Young Artists Embrace a New World," by Daniel Stone, National Geographic, December 12, 2016. "Rhythm in Your Blood: Meet the Young Artists Keeping Cuba's Traditional Music Alive," by Marisa Aveling, Pitchfork, June 13, 2016.